Financial Distress and Corporate Turnaround

Martin Schmuck

Financial Distress and Corporate Turnaround

An Empirical Analysis of the Automotive Supplier Industry

Springer Gabler

Martin Schmuck
TU München
München, Germany

Dissertation Technische Universität München, 2012

ISBN 978-3-658-01907-5 ISBN 978-3-658-01908-2 (eBook)
DOI 10.1007/978-3-658-01908-2

The Deutsche Nationalbibliothek lists this publication in the Deutsche Nationalbibliografie; detailed bibliographic data are available in the Internet at http://dnb.d-nb.de.

Library of Congress Control Number: 2013935439

Springer Gabler

Printed on acid-free paper

Springer Gabler is a brand of Springer DE.
Springer DE is part of Springer Science+Business Media.
www.springer-gabler.de

FOREWORD

Since its early days, business research has paid special attention to companies in distress situations. Its main focus has always been on the question of how distressed companies can successfully turn around. This issue is of major importance to academics as well as practitioners, but has only been partially answered so far. The reasons for the sparse and inconclusive research results are manifold. On the one hand, results are frequently hampered by the lack of exhaustive data and inappropriate research designs. On the other hand, the research samples under examination are often very heterogeneous, making it impossible to draw valid conclusions.

In his dissertation, Martin Schmuck analyzes the effectiveness of restructuring measures of companies in financial distress. In order to overcome the limitations of prior studies, he focuses on a sample of automotive suppliers; a distinctive, but nevertheless highly important industry segment. The international sample also makes it possible to accommodate regional differences. One of the main contributions of this doctoral thesis is that it includes a set of healthy companies in the research sample and, thereby makes it possible to identify how individual restructuring measures contribute to the corporate success of distressed and non-distressed companies.

This dissertation is underpinned by an excellent review of existing research efforts, a carefully constructed framework of hypotheses, and an extensive data set. The empirical analysis, conducted specifically for the purpose of this thesis, is based on advanced econometric methods, as well as an extremely well-structured approach. Both the research design and research results are a valuable and innovative contribution to national and international research on corporate turnaround. Martin Schmuck's dissertation on financial distress and corporate turnaround provides important new insights into this field, and future research workers as well as corporate decision-makers in the automotive industry will be able to significantly benefit from his work.

Munich, February 2013 Gunther Friedl

PREFACE

This book is the product of more than three years of my intensive research as an external doctoral student at the Department of Business Administration – Controlling at Technische Universität München. This dissertation is a result of my passion for business management, my scientific curiosity and, last but not least, my preference for working to a flexible time schedule. However, it would never have been written without the support and advice of numerous people, who provided both academic guidance and moral support, and thus played a substantial role in the completion of my dissertation.

First of all, I am extremely grateful to my academic advisor Prof. Dr. Gunther Friedl for his encouragement and trust during the past years. While he granted me a remarkable degree of freedom in defining and pursuing my research, my work would not have been possible without his invaluable advice and guidance. I would also like to thank the entire team of Prof. Dr. Gunther Friedl's chair for welcoming me to their team as an external doctoral candidate. Furthermore, I would like to thank the two other members of my dissertation committee, Prof. Dr. Dr. Ann-Kristin Achleitner for kindly agreeing to provide a second opinion, and Prof. Dr. Kaserer for chairing the examination board. I am very thankful for their efforts and the time they spent serving on my committee.

Special thanks go to my employer Oliver Wyman for generously supporting my Ph.D. leave. In particular, I would like to thank my advisor Dr. Tobias Eichner, who laid the academic foundation for my work, and also Dr. Lutz Jaede, who had already sponsored my diploma thesis. I am especially indebted to my former colleague Peter Bosch, who supported my move from consulting into academia early on, and without whom I would still be looking for the right moment to start this venture.

I would also like to thank my fellow doctoral student Marcel Naujoks for his thoughtful feedback and our ongoing discussions. I am thankful to Doug Boyle, Patrick Rohrmeier, and Tobias Wiesner for reading my thesis and for their helpful feedback. I would also like to thank all my friends who shared distractions from academia with me during the last three years. Finally and most importantly, my deepest gratitude goes to my family. I would like to thank my parents Maria and Hajo Schmuck for unconditionally supporting my education at all times, as well as my brother Stefan, whom I could always rely on. I would also like to express my utmost gratitude to my fiancée Sonja for her unreserved faith and support from day one of the dissertation project.

I wish to dedicate this thesis to my parents.

Munich, February 2013 Martin Schmuck

Synopsis

TABLE OF CONTENTS

List of figures

LIST OF TABLES

List of abbreviations

Adj.	Adjusted
AG	Aktiengesellschaft
AM	Americas
ANCOVA	Analysis of covariance
ANOVA	Analysis of variance
AP	Asia-Pacific
AR	Asset restructuring
CAGR	Compounded annual growth rate
CAP/CAPEX	Capital expenditures
CD	Cook's distance measure
CEO	Chief executive officer
Cont.	continued
Corp.	Corporation
CTX	Context
DBT	Total debt
CE	Common equity
df.	Degrees of freedom
DIV	Common dividends
DS	Distress severity
DY	Distress year
EA	Europe and Africa
EBITDA	Earnings before interest, taxes, depreciation, and amortization
EQU	Equity issue
ER	Early restructuring
EXP	Total operating expenses
FAS	Fixed assets
FC	Financial capacity
FR	Financial restructuring
FS	Financial slack
FTSE	Financial Times Stock Exchange Index
H-L	Hosmer-Lemeshow
ICB	Industry Classification Benchmark
IN	Industry subsector
Inc.	Incorporated
INT	Interest expense on debt
LL	Log-likelihood function
LN	Natural logarithm

LRT .... Likelihood-Ratio-Test
Ltd. .... Limited
MANCOVA .... Multivariate analysis of covariance
Manuf. .... Manufacturing
MR .... Managerial restructuring
MRA .... Top executive change – All
MRN .... Top executive change – Non-routine
ND .... Non-distressed
No. .... Number
NT .... Non-turnaround
OEM .... Original equipment manufacturer
OLS .... Ordinary least squares
OR .... Operational restructuring
p./pp. .... page/pages
PIMS .... Profit Impact of Marketing Strategies
PLC .... Public limited company
PP .... Prior profitability
R&D .... Research and development
REV .... Net revenue
RG .... Region
ROA .... Return-on-assets
ROE .... Return-on-equity
ROI .... Return-on-investment
s.d. .... standard deviation
s.e. .... standard error
SA .... Société anonyme
Sig. .... significance level
TA .... Turnaround
TAS .... Total assets
UK .... United Kingdom
US .... United States
USD .... United States Dollar
VIF .... Variance Inflation Factor
Vol. .... Volume
WC .... Working Capital
Y .... Year

1. INTRODUCTION AND PROBLEM STATEMENT

This research empirically investigates the phenomena of financial distress and corporate turnaround in the automotive supplier industry. CHAPTER 1.1 outlines the dissertation's general research objectives, including its research problem, underlying research questions, and intended contribution to the literature. The motivation and significance for the research object 'automotive supplier industry' and the identification of successful turnaround strategies are provided in CHAPTER 1.2. CHAPTER 1.3 presents the general research design, including research strategy, methodology, and methods. The first part concludes by outlining the dissertation's structure in CHAPTER 1.4.

1.1 Research objectives

1.1.1 Research problem

Corporate distress and turnaround long have been issues integral to business research. Already in the late 1920s, EMMERICH (1929) discussed different forms of turnaround for distressed companies, and SCHMALENBACH (1932) analyzed financing aspects of corporate turnarounds. The general goal of turnaround research has not changed since then: to identify how companies can overcome distress situations. The question of how distressed companies can successfully turn around is important for practitioners and scholars and has received considerable attention in the finance and strategy literature.[1]

Today, corporate turnaround remains one of the most important fields in business research.[2] Nonetheless, no complete and coherent theory of corporate turnaround exists.[3] Research has intensified since the 1970s,[4] but understanding of corporate turnaround remains incomplete, and empirical evidence for the effectiveness of turnaround actions is limited.[5] Insufficient research designs and limited theoretical grounding of existing findings constrict many research efforts in this field.[6] In addition, research themes in distress and turnaround studies have shifted from decade to decade, and the topic of effective distress resolution has been neglected in the recent past.[7] Although scholarship established early that the key to reversing a decline in firm performance is explicit action by management and that ability to formulate appropriate strategic responses is of prime consideration for management,[8] recommendations for practitioners have been only partially forthcoming from academics.[9] Researchers have investigated many critical questions, and an impressive body of literature concerning turnarounds has accumulated over several decades, but the subject remains largely idiosyncratic, and many open issues remain unsettled and contradictory.[10] That said, scholars

---

1 E.g., SUDARSANAM/LAI (2001, p. 183), HAMBRICK/SCHECTER (1983, p. 247), or SCHENDEL ET AL. (1976, p. 3).

2 See HAUSCHILDT ET AL. (2006, p. 7).

3 Compare FRANCIS/DESAI (2005, pp. 1203-1204), PAJUNEN (2005, p. 14), and PEARCE/ROBBINS (1993, p. 614).

4 BUSCHMANN (2006, p. 1) quotes the work of SCHENDEL/PATTON (1976) and SCHENDEL ET AL. (1976) as initial work. HAMBRICK/SCHECTER (1983, p. 232) quote HOFER (1980) and BIBEAULT (1982).

5 See for the following LIN ET AL. (2008, p. 540), SUDARSANAM/LAI (2001, p. 183), and PANDIT (2000, p. 31). For a review of shifting research themes, compare LAI (1997, p. 1).

6 Compare PANDIT (2000, p. 31).

7 Compare LAFRENZ (2004, p. 3).

8 See for example ABEBE (2009, p. 201), OFEK (1993), or SCHENDEL ET AL. (1976, p. 10). At the same time, D'AVENI (1989b, p. 600) states that managerial actions are not solely responsible for turnaround.

9 See FRANCIS/MARIOLA (2005, p. 1), CHOWDHURY (2002, p. 249), and WINN (1993, p. 48).

10 See e.g. LIN ET AL. (2008, p. 540), LIOU/SMITH (2007, p. 74), or FRANCIS/DESAI (2005, pp. 1203-1204).

generally agree that industry-specific research is one palliative for the disjointed state of current research and a path to better understanding of corporate turnaround.[11]

The major research objective of this dissertation is to analyze the effectiveness of restructuring activities in overcoming situations of financial distress in the international automotive supplier industry.[12] It is based on the analysis of managerial, operational, financial, and asset restructuring of 194 publicly listed automotive suppliers between 1999 and 2008.

1.1.2 Research target and questions

The dissertation contributes to the current academic debate over financial distress and corporate turnaround and provides recommendations for managerial decisions in one of the most relevant industry segments.[13] Its purposes are to integrate the existing turnaround literature and to evaluate empirically the effectiveness of turnaround actions by financially distressed automotive suppliers.

Three questions guide this inquiry. They concern the effectiveness of restructuring actions, the differentiation between distressed and non-distressed companies, and the archetypes for successful turnarounds.

Research question 1: Effectiveness of restructuring actions

- How effective are frequently recommended restructuring strategies in resolving financial distress among automotive suppliers?
  - Which of the known restructuring actions are applied in this industry segment?
  - How effective are the four categories of restructuring (managerial, operational, financial, and asset restructuring), and what is their relative contribution to turnarounds?

Research question 2: Strategies of turnaround and non-distressed companies

- What sets apart successful turnaround strategies from successful strategies of companies not in distress?[14]

---

11 Compare PEARCE (2007), MORROW ET AL. (2004), or SUDARSANAM/LAI (2001).

12 Financial distress is one specific form of corporate distress and is defined as "a condition when a firm incurs more debt than its firm size, profitability, and asset composition can sustain" (LIN ET AL., 2008, p. 542). Financial distress lies within the bounds of this study. See SECTION 3.1.1 for a differentiation among stages of distress and the positioning of financial distress within the corporate crisis progression.

13 For the selection of the research object "Automotive supplier industry," compare SECTION 1.2.1.

14 The focus is on successful turnarounds even if unsuccessful turnarounds are included in the comparison to identify more meaningful differences; compare CHAPTER 5.3 for details.

- Do restructuring actions in successful turnarounds significantly differ from actions of healthy firms?
- Are there timing differences between strategies of turnaround firms and non-distressed firms?

Research question3: Turnaround archetypes

- Are there archetypes for successful turnarounds among automotive suppliers?
  - Which restructuring actions are combined in successful turnarounds?
  - What is the relevant sequence of these restructuring actions?

These guiding questions address two important issues. First, they relate to important managerial decisions about which actions to consider during situations of financial distress. Second, they link these actions to performance consequences for the firm.[15] In a hypothesis-driven approach, key hypotheses are derived from existing theory and are empirically tested.

1.1.3 Intended contribution and originality

Although the research objective of identifying successful turnaround strategies is not new per se, questions that guide this dissertation differ from those that guided earlier studies of corporate turnaround and they contribute to existing literature in two distinct ways: (1) by focusing narrowly on one of the most affected industries[16] with an international sample and (2) by comparing turnaround strategies with strategies of non-distressed companies.

The importance of industry-specific characteristics in corporate turnarounds is widely acknowledged but often overlooked by scholars.[17] Prior research shows that the effectiveness of different turnaround strategies depends on specific industry settings.[18] PEARCE/ROBBINS (1993) early on pointed out “that differences in turnaround candidates and in their environmental contexts may necessitate different turnaround models.”[19] Research on generic turnaround strategies covering multiple industries provides limited results because it “may not fully capture the dynamics of performance decline and recovery in specific industries”[20]. With

---

15 Compare SINGH (1993, p. 162), who outlines the requirements for research questions in the context of corporate restructuring.

16 Compare OLIVER ET AL. (2008, p. 563). MOLDENHAUER/SEAGON (2008, p. 35), and FOLEY & LARDNER (2008).

17 E.g., PEARCE (2007), MORROW ET AL. (2004), or SUDARSANAM/LAI (2001) who outline this research deficit.

18 Compare for example SCHENDEL/PATTON (1976), CHOWDHURY/LANG (1993, p. 11), or MCGAHAN/PORTER (1997, p. 16).

19 PEARCE/ROBBINS (1993, p. 623). PEARCE (2007) restates this claim by requiring further research to investigate turnaround in single industries and in narrowly defined economic sectors with larger samples; see PEARCE (2007, p. 268).

20 SUDARSANAM/LAI (2001, p. 198).

respect to future research, SUDARSANAM/LAI (2001) emphasize "the need to identify turnaround strategies beyond the generic ones. How firms in specific industries achieve turnaround in response to industry-specific causes of financial distress is an interesting area for future research, requiring a rigorous conceptual development."[21] The need for industry-specific research stems from the fact that to generate valid conclusions the sample analyzed must be as homogeneous as possible.[22]

Many empirical large-sample turnaround studies have increased the homogeneity of their research samples. First, financials and utilities were excluded because of their singular business characteristics and the regulatory surroundings in distress situations.[23] Then broader industry groups were selected, albeit still covering multiple sectors in most cases.[24] A review of existing research shows that so far no large-sample empirical study of financial distress and turnaround has focused on one, single, specific industry sector.[25] This research on the automotive supplier industry minimizes extraneous variance and known distortions from industry effects such as differing growth rates.[26] Selecting an industry sector with similar operating and competitive conditions increases the validity and accuracy of any conclusion and offers the potential to resolve contradictory results in the existing research concerning financial distress and corporate turnaround.[27]

Related to the narrow industry setting is another distinctive feature in this research: its international sample. Most studies have examined single countries, primarily the US, or have partially combined two or three countries.[28] Due to the global nature of the automotive industry, automotive suppliers, in, for example, Japan, Europe, and the US, are affected alike, and a true international sampling of companies from important regions distinguishes this study.[29]

---

21 SUDARSANAM/LAI (2001, p. 198).

22 See BRYMAN/BELL (2007, pp. 195-197) for large-sample research in general, and see BARKER/DUHAIME (1997, p. 15) and ROBBINS/PEARCE (1992, p. 292) for turnaround research in particular.

23 See for example JOHN ET AL. (1992, p. 894), OFEK (1993, p. 7), ASQUITH ET AL. (1994), and SUDARSANAM/LAI (2001, p. 190).

24 See for example SMITH/GRAVES (2005), FURRER ET AL. (2007), or MORROW ET AL. (2007).

25 So far even studies focusing on manufacturing include companies within different value chain segments, hence Original Equipment Manufacturers (OEMs) and suppliers in their samples.

26 See for the following CHOWDHURY/LANG (1993, p. 11). Industry-adjusted performance measures are one form of adjustment used in other empirical studies; see for example YAWSON (2009, p. 218), DENIS/KRUSE (2000, p. 398), or CHOWDHURY/LANG (1996, p. 172). Because this approach captures only the effects from different industry performance levels, not industry dynamics, it is considered inferior compared to using an industry-specific sample.

27 ROBBINS/PEARCE (1992, p. 1992). One recurring issue is the role of retrenchment; compare BARKER/MONE (1994).

28 Compare LIOU/SMITH (2007, p. 101). See CHAPTER 2.2 for an overview of the geographic focus of corporate turnaround studies.

29 See OLIVER ET AL. (2008, p. 563).

The second original feature of this research is its inclusion of non-distressed firms in comparison to turnaround firms. Prior literature delineates that distressed companies are forced to consider substantive changes and that business-as-usual methods are no longer appropriate.[30] But even if declining firms execute identical restructuring actions as healthy firms, the intensity is often higher than for the firm population at large.[31] Post-distress firms are "paralyzed"[32] strategically and therefore should display behaviors distinguishable from healthy firms. At the same time, some restructuring actions such as cutbacks may be necessary even for healthy corporations due to competitive pressures.[33] Few research studies have compared distressed firms with a matched sample of non-distressed firms.[34] FURRER ET AL. (2007) pioneer in this regard by comparing continuously declining firms that later turn around with non-declining firms. Still, FURRER ET AL. (2007) do not analyze the magnitude and impact of single restructuring actions, only the overall impact on shareholder value. So far, no research has compared single restructuring actions of financially distressed and healthy firms within a single industry sector. By including healthy companies that avoided financial distress, this research can distinguish true turnaround actions from actions of non-distressed automotive suppliers.[35]

1.2 Motivation and significance of the topic

1.2.1 Research object 'Automotive supplier industry'

The need to concentrate on one industry sector to enhance validity of the results was outlined in the previous chapter. This chapter briefly introduces the automotive supplier industry as the research object and discusses the rationale for its selection.

MENTZ (2006) defines an automotive supplier as any economic entity directly or indirectly delivering products to car producers, so-called Original Equipment Manufacturers (OEMs), that are included in the production of automobiles or intended to become part of the automobile itself.[36] The scope of the dissertation is confined to genuine suppliers and consequently, OEMs and raw materials companies, which represent respective ends of the

---

30 See WEITZEL/JONSSON (1989, p. 102).

31 See LAI/SUDARSANAM (1997, p. 217).

32 D'AVENI (1989b, p. 580).

33 See WEITZEL/JONSSON (1989, p. 95).

34 See for the following FURRER ET AL. (2007, p. 376) or ROUTLEDGE/GADENNE (2004, p. 35).

35 Compare FAN ET AL. (2011, p. 15), who introduced healthy companies as a control group in their research involving institutions, ownership structures, and firm distress.

36 See for the following MENTZ (2006, pp. 8-10) and LAABS (2009, pp. 9-10). Service companies, which are included under MENTZ (2006), are explicitly excluded because of their different business designs; see BARKER/DUHAIME (1997, p. 21), O'NEILL (1986b, p. 85), and FURRER ET AL. (2007, p. 380).

automotive value chain, are excluded. In general, the development of the automotive supplier industry is closely tied to its customers, the automotive OEMs.

The automobile industry has been characterized by several major trends during the past 15 years, including globalization, a shift in the value chain, and shorter product cycles, all of which directly affect automotive suppliers.[37]

Globalization of the automotive OEMs, notably a shift from North American production to Asia, has led to an increase in the global footprint of automotive suppliers (see FIGURE 1).[38] Worldwide follow-sourcing alongside requirements like customs and in-country quotas pressured automotive suppliers to establish a global presence to compete in a global market.[39] In 2008, 85%, 74%, and 68% of production facilities of Western European, Asian, and North American suppliers, respectively, were located abroad.[40]

Figure 1: Global light vehicle production by region 1999-2008.

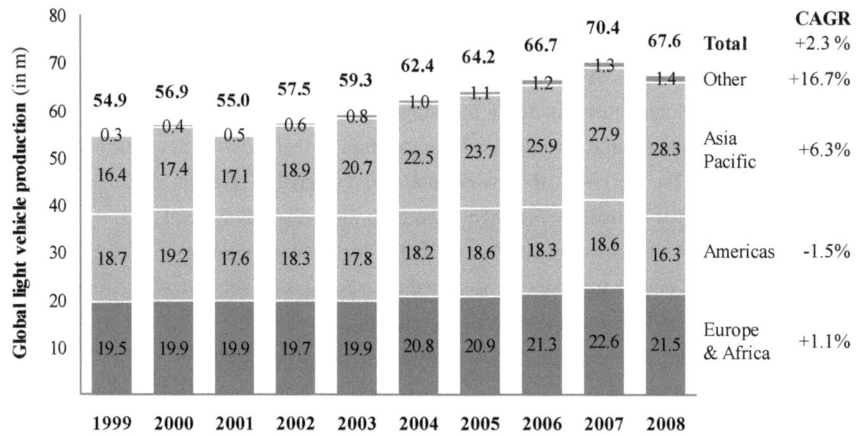

Source: Own illustration based on J.D. Power and Associates (2010).

Along with globalization are the trend of automotive OEMs to outsource production and their preference for purchasing systems of components rather than individual parts.[41] This means that automotive suppliers' value-added is increasing. Although they long have had the largest share of value-added in the automotive industry, it further increased from 65% in 2000 to about 75% in 2010.[42] Not only did suppliers' value-added for manufacturing increase from

37 For an overview of current trends compare LAABS (2009, pp. 10-14).
38 See WAD (2008, p. 56) and DIEZ/REINDL (2005b, pp. 116-125).
39 See LAABS (2009, p. 11).
40 See KPMG (2009, p. 3).
41 See for the following WAD (2008, pp. 56-57) and DIEZ/REINDL (2005a, pp. 79-80, 91-96).
42 See for the following estimates WAHRENDORFF (2008, p. 7) and KALMBACH (2007, p. 35).

72% to 80%, but also the value-added for research and development increased from 30% to 50% during the same period. This development highlights the increasing importance of automotive suppliers for the entire automotive industry.

At the same time as suppliers increased their already large share of value-added, product lifecycles within the automotive industry shortened. The current product lifecycle is estimated at two to three years, compared to four to seven years a few years ago.[43] Based on their larger share of value-added, accommodating shorter product lifecycles requires a commitment to innovation from the suppliers, as they must take over responsibility for product renewal and upgrade systems and components more frequently.

Overall, automotive supply is a highly competitive industry. Profit margins are under pressure because of OEMs' cost-cutting and the rising cost of raw material inputs.[44] This competitive environment has led to consolidation: the number of suppliers declined from above 8,000 in 1998 to 5,600 in 2000. A further decrease to 2,800 is estimated in 2015.[45]

For research on corporate turnaround, the automotive industry is especially relevant for academics and practitioners. Academics outline two main reasons: the level of distress and the severity of distress. First, "manufacturing industries such as [...] automotive [...] were the first to face widespread turnaround situations".[46] Competition in this industry has "reached a level where it threatens the survival of new-entrant and established players alike"[47] and the prevalence of financial distress is expected to be high. Second, mature industries such as the automotive industry "face particularly difficult turnaround situations"[48]. Therefore restructuring actions and instruments are assumed to be more sophisticated and advanced than in less-competitive industries, and results of empirical studies are expected to be more meaningful and potentially transferable, even beyond industry boundaries.[49]

In addition, practitioners regard the automotive industry as among those having the highest risk of financial distress.[50] With the financial difficulties confronting the automotive industry, it is important that decision makers in the automotive supplier industry understand these

---

43 See for the following CEGLAREK ET AL. (2004, p. 12).

44 See LAABS (2009, p. 13).

45 Compare WALLENTOWITZ ET AL. (2009, p. 41) and KALMBACH (2007, p. 38), including public and non-public companies. This consolidation trend can be observed for Tier-1 (systems), Tier-2 (modules and sub-systems), and Tier-3 (components) suppliers alike, see WALLENTOWITZ ET AL. (2009, p. 37-43) for a detailed discussion.

46 PEARCE/ROBBINS (1993, p. 613).

47 OLIVER ET AL. (2008, p. 563).

48 HAMBRICK/SCHECTER (1983, p. 231). Compare with OLIVER ET AL. (2008, p. 563), who define the automotive industry as a "very mature industry".

49 See EICHNER (2008, p. 60) and CHRISTIE ET AL. (2003, p. 17).

50 MOLDENHAUER/SEAGON (2008, p. 35) quotes a study of Roland Berger Strategy Consultants, which sees automotive suppliers as the industry segment with the highest demand for corporate restructuring after the banking industry.

distress situations and the variety of turnaround strategies available to help them.[51] Still, many managers find that "the problems of company survival, down-sizing, and regeneration are ones for which they are often ill-prepared"[52].

1.2.2 Success factor research on corporate turnaround

Business performance is at the center of any research on corporate turnaround.[53] As part of the ongoing rigor-relevance debate in management research, there is broad discussion about success factors and use of organizational performance as a dependent variable.[54] Despite the multi-dimensionality and multi-causality of organizational performance, research on corporate turnaround centers on identifying a few key factors underlying success or failure.[55] Like most empirical studies of corporate turnaround, this research uses "performance as a dependent variable and seek[s] to identify variables that produce variations in performance"[56]. A short introduction to the academic debate follows, and the remainder of this section provides a rationale for empirical success factor research on corporate turnaround.

Research on success factors has its roots in the early 1960s within the PIMS-Program (Profit Impact of Marketing Strategies) in the US, where yearly data for about 300 companies are systematically collected.[57] The PIMS-Program explained 80% of the Return-on-investment (ROI) with about 30 internal and external factors within a multiple regression analysis. Since then, the orientation towards organizational performance and the search for success factors have been considered central to strategic management: researchers want to know what drives corporate success and failure.[58]

Despite the popularity of success factor research, this research stream is exposed to harsh criticism. Some of the major criticisms are summarized below:

---

51 Compare FOLEY & LARDNER (2008).

52 HARKER (2001, p. 198).

53 See CHOWDHURY (2002, p. 250). VENKATRAMAN/RAMANUJAM (1986, p. 802) in their general work on firm performance explicitly list research on corporate turnaround as one field where performance measures are especially important.

54 For a summary of the discussion in Germany see RÖDERSTEIN (2009) and WOYWODE (2004). For the Anglo-American discussion see GULATI (2007, pp. 775-777).

55 See SCHMALEN ET AL. (2005, pp. 1-2).

56 MARCH/SUTTON (1997, p. 698).

57 See WOLFF ET AL. (2004). Because of problems with time series, the program was ended in 1999. The importance of success factor research also was shown by a literature review of the *Strategic Management Journal*, the *Academy of Management Journal*, and the *Administrative Science Quarterly* between 1993 and 1995, when 28% of all articles published used performance as the dependent variable; see MARCH/SUTTON (1997, p. 706). For a detailed review of different streams of success factor research and their evaluation see HAENECKE (2002).

58 See HAUSCHILDT (2006, p. 62).

- Success factor research suffers from over-simplification, and therefore insufficient problem-solving, by limiting success to a few selected variables.[59] The different interdependencies among variables do not allow for isolating the influence of a single factor on corporate success. Thus, success factor research cannot be considered meaningful.
- Success factor research has provided no accumulated and consistent insights. NICOLAI/KIESER (2002) complain that no single significant success factor exists about which normative conclusions could be drawn.[60] This argument also holds true for research on corporate distress and turnaround, where study results are considered heterogeneous and inconclusive.[61]
- Empirical research can identify only success factors that have applied in the past, and reliance on information from the past does not allow normative interpretations.[62] In addition, success factors, which are known, can be copied by competitors and therefore lose their effectiveness.[63] MARCH/SUTTON (1997) describe this process as "self-destructive"[64].
- Finally, critics argue that results of success factor research find no application in management, and therefore it fails its own ambition of bridging the gap between rigor and relevance.[65]

Critics conclude that "rigorous and relevant research represent distinct types of knowledge"[66] and that "increasing [the] relevance of management research is only possible at the expense of scientific rigor and vice versa"[67]. KIESER/NICOLAI (2005) base this view on "the sociology of science that conceptualizes science as a self-referential social system"[68]. The rigor-relevance gap lies in the difference between the social systems of academia and practice, and success factor research is not able to bridge these gaps.[69]

---

59 See for the following RÖDERSTEIN (2009, p. 36).
60 See NICOLAI/KIESER (2002, p. 582).
61 See PRETORIUS (2009, p. 1) and WINN (1993, p. 48).
62 See NICOLAI/KIESER (2002, p. 587).
63 See MARCH/SUTTON (1997, p. 699).
64 MARCH/SUTTON (1997, p. 699).
65 Compare AGUINIS ET AL. (2010, p. 516), who reviewed several studies analyzing the audience of several academic publications.
66 GULATI (2007, p. 776).
67 KIESER/NICOLAI (2005, p. 276). This view was already expressed by HAMBRICK (1994), who stated that to gain more of one we must lose some of the other in an zero-sum game; see HAMBRICK (1994, pp. 11-16).
68 KIESER/NICOLAI (2005, p. 276).
69 See KIESER/NICOLAI (2005, p. 276). WOYWODE (2004, p. 21) argues that the exclusion of organizational performance as a dependent variable would a priori exclude one of the most central question in business science.

Notwithstanding these criticisms, researchers who favor success factor research argue that "the rigor-relevance debate is misguided and ultimately damaging"[70] and that demand exists for research creating "academic and practice-focused synergy"[71]. The presumption is that someone writing for practitioners is by definition producing work that is not rigorous and that someone writing primarily for academe is producing work of limited practical relevance.[72]

HAMBRICK (1994) points out that researchers' responsibility is "[...] to the institutions around the world that are in dire need of improved management"[73]. Many researchers have acknowledged the importance of bridging the science-practice gap and see this harsh critique as a call for even more intense research on corporate success factors.[74] Existing research has outlined several requirements for overcoming the most common criticisms:

- Research questions for 'problem-oriented' research should select research objects that derive from real-world challenges where theory and knowledge are inadequate.[75]
- Research on corporate success factors depends on relevant context.[76] Results can only be interpreted as potentially successful within a specific context, not as guarantees for success. Dependency on context also implies that ongoing research is required when past success factors may not necessarily be those of the future.[77] But even if only inferences about the past are justifiable, success factor research can indicate which variables are important. Emphasis on industry-specific research is proposed here.[78]
- For meaningful results, researchers "should try to ground ideas in existing theory"[79]. Only theory-based research designs allow systematic research on success factors and facilitate interpretation of results compared to arbitrary data mining.[80] Still, theory has only a serving role, not a ruling one, in problem-oriented business research.[81]
- Empirical research on success factors must be based on well-grounded methods and must make clear that no general, causal relationships can be inferred. Even if methodologically

70 GULATI (2007, p. 779).
71 GULATI (2007, p. 779).
72 See GULATI (2007, p. 777).
73 HAMBRICK (1994, p. 13).
74 See WOYWODE (2004, p. 21).
75 See LAWRENCE (1992, pp. 140-141). KIESER/NICOLAI (2005, pp. 276-277) state that the focus on real-world problems is useless because over time additional problems will be identified and the initial problem will be lost in the scientific discourse. Although this criticism might be apt, it cannot be accepted as an argument against choosing real-world research problems. Instead of rejecting real-world problems as research subjects, researchers should refocus on the initial problem when their research strays from the initial problem.
76 See for the following RÖDERSTEIN (2009, pp. 37-40), who differentiates between context-specific and context-unspecific success factors.
77 See WOYWODE (2004, p. 23).
78 See RÖDERSTEIN (2009, p. 44).
79 GULATI (2007, p. 780).
80 See WOYWODE (2004, p. 39).
81 See HAUSCHILDT (2006, p. 63).

challenging, a variety of statistical instruments is available to provide econometrically correct results.[82]

- To assure knowledge transfer between academics and practitioners, academic researchers must be willing to translate their insights.[83] AGUINIS ET AL. (2010) outline several recommendations for reporting research results to overcome the science-practice gap.[84]

Based on the foregoing requirements, this research adopts the view that research on success factors, and in this case research on success factors in corporate turnarounds, can report "significant research results in a way that is rigorous and relevant and therefore meets the needs of both academics and practitioners"[85]. Even MARCH/SUTTON (1997), who criticize success factor research emphatically, say "the essential point is that scholarship is probably better served by maintaining a tension between saying more than we know and understanding how little we can know, rather than by a definite resolution of conflict"[86].

1.3 Research design

This chapter introduces the research design and the overall configuration of this research. The design is based on the research target and questions and includes the research strategy, methodology, and methods.

Research target

Selection of a research design primarily depends on the presiding research questions and corresponding research target. The research target in turn depends on the understanding of management research in general and the current state of research on corporate turnaround in particular. By following an understanding of management and business research as an applied science, the research target becomes pragmatic and normative.[87] This dissertation aims to contribute to the current academic debate over corporate turnaround and to make theoretical evidence from academic research useful through recommendations for managerial decision-making in an industry segments highly relevant for studying corporate distress.[88] The research

---

82 See WOYWODE (2004, pp. 31-39). For example ALBERS/HILDEBRANDT (2006) provide a detailed discussion of the application of structural equation models in success factor research. SCHMALEN ET AL. (2005, pp. 6-7) discuss factor analysis, regression analysis, and discriminant analysis.

83 See GULATI (2007).

84 Compare AGUINIS ET AL. (2010).

85 AGUINIS ET AL. (2010, p. 517).

86 MARCH/SUTTON (1997, p. 704).

87 See BRYMAN/BELL (2007, p. 6). For a detailed explanation compare WITTE (1981b, p. 13), who formulates this in reference to all empirical research in business and management.

88 Compare CARLILE/CHRISTENSEN (2005, p. 1). Even if the research target is considered partially normative, it is important to acknowledge that „it is simply impossible to establish the external validity of a theory by testing it on data. There will always be another set upon which it hasn't yet been tested, and the future will

questions address important managerial decisions concerning which actions to pursue to achieve successful turnaround and explicitly consider the organizational and performance consequences of these decisions. Based on the knowledge accumulated but recognizing the still incomplete nature of corporate turnaround theory, a primarily[89] explanative research design of testing hypothesis is preferable to explorative or descriptive designs.[90]

Research strategy

There are three generic research strategies in the field of management research: conceptual, analytical, and empirical.[91] Conceptual research is grounded in considerations of validity, sometimes with the help of empirical examples. It often is applied early in a research stream when no testable hypotheses exist. Analytical research is characterized by describing problems in simplifying abstraction, often using mathematical models, through a logical approach toward problem-solving.[92] An empirical research strategy is in general concerned with systematic collection and analysis of empirical data and careful examination of patterns in the data to understand and explain the phenomena of interest.[93] The empirical strategy chosen accords with the research target and with current theory about corporate turnaround. This dissertation aims to move the current, primarily descriptive, theory of corporate turnaround forward to a more normative character through "careful field-based research"[94] as recommend by CARLILE/CHRISTENSEN (2005).

Research methodology

Two primary research methodologies exist within empirical research: quantitative and qualitative.[95] The type of data used is the main differentiating criterion: qualitative research verbalizes real-world phenomena, whereas quantitative research describes these phenomena as numbers.[96] There are other distinct features to both research methodologies, but generally

---

always lie just beyond the reach of data"; CARLILE/CHRISTENSEN (2005, p. 16).

89 The research target is considered primarily explanative, as the second and third research questions concerning turnaround strategies also include an explorative character based on answers to the first research question.

90 BORTZ/DÖRING (2006, pp. 50-53). Descriptive and explorative approaches are insufficient because empirical evidence already exists. Only at an early stage of theory-building will a description and categorization of phenomena suffice for the researcher. At the same time, each investigation will include at least some descriptive elements in describing the phenomenon of interest.

91 See for the following RIESENHUBER (2007, p. 3).

92 So far, application of analytical methods is rare in the context of corporate turnaround. See LIN ET AL. (2006) for an example.

93 See NEUMAN (2005, pp. 151, 458).

94 CARLILE/CHRISTENSEN (2005, p. 6). CARLILE/CHRISTENSEN (2005) provide a broad discussion of the process of theory-building and the development of descriptive theory to normative theory through field-based research.

95 Research methodology here includes data collection and data analysis, although the two elements cannot always be differentiated; compare SCHNELL ET AL. (2005, p. 407).

96 For a differentiation of quantitative and qualitative research streams compare in detail KELLE (2008),

qualitative research is more inductive, occupied with generating theory, and works with small to very small samples, whereas quantitative research is more deductive, focused on testing of theory, and works with large samples.[97]

While a qualitative research methodology is often used at an early stage of theory development and fits a descriptive or explorative research setting, the quantitative research methodology chosen here fits both the current state of research and the explanative research setting.[98] Large-sample quantitative research provides results which are often more reliable, representative, and testable. As such, the results often allow the researcher to, if applicable, falsify hypotheses and derive recommendations.[99] The generic steps in a quantitative research methodology applied here include the development of a theoretical research framework[100] based on a detailed analysis of existing research, the formulation and operationalization of corresponding research hypotheses, the empirical testing of these hypotheses with the sample of publicly listed automotive companies, and finally the improvement of the initial theoretical framework.[101]

Research methods

Numerous research methods exist in the empirical, quantitative research methodology. The most common are experiments, surveys, case-studies, cross-sectional methods, longitudinal studies, and panel studies.[102] Having access to a large sample of secondary data,[103] the focus

---

BRYMAN/BELL (2007), and SHAH/CORLEY (2006).

97 Qualitative and quantitative research should not be seen as dichotomous streams. With increasing frequency, both are included in single research projects; this is called ‚mixed methods research‘. For an introduction into ‚mixed methods research‘, see e.g. BRYMAN/BELL (2007, pp. 28-29), CRESWELL (2009, pp. 14-18), or KELLE (2008).

98 Compare the literature review of case studies and anecdotal evidence by PANDIT (2000) for an overview.

99 See RIESENHUBER (2007, pp. 6-7) and SCHWAIGER/ZIMMERMANN (2009, p. 421).

100 The wording 'research framework' is explicitly used to differentiate it from a theory. A framework can be considered preliminary to a theory and contains a variety of theoretical definitions which are expected to become part of a theory later; compare KIRSCH (1981, pp. 193-200).

101 RIESENHUBER (2007, p. 4).

102 See for the following BRYMAN/BELL (2007, p. 361), NEUMAN (2005, pp. 246-340), and CRESWELL (2009, pp. 145-171). Each of these research methods also can be applied in different forms in a qualitative research methodology; see BRYMAN/BELL (2007, p. 71) for an overview.
Experiments are rare in management research, primarily because the requisite level of control when dealing with organizational behavior is insufficient. Although the experiment is a powerful way to isolate causal relationships, it is better suited for micro-level than for macro-level theoretical concerns or issues; see NEUMAN (2005, p. 247). The same is true for research on corporate turnaround: in a review of the majority of empirical turnaround studies conducted after 1970 did not reveal one experiment.
A survey design provides a quantitative or numeric description of trends, attitudes, or opinions of a population by studying a sample of that population; see CRESWELL (2009, p. 143). Because of the negativity surrounding distress situations, objectivity is not assured, as a survey design is expected to show key informant bias; compare HURRLE/KIESER (2005) for a detailed discussion.
The basic case study entails the detailed and intensive analysis of one or more cases and is concerned with the complexity and particular nature of the cases in question; see BRYMAN/BELL (2007, pp. 62-64). Case studies have been popular in examining turnarounds in the past, and single turnaround cases and anecdotal evidence dominated the field; compare MAHESHWARI (2000, p. 42) and PANDIT (2000) for an overview.

is on cross-sectional, longitudinal, and panel methods. Given that prior research shows no statistical influence for the calendar year of distress versus the turnaround outcome, a cross-sectional research method is proposed here.[104]

A cross-sectional design can be described as "the collection of data on more than one case (usually a lot more than one) at a single point in time in order to collect a body of quantitative or quantifiable data in connection with two or more variables (usually many more than two) which are then examined to detect patterns of association."[105] A comparative design, a special form of cross-sectional research, is especially suited for researching corporate turnaround.[106] In a comparative design, two or more cross-sectional studies are carried out at more or less the same point in time. The logic of comparison perfectly suits the turnaround versus non-turnaround as well as the distressed versus non-distressed level of analysis. In terms of reliability, validity, replicability, and generalizability, the comparative study is no different from the cross-sectional design. Even if no causality can be shown because of the limitations of cross-sectional methods, the usual approach is to draw inferences about causal directions based on assumptions and the underlying theoretical foundations.[107]

In summary, the research design in this study includes a pragmatic, normative research target with the intent of enhancing theory and providing recommendations for practitioners. An empirical, theory-based research strategy is chosen with a quantitative research methodology and a cross-sectional research method. CHAPTER 4.3 discusses statistical methods in detail.

1.4 Study outline

Following the introductory overview, this dissertation is structured into five parts. PART 2 reviews research streams within the general field of corporate crisis (CHAPTER 2.1) and empirical research on corporate turnaround in particular (CHAPTER 2.2). The dissertation is positioned within existing research and linked to related empirical studies.

In PART 3 the theoretical framework and hypotheses are developed. The discussion includes the initial definition and differentiation of key terms used in this study (CHAPTER 3.1) and the

---

The case study approach plays a minor role in quantitative research since the research already moved from descriptive, explorative to explanative it is rejected here.

103 Secondary analysis reanalyzes previously collected data; see NEUMAN (2005, p. 333). This research uses the Thomson ONE database, which provides detailed financial statement data and profile data for 58,000 public companies covering approximately 95% of global market capitalization at the end of 2008.

104 Compare EICHNER (2008) and see CHAPTER 5.1 for the same result.

105 BRYMAN/BELL (2007, p. 55). This differentiates it from longitudinal research methods in which a phenomenon is examined at least at two points in time. A special form of the longitudinal research method is the panel study, in which data on more than one case are examined over time; see BRYMAN/BELL (2007, pp. 60-61).

106 See for the following BRYMAN/BELL (2007, pp. 66-70).

107 Compare BRYMAN/BELL (2007, p. 361) and WOYWODE (2004, p. 23).

development of the theoretical framework (CHAPTER 3.2). The theoretical framework includes the restructuring content, including managerial, operational, financial, and asset restructuring as well as process- and context-related aspects. Key hypotheses for the empirical analysis are derived in this chapter. PART 3 closes with a summary of the complete theoretical framework (CHAPTER 3.3).

PART 4 introduces the basics of the empirical study, including a description of the sampling procedure (CHAPTER 4.1), the operationalization of the variables and measures used (CHAPTER 4.2), and the discussion of the statistical methods applied (CHAPTER 4.3).

PART 5 includes the empirical analysis of restructuring actions of automotive suppliers. At the beginning, an overview of the sample and important sample characteristics are provided (CHAPTER 5.1). The remainder of this part is structured in line with the three research questions and provides empirical results for the effectiveness of various restructuring actions (CHAPTER 5.2), the differences between distressed and non-distressed companies (CHAPTER 5.3), and the patterns of successful turnarounds (CHAPTER 5.4).

PART 1 concludes the dissertation, summarizing its main results (CHAPTER 6.1) and limitations and posing directions for future research (CHAPTER 6.2).

2. LITERATURE REVIEW: EARLIER RESEARCH AND STATUS OF THE AREA

This part reviews previous research on corporate crisis management generally and corporate turnaround in particular. CHAPTER 2.1 introduces the five main streams within corporate crisis research and positions research on corporate turnaround within this main research field. CHAPTER 2.2 is a detailed discussion of existing large-sample empirical studies of corporate turnaround.

2.1 Research on corporate crisis

In this dissertation, corporate crisis is defined as "an unwanted event which always seriously threatens the continued existence of the firm."[108] Corporate crisis can have several distinct manifestations and refers to any pattern of deteriorating performance.[109] Despite the threat posed to a firm by any type of crisis, it usually appears possible to save the firm or considerable parts of it.

According to WITTE (1981A), a theory of corporate crisis must include five building blocks (see FIGURE 2): the progression of corporate crisis, its causes, its effects, its identification, and its resolution.[110]

Figure 2: Research streams on corporate crisis.

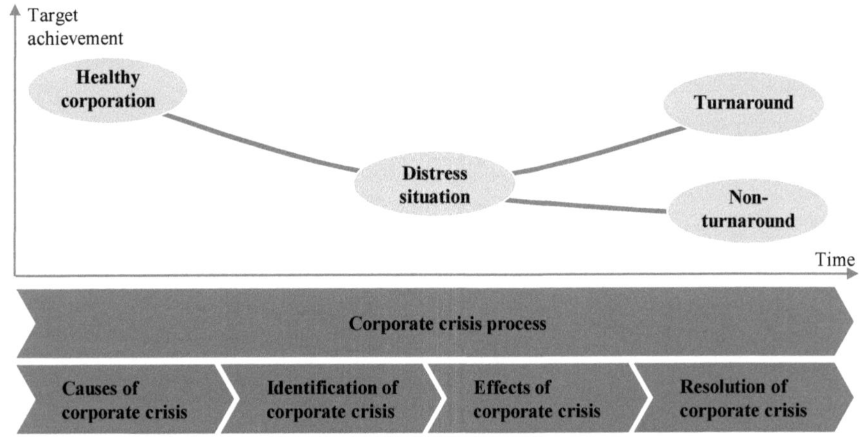

Source: Own illustration based on KALL (1999, p. 10).

The remainder of this chapter introduces the five building blocks of a theory of corporate crisis, including the main research targets, representative research, and – when applicable – a link to the empirical turnaround research within this study.

---

108 MÜLLER (1985, p. 39). 'Corporate crisis' is an umbrella term for the assorted nomenclature used in existing literature like decline, deterioration, distress, collapse, demise, etc. Compare PRETORIUS (2009, pp. 5-8) for an extensive survey of definitions appearing in existing research. The exact definition of financial distress, which is the distinct form of corporate crisis analyzed in this research, is provided in SECTION 3.1.1.

109 Compare for the following MÜLLER (1985, pp. 39-42).

110 Compare WITTE (1981a, pp. 14-21), who initially defined these five elements. This framework is then repeated multiple times. See for example KRYSTEK (1987, pp. 2-3), KALL (1999, pp. 8-11), BUSCHMANN (2006, pp. 11-24), or SCHLEY (2010, p. 16).

Corporate crisis process

Research on the progression of corporate crises attempts to identify patterns in the sequence of crises. Numerous differing models explain the progression and can be differentiated by noting the corporate objectives threatened, the degree of threat, and the pressure to act as well as the freedom of action.[111]

One of the most popular models, MÜLLER (1985), will be introduced shortly.[112] MÜLLER (1985) describes four generic phases of corporate crisis: strategic crisis, performance crisis, liquidity crisis, and insolvency. A strategic crisis is a threat to the potential of the firm and can occur from the firm's failure to build up or maintain its foundations in the market in such areas as product differentiation, know-how, or cost advantage. A performance crisis threatens the firm's profitability and is defined as a consistent failure to meet sales or profitability targets. Threat of insolvency when a firm can no longer meet its obligations defines a liquidity crisis. The final phase is insolvency[113], the threat of dissolution. The number of possible counteractions decreases within each phase while the pressure to take counteractions simultaneously increases. Identifying a crisis is most difficult during its earlier phases.

Process models often lack exact definitions of different phases, rendering distinctions between phases impossible.[114] The corporate crisis process is important for turnaround management because each phase requires different actions for overcoming its particular distress. It is essential that turnaround research be able to identify and compare companies occupying the same stage of distress.

Causes of corporate crisis

Studying the causes of corporate crisis is a first step in understanding cause-effect relationships to explain the existence of corporate crisis in a generally acceptable form.[115] The main research question is: Why do firms decline?[116] Two classification schemes for the analysis of causes of corporate crisis are introduced briefly: by origin and by nature of distress. A first possible distinction is by the *origin of distress*: external and internal.[117] The

---

[111] Compare for a comprehensive overview KRYSTEK (1987, pp. 10-32). Three exemplary models are listed: the latent/manifest distinction by HAUSCHILDT (2000, p. 3); the crisis denial, hidden crisis, disintegration of organization, and organizational collapse framework based on typical behavioral patterns during situations of corporate distress by SLATTER/LOVETT (1999, p. 61); and the five-stage model of organizational decline (blinded, inaction, faulty action, crisis, and dissolution) by WEITZEL/JONSSON (1989, p. 97).

[112] See for the following MÜLLER (1985). The same process model is used for example by GLESS (1996, pp. 128-130), KRAUS/HAGHANI (2004, pp. 15-18), or HOPFMUELLER (2010, pp. 30-31).

[113] "Insolvency" is an umbrella term comparable to bankruptcy because the latter is a juridical definition of business failure. Compare also BALCAEN (2009, pp. 5-6).

[114] See for the following BUSCHMANN (2006, p. 14).

[115] See KRYSTEK (1987, p. 32).

[116] Compare MAHESHWARI (2000, p. 40).

[117] Compare for the following BALGOBIN/PANDIT (2001, pp. 302-303) who summarize the findings of six

main external causes of distress are decreases in demand, increases in competition, and increases in input costs. Principal internal causes of distress include poor management, inadequate financial controls or policies, and high cost. A second possible distinction is by the *nature of distress*: operational and strategic.[118] Operational causes include, amongst others, inefficiencies, unprofitable cost relationships, incorrect resource applications, or managerial deficiencies. Strategic causes can emerge from the external environment and include, for example, weak positioning in the market or technological changes.

Research on causes of corporate crisis also can be divided into qualitative and quantitative research.[119] *Quantitative research* is based on the analysis of statistical data to identify causes of corporate crises. The explanatory power of these studies is often limited because no clear separation between causes and symptoms can be reached.[120] *Qualitative research* tries to identify general conclusions about causes of corporate crises by surveying, for example, insolvency administrators, involved management, or consultants. These primary informational sources are often inaccessible, and if such experts can be surveyed, their explanations likely suffer from self-reporting and retrospective biases.[121] Overall, research on causes of corporate crises is highly complex due to multi-causality, multi-stage cause-effect relationships, and inability to identify single origins for corporate distress.[122]

The causes of distress are also important for research into the resolution of corporate crises because different causes often require different restructuring actions. Therefore, the two research streams are intertwined.

Identification of corporate distress

Research on the identification of corporate distress has received the broadest attention among the research fields outlined. This research stream aims to forecast corporate distress at a very early phase of the crisis progression to initiate appropriate counteractions.

A range of models predict corporate distress, and they differ in respect to input factors and statistical methods. Broadly, models use one of two sets of inputs: accounting-based models use information contained in financial statements, and market-based models estimate distress

popular studies SCHENDEL ET AL. (1976), BIBEAULT (1982), THAIN/GOLDTHORPE (1989), SLATTER (1984), GRINYER ET AL. (1990), and GOPAL (1991). BALGOBIN/PANDIT (2001, p. 303) speak of „high cost structures“ while the original work by SCHENDEL ET AL. (1976, p. 6) describes simply „higher costs“ without emphasizing specifics for the cost structure.

118 See for the following PRETORIUS (2010, p. 224) and PEARCE/ROBBINS (1993, p. 626).

119 Compare KRYSTEK (1987, p. 33).

120 See BUSCHMANN (2006, p. 15) and HOPFMUELLER (2010, p. 32).

121 See PRETORIUS (2010, p. 219).

122 See KRYSTEK (1987, p. 67).

risk by combining the firm's liability structure with market prices of its assets.[123] Statistical models use both univariate and multivariate methods.

Among the most popular accounting-based models for identifying corporate distress is the Z-Score developed by ALTMAN (1968),[124] which explicitly measures the likelihood of a firm's bankruptcy. Its significance for turnaround management stems from its frequent use as an indicator of distress, and, during distress situations, as a metric to assess whether the company is a likely turnaround candidate.[125] In addition, it can indicate the severity of distress.[126] The generic Z-Score is the distillation into a single measure of a number of appropriately chosen accounting and market-based ratios, weighted and added (see EQUATION 1).[127] The result is a clear cut-off for financially healthy firms or potential failures: companies with a Z-Score below 2.67 (or, more conservatively, 1.81) are classified as going bankrupt by ALTMAN'S model. This multivariate approach has predictive ability up to two years.

Equation 1: Altman Z-Score.

$$Z = 0.012X_1 + 0.014X_2 + 0.033X_3 + 0.006X_4 + 0.999X_5$$

where:

X_1 = working capital^a/total assets; *with* ^{a} working capital = current assets - current liabilities,

X_2 = retained earnings/total assets,

X_3 = earnings before interest and taxes/total assets,

X_4 = market value equity/book value of total liabilities,

X_5 = sales/total assets, and

Z = overall index

Source: ALTMAN (1968, p. 594).

In the past, the Z-Score model was recognized as a highly reliable predictor of corporate failure.[128] Today, scholars criticize that a theoretical foundation for cutoff values–when a firm is in distress and when it is considered to be financially healthy–is missing.[129] In addition, researchers argue that the model has lost some of its classification power over recent

---

123 Compare for an overview OUTECHEVA (2007, pp. 87-104) and ALTMAN/HOTCHKISS (2006, pp. 233-259).

124 See for the following LAI (1997, p. 6) and SUDARSANAM/LAI (2001, pp. 187-188). In the UK, a deviation of Altman's Z-score model was developed; see TAFFLER (1983) and TAFFLER (1984). ALTMAN ET AL. (1977) developed ZETA, a second-generation model with several enhancements to the original Z-score approach.

125 See for example SMITH/GRAVES (2005), KANE/RICHARDSON (2002), or SUDARSANAM/LAI (2001).

126 See for example SMITH/GRAVES (2005), FRANCIS/DESAI (2005), or ROBBINS/PEARCE (1992).

127 Compare for the following ALTMAN (1968) and AGARWAL/TAFFLER (2007). For a detailed discussion of the elements of the Z-Score see ALTMAN (2000, pp. 9-12).

128 See SMITH/GRAVES (2005, p. 309), who focus on Taffler's Z-Score for the UK.

129 See LAI (1997, p. 24). BARKER/DUHAIME (1997) for example propose a cut-off of 3.0 "as the presence of a Z-Score below 3.0 suggests that one cannot predict with a high level of certainty that a firm will not go bankrupt in the near term." BARKER/DUHAIME (1997, p. 22). A Z-score below 3.0 serves as a screen to assure that there was a threat to firm survival and that firms with merely stagnating performance where not included in the sample.

decades.[130] Through its frequent use in turnaround research, there is a direct link to this research setting. But the main application for the Z-Score remains the prediction, and not the resolution, of financial distress.[131]

Effects of corporate crisis

Related to research into causes of corporate distress is research into its effects. The main research question is: What are the consequences of a firm's decline within and outside the organization?[132] Researchers have concentrated on delineating the impact of corporate crisis on the behavior of, for example, suppliers, customers, and employees.

In most cases, research on the consequences of decline examines negative effects, hence the focus on the cost of corporate distress.[133] These include direct costs, such as renegotiating debt or professional fees, and indirect costs, defined as lost opportunities such as lost sales, decreased productivity, or loss of market position. Besides the cost of distress, positive effects like increased motivation, increased willingness for change, or faster decision-making are also assumed in situations of corporate distress.[134] In combination, these effects can offer opportunities for change, but primarily they are assumed to threaten the firm's existence.[135]

This research stream is an essential part of a theory of corporate crisis, but only limited research has inquired into the effects of corporate crisis.[136] Even if literature by practitioners highlights the topic's importance, its complexity and scarcity of relevant data have limited research work.[137] In addition, "the lines between what is cause and what is consequence become increasingly blurry"[138] within a crisis setting.

Resolution of corporate crisis

The main objective of this research stream is to understand how companies, once distressed, can turn themselves around.[139] At present, no common "definition, classification, or

---

130 Compare the study of BEMMANN (2005) for details.

131 See CHAKRAVARTHY (1986, p. 446).

132 See for the following MAHESHWARI (2000, p. 41).

133 See for the following OUTECHEVA (2007, p. 61) and AROGYASWAMY ET AL. (1995, pp. 498-501). An alternative differentiation is between financial symptoms (for example, reduced reserves, increasing cost of capital, or reduced profitability) and organizational and structural symptoms (centralization of decision processes, reduced internal and external communication, or increased potential for conflict); see HOPFMUELLER (2010, p. 32) for details.

134 See ZIMMERMANN (1989, p. 114).

135 See D'AVENI (1989a, pp. 1120-1124).

136 Compare PANDIT (2000).

137 See OUTECHEVA (2007, p. 60) and BUSCHMANN (2006, p. 19).

138 HOPFMUELLER (2010, p. 32).

139 Resolution of corporate crisis is the same as corporate turnaround management.

vocabulary regarding turnaround" [140] exists. Turnaround in general can be described as "recovery of a firm's economic performance following an existence-threatening decline"[141].

Based on the framework of PETTIGREW (1987), research on corporate turnaround analyzes three dimensions: context, content, and process.[142] *Context* addresses the question of "why" and includes topics such as the analysis of market and competition, resources, stakeholder relationships, causes of decline, or severity of the distressed state. Activities used to overcome corporate crisis are analyzed under *content.* Operational, managerial, financial, and asset restructuring actions can be differentiated.[143] The third dimension of the framework, *process*, analyzes turnaround as a sequence or progression of events.[144] Separate sequences like distress, retrenchment, recovery, and finally turnaround are studied. Intensity, speed, and timing are relevant aspects of the turnaround process[145].

Resolution of corporate distress is at the heart of this dissertation. The next chapter reviews empirical research in this area.

2.2 Empirical research on corporate turnaround

This chapter surveys the large-sample studies of corporate turnaround. It explains the relevant research disciplines, summarizes the research subject, and describes the samples used. A detailed analysis of the distinct studies will be integrated into development of the theoretical framework in PART 3.

FIGURE 3 shows the most important empirical studies in the field of corporate turnaround. The focus is on 22 empirical large-sample studies published in academic journals, frequently cited in the literature, and considered to add significant value to the empirical literature concerning corporate turnaround.[146] For a supplementary overview of corporate turnaround literature, the work of LIOU/SMITH (2007) is recommended.[147]

---

140 HOPFMUELLER (2010, p. 34).

141 PANDIT (2000, p. 32).

142 See for the following PANDIT (2000, p. 37) and PETTIGREW (1987, pp. 3-7). This framework is popular for research on corporate turnaround; compare for example SCHLEY (2010), EICHNER (2008), or BUSCHMANN (2006) as recent applications.

143 See for the following SUDARSANAM/LAI (2001, pp. 184-187) and EICHNER (2008, pp. 42-43).

144 See for the following CHOWDHURY (2002, p. 250).

145 The analysis of the turnaround process is based on successful turnarounds. If unsuccessful turnarounds and non-distressed companies are considered, the more general term 'restructuring process' is preferred.

146 Case studies and anecdotal evidence are excluded from the literature review because the focus is on large-sample studies. Some additional large-sample studies often referred to are excluded for the following reasons: HAMBRICK/SCHECTER (1983), THIÉTART (1988), and CASTROGIOVANNI/BRUTON (2000) because of their focus on business units; CHOWDHURY/LANG (1994) and CHOWDHURY/LANG (1996) because of their focus on small companies; O'NEILL (1986a) because of his industry focus on commercial banking. A related research subject is bankruptcy or voluntary administration; see e.g. D'AVENI (1989a), D'AVENI

Since empirical research on corporate turnaround began in the mid-1970s, the subject has received considerable attention in the literature of strategy and finance, depending on the underlying theoretical framework.[148] These research streams differ in their center of attention (i.e., type of strategies examined), approach, and definition of performance decline, but clear distinctions among research streams cannot be drawn.[149] Both grounding theories are included in this dissertation because doing so can establish the internal validity of a theory of corporate turnaround by examining the distress and turnaround phenomena through the lenses of many disciplines.[150] Plausible alternative explanations for the effectiveness of various restructuring actions can only appear through application of alternative academic disciplines.

(1989a), and ROUTLEDGE/GADENNE (2004). Here the research focus is on distress because distress is a "much more common phenomenon than bankruptcy"; KANE/RICHARDSON (2002, pp. 3-4).

147 For a literature review, including anecdotes and case studies, see PANDIT (2000). Earlier literature reviews are provided by HOFFMAN (1989) and WEITZEL/JONSSON (1989). In addition, EICHNER (2008, p. 26) surveys empirical contributions, and SCHLEY (2010) provides an overview of results of empirical studies along the various research dimensions of corporate turnaround.

148 Compare EICHNER (2008, pp. 15-24) for an overview.

149 See SUDARSANAM/LAI (2001, p. 183).

150 Compare CARLILE/CHRISTENSEN (2005, p. 15), who recommend a multi-lens approach for any business research.

Figure 3: Empirical large-sample studies on corporate turnaround.

Study	Discipline	Research subject						Sample		
Author (Year)		Content				Process	Context	Size	Geo.	Industry
		MR	OR	FR	AR					
Schendel et al. (1976)	Strategy	x	x		x		x	54	US	Manuf.
Schendel/Patton (1976)	Strategy		x		x			72	US	Manuf.
Gilson (1989)	Finance	x					x	381	US	Multiple
Pant (1991)	Strategy						x	137	US	Multiple
John et al. (1992)	Finance	x	x	x	x	x	x	46	US	Multiple
Robbins/Pearce (1992)	Strategy		x		x	x	x	38	US	Manuf.
Ofek (1993)	Finance	x	x	x	x		x	358	US	Multiple
Barker/Mone (1994)	Strategy		x		x			32	US	Manuf.
Asquith et al. (1994)	Finance		x	x	x		x	102	US	Multiple
Kang/Shivdasani (1997)	Finance	x	x		x		x	92	AP	Manuf.
Barker/Duhaime (1997)	Strategy	x	x		x		x	120	US	Manuf.
Lai/Sudarsanam (1997)	Finance	x	x	x	x	x	x	297	UK	Multiple
Whitaker (1999)	Finance		x				x	267	US	Multiple
Denis/Kruse (2000)	Finance	x	x		x	x	x	339	US	Multiple
Sudarsanam/Lai (2001)	Strategy	x	x	x	x	x	x	188	UK	Multiple
Bruton et al. (2003)	Strategy	x	x		x		x	90	AP	Multiple
Francis/Desai (2005)	Strategy		x		x		x	97	US	Manuf.
Smith/Graves (2005)	Finance	x			x		x	102	UK	Manuf.
Morrow et al. (2007)	Strategy				x		x	178	US	Manuf.
Furrer et al. (2007)	Strategy		x				x	68	US	Manuf.
Lin et al. (2008)	Strategy		x	x	x		x	254	US	Multiple
Yawson (2009)	Finance	x	x	x	x	x	x	269	AP	Multiple

Abbreviations:
Geography: United States (US), United Kingdom (UK), Asia-Pacific (AP)
Restructuring content: managerial (MR), operational (OR), financial (FR), asset (AR)

Source: Own illustration.

The research setting of the selected empirical studies shows various differences with respect to the research subject as well as the samples used. The *research subject* is a single aspect in some studies, such as Furrer et al. (2007), who review only operational restructuring strategies. Other studies, such as Yawson (2009), provide comprehensive models featuring all three dimensions of corporate turnaround and all four categories of restructuring content. Due to the research setting, all but one study focus on the content of various restructuring strategies. The focus for the different categories of restructuring actions is on operational and asset restructuring; these are included in 18 studies. In most cases (16 studies) both categories are considered together. Managerial restructuring is included in the majority of studies (12 studies). Financial restructuring issues often have been neglected: so far only seven studies discuss some form of financial restructuring. Twenty studies include context factors in their analysis, thereby providing information about 'pre-conditions' for turnarounds. PANT (1991) even looks only at internal and external context factors of successful turnarounds. The final dimension, process, also has been neglected in turnaround research.[151] Even today, studies fail to take inter-temporal interdependencies into account.[152] Like YAWSON (2009), SUDARSANAM/LAI (2001), LAI/SUDARSANAM (1997), or JOHN ET AL. (1992), this dissertation chooses, in line with the three research questions outlined, a framework that includes all dimensions of corporate turnaround and all categories of restructuring content. This framework permits analyzing the effectiveness of different restructuring actions and the interactions among them and over time.

The *research samples* in the selected empirical studies differ in size, geography, and industry. Sample size ranges from 38 companies to large samples exceeding 380 firms. Most sample US companies (16 studies), although three studies analyzed companies from the UK and Asia-Pacific.[153] Industries examined vary: whereas eight studies examine manufacturing, 14 analyze multiple industries within one research setting.[154]

As outlined in SECTION 1.1.3, research on corporate turnaround is heterogeneous, and the reviewed large-sample studies have reached mixed conclusions so far.[155] An initial integration of the existing literature is provided in the next part of the dissertation.

151 Compare for the same conclusion PANDIT (2000).

152 Compare CHOWDHURY (2002, p. 250) and BALGOBIN/PANDIT (2001) for a similar conclusion.

153 Because of the selection of academic journals for the review, the geographic focus on the US is partially overstated. For studies with, for example, German companies see the dissertations of SCHLEY (2010), JOSTARNDT (2007), BUSCHMANN (2006), and NOTHARDT (2001). For an international approach including German, UK, and US companies see the dissertation of EICHNER (2008).

154 In most cases, industry selection is based on SIC codes, covers multiple industry sub-segments, and is not differentiated between OEMs and suppliers.

155 Compare PANDIT (2000, p. 31) and LIN ET AL. (2008, p. 540).

3. RESEARCH FOUNDATIONS: THEORETICAL FRAMEWORK AND HYPOTHESIS

This part establishes the theoretical basis for the later empirical analysis. First, because the wording in the existing literature is seldom unambiguous, the terms 'financial distress', 'corporate turnaround' and 'corporate restructuring' are defined in CHAPTER 3.1. CHAPTER 3.2 integrates existing theory and empirical findings into the theoretical framework of corporate turnaround among financially distressed automotive suppliers. As explained, the framework is structured along the three dimensions of content, process, and context with a focus on managerial, operational, financial, and asset restructuring actions. Based on this framework, hypotheses for the effectiveness of each restructuring activity within the turnaround process are derived. CHAPTER 3.3 summarizes the theoretical framework and corresponding hypotheses.

3.1 Definitions

3.1.1 Financial distress

The definition of distress in general and the selection of a distress criterion have major implications on research results, particularly in empirical research.[156] Definitions of what constitutes good and poor performance, which are determinative in the finding of a distress situation, have been imprecise since the earliest research on corporate turnaround, and researchers have markedly different understandings of distress.[157] This research concerns companies in financial distress, and in this section, financial distress is first positioned within the corporate crisis process. Then key requirements for distress criteria and an overview of generic performance measurement concepts are provided before the appropriate criterion to define financial distress is selected.

Positioning within crisis process

Figure 4: Stages of corporate distress.

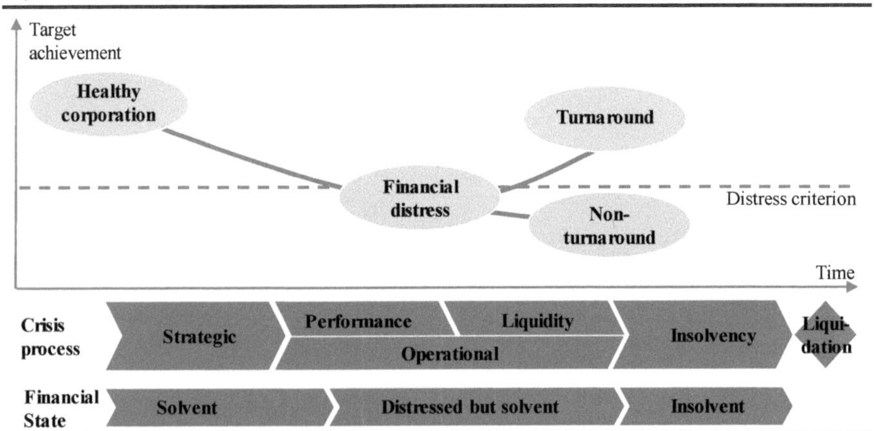

Source: Own illustration based on OUTECHEVA (2007, p. 24) and MÜLLER (1985, p. 40).

To identify financial distress and to create a sample of firms occupying the same discernible level of distress, various forms of distress must be considered. In the progression of corporate crisis (see FIGURE 4), financial distress is positioned at the onset of a liquidity crisis.[158] Per LIN ET AL. (2008), financial distress is defined as "a condition when a firm incurs more debt

156 Compare WINN (1993, p. 48) and PRETORIUS (2009, p. 1), who state that past researchers often did not examine the appropriateness of their performance measures used to define distress and instead chose measures to fit their data.

157 See BALCAEN (2009, p. 6) and HAMBRICK/SCHECTER (1983, p. 234). This leads to overlapping research populations and results with inconclusive results; compare WINN (1993, p. 48) and PRETORIUS (2009, p. 1).

158 Compare CHAPTER 2.1, which describes distress situations in general compared to the more specific situation of financial distress. Financial distress is one specific distress situation.

than its firm size, profitability, and asset composition can sustain. With declining ability to generate revenue coupled with inadequate cash flow from operations, a financially distressed firm will be trapped into severe liquidity problems, consequently affecting its solvency"[159]. Liquidity is the firm's ability to meet short-term obligations; solvency is its ability to pay long-term debts and long-term fixed expenses.

In this dissertation, the selection of financially distressed firms assures meaningful results because the distress level is severe enough to trigger managerial action but not so severe as to preclude recovery.[160] Managers of companies in financial distress can be expected to act soon after its onset, or the firm will cease to exist. Financial distress cannot persist for several years.[161] A homogeneous sample is established, and by identifying companies having the same intense need for change in order to recover, a comparison of turnaround actions is possible.[162] This study's attention to the financial distress phase differentiates it from research focused on continuous decline or poor performance, both of which can persist for years and do not necessarily trigger immediate remedial action.[163]

Key requirements

To identify companies in distress, the chosen distress criterion must fulfill three requirements: it must be clear without ambiguity, objective, and linkable to existing research.[164] *Clear without ambiguity* means the distress criterion must be easy to operationalize and that distractions, such as those caused by differing accounting standards or management manipulations, should be minimized to the extent possible.[165] The distress criterion must be *objective* to permit reliable replication among researchers and generalizability.[166] Also, objectivity of the performance measure is required in order to convert a distress criterion directly into a turnaround criterion.[167] *Linkability* to prior research allows the generalization of findings.[168] The distress criterion should have been found suitable within prior studies and, for an international context, have been applied in different geographies.[169]

---

159 LIN ET AL. (2008, p. 542). See for the following LIN ET AL. (2008, p. 549).

160 See SCHENDEL/PATTON (1976, p. 240) and BARKER/DUHAIME (1997, p. 15).

161 See WINN (1993, p. 54).

162 See BARKER/DUHAIME (1997, p. 15), CHOWDHURY (2002, p. 250), BRUTON ET AL. (2003, p. 526), and FALKENBERG ET AL. (2004, p. 22).

163 E.g., LEE ET AL. (1998) and THIÉTART (1988).

164 A fourth requirement, ability to identify a defined level of distress, is already included by selecting financially distressed companies.

165 See for the following EICHNER (2008, pp. 45-47) and WOYWODE (2004, p. 23).

166 See BRUTON (1989, pp. 18-23), BARKER/MONE (1994, p. 399), and WOYWODE (2004, p. 40). Subjective or impressionistic measures often will not assure that results can be compared among researchers or replicated; see ROBBINS/PEARCE (1992, p. 295).

167 See CHOWDHURY (2002, p. 256) and EICHNER (2008, p. 46).

168 See WINN (1993, p. 49).

169 See O'NEILL (1986a, pp. 167-168) and EICHNER (2008, p. 47).

Performance measurement concepts

Selection of the appropriate criterion to define financial distress is based on three generic concepts of performance measurement: the domain for performance measurement, the mode of assessment, and the source of data. The dominant *domain for performance measurement* in empirical strategy research, not only for distress and turnaround, is financial performance.[170] Financial performance is the narrowest conception of business performance and centers on the use of simple outcome-based financial indicators that are assumed to reflect the fulfillment of the firm's economic goals. It assumes the dominance and legitimacy of financial goals in a firm's system of goals. Prior research shows that financial measures are useful as a basis for understanding phases of corporate decline and subsequent turnaround.[171]

The *mode of assessment* may be perceptual or objective.[172] In the turnaround literature, a variety of perceptual distress definitions, hence definitions by judgment of corporate performance, are found to identify distressed companies.[173] But due to the unspecific, qualitative approach, perceptual performance measures suffer from bias.[174] Objective performance measures are record-based and can be differentiated by their *source of data*: primary or secondary. But even for objective data reported from primary sources, the possibility of bias cannot be ruled out.[175] In comparison, secondary sources are common sources for financial data.[176] Objective performance measures from secondary sources offer the advantages that they permit replication and they are suited for the context of corporate-level research. The remainder of this chapter focuses primarily on objective performance metrics from secondary sources in the financial domain of corporate performance.

Distress criterion

This paragraph addresses the important question for research on corporate distress and turnaround of "What is an appropriate performance criterion to identify financial distress?"[177]

---

170 Compare for the following VENKATRAMAN/RAMANUJAM (1986, pp. 803-804), who differentiates three domains for performance measurement: financial performance, business performance, and organizational effectiveness.

171 See PEARCE/DOH (2002, p. 5). This is especially true for large companies; compare KEASEY/WATSON (1987, p. 336).

172 Compare VENKATRAMAN/RAMANUJAM (1987, p. 110).

173 Compare NOTHARDT (2001, pp. 146-150) for an overview. This literature mainly stems from practitioners like consultants, interim managers or bankers and the performance definitions are often global and impressionistic; see BRUTON (1989, pp. 18-23).

174 See HURRLE/KIESER (2005) for a discussion of key informant bias.

175 See VENKATRAMAN/RAMANUJAM (1986, p. 808).

176 See VENKATRAMAN/RAMANUJAM (1986, p. 808). Secondary published data are easy to access, and popular databases which have proven reliable in this research context include for example Compustat, Worldscope, or Datastream; compare CHOWDHURY (2002, p. 249).

177 SUDARSANAM/LAI (2001, p. 184). After analysis of the literature concerning corporate turnaround LAI (1997) even concluded "there exist as many definitions of distress as there are empirical studies on this subject"; LAI (1997, p. 17).

The review of existing empirical studies shows that no consensus definition for a performance measure in distress-related research exists. Disparate accounting- and market-based distress criteria are used. This dissertation uses accounting-based criteria as its definition because market-based definitions cannot be considered objective: they incorporate expectations of the value of any restructuring or disciplinary action following a performance decline.[178] In addition, stock prices and returns are influenced both by company fundamentals and by supply and demand and market sentiment,[179] all of which hinder creation of a homogeneous sample.[180]

In line with EICHNER (2008) and ASQUITH ET AL. (1994), this study's definition of financial distress is based on interest coverage. A firm is considered financially distressed if "earnings before interest, taxes, depreciation, and amortization (EBITDA) less capital expenditure (CAPEX) – becomes insufficient to cover net interest payments"[181]. Negative interest coverage provides a natural breakpoint to identify distress and is an efficient means of identifying companies in financial distress.[182] EBITDA avoids distortions from varying depreciation policies or greater prudence in writing down assets and excludes extraordinary items like gains or losses on asset sales.[183] Changes in EBITDA capture much of the theorized effects of financial distress on firm performance and control somewhat for the impact of earnings management.[184] Further, interest coverage as a distress criterion is used by YAWSON (2009), EICHNER (2008), JOSTARNDT (2007), KANG/SHIVDASANI (1997), and ASQUITH ET AL. (1994). That is, the selected distress criterion has been applied in different regions like the US, UK, Germany, Australia, as well as Japan and provides a direct link to existing research.

---

178 See YAWSON (2009, p. 218) and DENIS/KRUSE (2000, p. 398).

179 See STARBUCK (2005, p. 282), who notes that stock prices as indicators of performance are more volatile than profit measures and information with no specific relationship to the single company may have a strong impact on stock prices.

180 See for the following ASQUITH ET AL. (1994, p. 628) and KANG/SHIVDASANI (1997, p. 34). Possible problems with accounting-based measures arise when management becomes aware of performance problems well before these problems become evident in accounting-based performance measures, and creative accounting or earnings manipulation are initiated in decline situations; see WEITZEL/JONSSON (1989, p. 101). Also there are differences among firms in the timing of the release of financial reports during the calendar year and in the timing of financial reports relative to other news resources; see JOHN ET AL. (1992, p. 893). This means that a distress definition based on accounting data may identify the starting point of distress incorrectly and the speed with which turnaround actions occur is overstated; see DENIS/KRUSE (2000, p. 401).

181 EICHNER (2008, p. 47). EBITDA is used a proxy for operating cash flow to assure a close link to existing research. The problem is that if a firm has sufficient liquid funds to meet interest payments, management action may not be triggered because there is no clear sign of distress; see ASQUITH ET AL. (1994, p. 628).

182 Compare also YAWSON (2009, p. 218) and KANG/SHIVDASANI (1997, p. 33), who use positive interest coverage as an indicator that the firm is not in distress.

183 See LAI (1997), WHITAKER (1999), and BUSCHMANN (2006).

184 See YAWSON (2009, p. 218).

Besides defining financial distress, the onset of financial distress must be correctly identified to capture the trigger function.[185] This trigger requires not only distress as a static state, but must capture the step of deterioration.[186] It is the year-on-year decline of performance that causes attention and triggers remedial restructuring. The fall of a firm from superior, stable, high performance normally points to fundamental problems with its management and strategies.[187] Firms experiencing abrupt performance declines are more likely to react quickly.[188] Therefore, a one-year pre-distress phase with positive interest coverage is established to enable a common starting point of the analysis and to serve as a temporal baseline.

3.1.2 Corporate turnaround

The definition of 'turnaround' is directly related to the definition of 'distress' since for objectivity demands the distress criterion has to be directly convertible into a turnaround criterion.[189] The definition of corporate turnaround includes the definition of the turnaround criterion itself and the duration of the restructuring process, hence at what point of time the criterion is applied.

In general, a corporate turnaround is a reversal in direction and can be described as "recovery of a firm's economic performance following an existence-threatening decline"[190]. This definition means that the company restores performance to its pre-distress levels and no longer meets the definition of being in distress.[191] For this research, a distressed company is considered a successful turnaround if it restores positive interest coverage. The duration of the turnaround criterion is recommended to be the same as for the distress criterion; therefore, a one-year period is used to define if the company is a turnaround or a non-turnaround.[192]

---

185 See DENIS/KRUSE (2000, p. 401).

186 See for the following EICHNER (2008, pp. 46-47).

187 See SUDARSANAM/LAI (2001, pp. 184, 207), this requirement also avoids sampling companies whose performance decline is due to short term volatility of their share prices if a market-based performance measure is used.

188 See DENIS/SHOME (2005, p. 446). A homogeneous sample requires that the stage of decline is aligned with the expected turnaround actions. The problem is that for gradually declining firms or lingering firms the clear starting point for their difficulties is hard to identify. Only with short-term distress, hence with sudden decline, is there a clearly identifiable trigger for management action. This directly influences the duration of the distress phase: The longer the timeframe to identify distressed firms, the more the sample will include continuously declining firms. If the aim is to study turnaround actions initiated because of the distress state, the focus should be on firms that experience sudden decline, not ongoing performance problems. Selecting firms with one year of poor performance assures identification of responses to short-term distress and makes it possible to evaluate the speed with which a firm reacts to a decline in value. Compare D'AVENI (1989b, p. 579), OFEK (1993, p. 7), DENIS/KRUSE (2000, p. 398), CHOWDHURY (2002, p. 255), FRANCIS/DESAI (2005, p. 1209) and DAS/LECLERE (2003, p. 3).

189 See CHOWDHURY (2002, p. 256) and EICHNER (2008, p. 46).

190 PANDIT (2000, p. 32). See also CHAPTER 2.1.

191 See SUDARSANAM/LAI (2001, p. 187), KANE ET AL. (2006, pp. 13-14), or CHOWDHURY (2002, p. 256).

192 Compare CHOWDHURY/LANG (1996, p. 172). The definition of the turnaround phase must assure that a

After defining a positive interest coverage ratio for one year as the turnaround criterion, the next question concerns after what period of time this criterion is applied.[193] HAMBRICK/SCHECTER (1983) point out that "the amount of time required for [the] turnaround [process] is of interest both for its practical significance and in developing a research design"[194]. Typically, turnarounds are defined as a recovery immediately following a period of decline, and many turnaround studies implicitly treat turnaround responses and improved results as almost simultaneous events.[195] An example would be to require a positive interest coverage ratio for the first year after the distress year.[196] In this paper, a transition or interval is introduced before firms are classified as turnarounds or non-turnarounds.[197] The rationale for this transition phase is that a substantial time must pass before results of turnaround strategies appear. Accordingly, there is no need to link the progression of decline and the beginning of the turnaround directly.[198]

The length of transition is important, as this choice must allow for the drawn-out nature of recovery and for the feedback effects of early-stage strategies.[199] If the period is too short, selected strategies might not improve performance, and potential candidates for turnaround may be prematurely categorized as failures. If the period is too long, the effects of some short-term strategies are likely to be masked by those of long-term strategies deployed later in the transition as turnaround actions subsequently decline in following years. The definition of the turnaround timeframe also relates to the research framework because different stages or sequences of moves occur during turnaround.[200] According to the existing literature, the effectiveness of restructuring efforts is usually apparent within three years following the onset of distress.[201] Therefore, a two-year transition period is used, and firms are categorized as turnarounds or non-turnarounds in the third year after the onset of distress.[202]

---

lasting improvement in performance is established and avoid that firms are prematurely considered successful or unsuccessful turnaround; see THIÉTART (1988, p. 44), CHOWDHURY (2002, p. 256), and PEARCE (2007, p. 255). To avoid bias, multiple distress situations were excluded from the sampling process; see CHAPTER 4.1.

193 The definition of the timing pattern is important because such a temporal analysis provides more insight into the dynamics of corporate recovery; see SUDARSANAM/LAI (2001, p. 197). Some of the mixed results of prior studies appear to derive from differences in the choice of timing pattern; compare HOLDER-WEBB ET AL. (2005, p. 322).

194 See HAMBRICK/SCHECTER (1983, p. 235).

195 See WINN (1993, p. 52) and CHOWDHURY (2002, p. 255).

196 This can also be labeled as a minus-plus pattern.

197 This view accords with the four-stage model of decline, response initiation, transition, and outcome by CHOWDHURY (2002). A slightly different model is proposed by BALGOBIN/PANDIT (2001), who distinguish the five stages as decline and crisis, trigger for change, recovery strategy formulation, retrenchment and stabilization, and return to growth.

198 See CHOWDHURY (2002, pp. 255-256) and PAJUNEN (2005, p. 426).

199 See for the following SUDARSANAM/LAI (2001, p. 197).

200 See HAMBRICK/SCHECTER (1983, p. 235).

201 Compare LIN ET AL. (2008), DENIS/KRUSE (2000), and KANG/SHIVDASANI (1997).

202 At the same time, a two-year transition period often will not allow all turnaround attempts (or their

3.1.3 Corporate restructuring

Corporate restructuring is the last construct to be defined in the context of corporate turnaround. Again, the literature offers no single definition.[203] It can be described as the process of turning around a weak firm or increasing the value of a strong firm.[204] Even if the focus here is on specific restructuring actions by distressed firms, this definition already emphasizes that the concept of corporate restructuring is not limited to distressed firms.[205]

For this research, the definitional scope of corporate restructuring is broad, encompassing numerous actions in the categories of managerial, operational, financial, and asset restructuring (see FIGURE 5).[206]

Figure 5: Corporate restructuring categories.

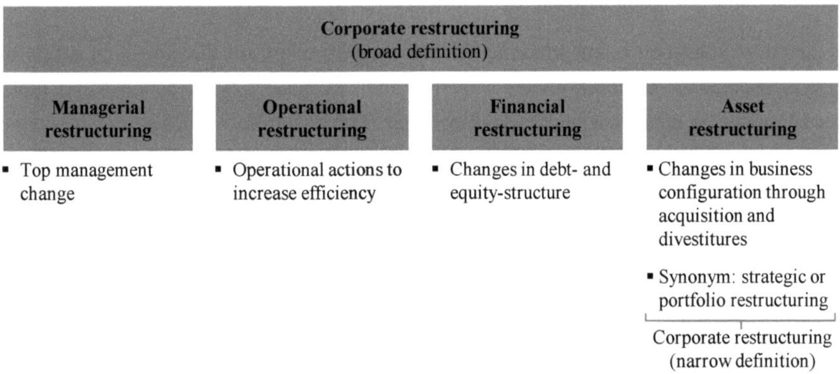

Source: Own illustration based on SUDARSANAM/LAI (2001, pp. 184-187).[207]

aftermaths) to be seen in their entirety and could limit the study; see HAMBRICK/SCHECTER (1983, p. 237). Some researchers argue that a five-year span may be too short to observe a lasting improvement, because the strategic actions identified may temporarily relieve a troubled business without solving the real problem; see THIÉTART (1988, p. 44). However, as long as general tendencies are not altered, the results should not be affected if a two-year transition period is chosen and the research results provide valid guidelines for appropriate actions; see HOLDER-WEBB ET AL. (2005, p. 322). This definition of the timeframe also aligns with the selection of the distress state because financial distress cannot persist for several years; see WINN (1993, p. 54).

203 Compare SCHMITT (2009, p. 37).

204 See HURRY (1993, p. 70).

205 This broad concept of corporate restructuring is the basis for comparing distressed and non-distressed firms for the second research question.

206 See YAWSON (2009, p. 216), DENIS/SHOME (2005, p. 427), and SUDARSANAM/LAI (2001, p. 183). A narrow view of corporate restructuring focuses exclusively on asset restructuring such as acquisitions or divestitures. Compare ACHLEITNER ET AL. (2003, p. 435), BOWMAN ET AL. (1999, pp. 34-36), and BOWMAN/SINGH (1993, pp. 6-12).

207 For a general overview of the corporate restructuring concept compare ACHLEITNER ET AL. (2003), BOWMAN ET AL. (1999), and BOWMAN/SINGH (1993). For an overview of corporate restructuring in the turnaround context compare SUDARSANAM/LAI (2001).

Managerial restructuring encompasses changes to the firm's top management. Although it pertains to changes to the senior management team in general, in most cases the CEO is the focus.

Operational restructuring comprises a variety of actions and aims at improving efficiency, controlling costs, and coping with the changing business environment.[208] This includes revenue growth strategies and cost-cutting or employee layoffs.

Financial restructuring is broadly related to the firm's debt-equity structure and its corresponding changes.[209] Equity issuance and changes in dividend payments affect the company's shareholders, whereas debt issuance and changes in interest or principal payments affect its debt holders.

Changes to the firm's business configuration are *asset restructuring* activities.[210] Asset restructuring is the narrowest definition of corporate restructuring. Strategic or portfolio restructuring are often used as synonyms. Asset restructuring includes contraction initiatives such as the sale of subsidiaries, disposal of plants, property and equipment, or the closing of business units.[211] It also includes asset expansions—for example, acquisitions, joint ventures or expansion of production facilities.

Most categories of restructuring include retrenchment activities, called belt-tightening, and activities of an entrepreneurial, growth-oriented nature, called recovery.[212] Each of the four restructuring categories is included in the theoretical framework for the empirical analysis, and the rationales for restructuring actions within single categories are detailed in the next chapter.

3.2 Research framework

3.2.1 Preliminaries

The research framework for corporate turnaround is based on the three dimensions of research on management and strategic change by PETTIGREW (1987) and analyzes the context, content, and process dimension (see FIGURE 6).[213] The research framework emphasizes the content

---

208 See for the following LIN ET AL. (2008, p. 540), SUDARSANAM/LAI (2001, pp. 184-187) and EICHNER (2008, pp. 52-53).

209 Compare for the following YAWSON (2009, p. 222).

210 Asset restructuring is a synonym for portfolio or strategic restructuring; see SUDARSANAM/LAI (2001, p. 186) and BOWMAN/SINGH (1993, pp. 8-10).

211 See for the following YAWSON (2009, p. 224).

212 See ROBBINS/PEARCE (1992).

213 See for the following PANDIT (2000, p. 37) and PETTIGREW (1987, pp. 3-7). This framework is popular for research on corporate turnaround; compare for example SCHLEY (2010), EICHNER (2008), or BUSCHMANN

dimension, hence the examination of automotive suppliers' actions to overcome financial distress. The process dimension analyzes the sequence and progression of turnaround actions. Context addresses the situational factors that might impact the effectiveness of the selected turnaround actions.

Figure 6: Overview research framework.

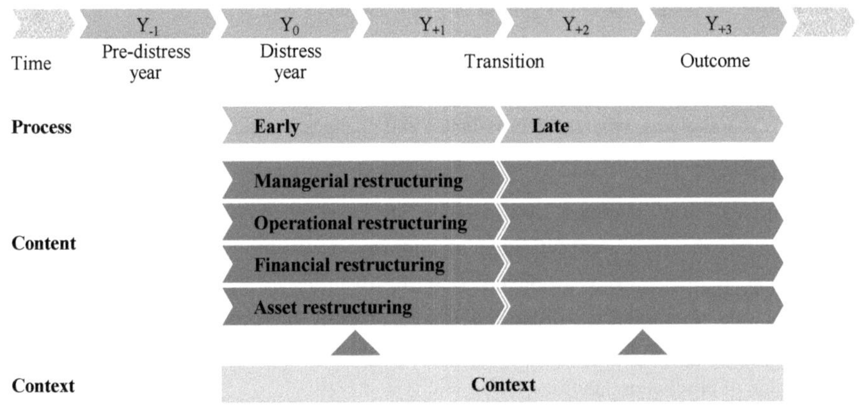

Source: Own illustration.

This empirical analysis weighs the effectiveness of various restructuring activities. Because each restructuring action is examined over time, the process aspects of corporate turnaround are discussed first (SECTION 3.2.2). The development of hypotheses for the four categories of restructuring content is at the center of the theoretical framework (SECTION 3.2.3). Situational context factors that might influence the effectiveness of restructuring actions are discussed afterward (SECTION 3.2.5). The organization of restructuring actions into turnaround archetypes is introduced in the last section (SECTION 3.2.6).

3.2.2 Process

The restructuring or turnaround process[214] is a central dimension in analyzing corporate turnaround and encompasses the "temporal pattern of deployment of recovery strategies"[215]. A literature review shows that the process dimension is neglected in turnaround research, even if many scholars acknowledge its importance in explaining corporate turnaround.[216] Restructuring actions are undertaken in part simultaneously and in part sequentially and have

(2006) as recent applications. See also CHAPTER 2.1.

214 In the context of successful turnarounds, the process can be labeled 'turnaround process'. In a more general setting including the process of unsuccessful turnarounds, the term 'restructuring process' is preferred; compare also FOOTNOTE 145.

215 SUDARSANAM/LAI (2001, pp. 197-198).

216 Compare BALGOBIN/PANDIT (2001), who quote PANDIT (2000) and HOFFMAN (1989).

joint and overlapping effects on the probability of turnaround.[217] Therefore, not only the choice of restructuring actions themselves but also chronology contributes to the difference between successful and unsuccessful turnarounds.[218] Prior research shows that although turnaround and non-turnaround firms explore the same restructuring actions, priorities between these two groups shifted over time.[219] When, for example, short-term measures are implemented too late, the decline cannot be reversed.[220] Only the joint empirical observation of process and content can help to explain relationships in the corporate turnaround phenomenon.[221]

Based on the chosen turnaround definition, companies are categorized as turnaround or non-turnaround in the third year (Y_{+3}) after the onset of distress (Y_0). By including the year of onset, a four-year timeframe of corporate restructuring actions is analyzed. This four-year timeframe provides an equal length period for comparison and accords with existing research that shows extensive restructuring under way during the year of distress (Y_{-0}) and the following year (Y_{-1}), and a slightly lower but still considerable amount of restructuring in the second and third years after onset (Y_{+2} and Y_{+3}).[222] The onset year (Y_0) is explicitly included because firms typically respond to distress when difficulties become obvious.[223]

For the necessary multi-period examination of the restructuring process, the definition of generic stages is required.[224] Existing research differentiates two main phases within the turnaround: retrenchment and recovery.[225] The first stage, retrenchment, targets the immediate stabilization of declining performance and includes reductions in costs and assets.[226] The objectives are survival of the company and reestablishment of positive interest coverage. Restructuring actions are often efficiency-oriented. Recovery, the second and partially

217 See SUDARSANAM/LAI (2001, p. 187).

218 Compare CHOWDHURY (2002, p. 256), who quotes HOFFMAN (1989) and SCHENDEL/PATTON (1976).

219 Compare SUDARSANAM/LAI (2001, p. 192).

220 See CHOWDHURY (2002, p. 255).

221 See CHOWDHURY (2002) and PETTIGREW (1992). CHOWDHURY (2002, p. 250) states that the linkage of content and process “lays at the heart of a good theory”.

222 Compare DENIS/KRUSE (2000), OFEK (1993), and KANG/SHIVDASANI (1997). JOHN ET AL. (1992) point to the fact that some policy changes in response to distress could have begun before the initial onset of distress; compare JOHN ET AL. (1992, p. 897). This is especially important when the definition of distress covers multiple years. The problem is minimized in this dissertation by the plus-minus pattern in the distress definition and by excluding companies with multiple distress situations from the sample; see CHAPTER 4.1.

223 Compare DEANGELO/DEANGELO (1990, p. 1420), who show this with respect to dividend reductions.

224 See SUDARSANAM/LAI (2001, p. 183).

225 This differentiation was introduced by ROBBINS/PEARCE (1992), and the role of retrenchment is still discussed heatedly. Compare MORROW ET AL. (2004), FRANCIS/PETT (2004), or PAJUNEN (2005). Several variations of this two-stage model exist; compare for an overview EICHNER (2008, p. 56), who discusses the models of BIBEAULT (1982), HAMBRICK/SCHECTER (1983), AROGYASWAMY ET AL. (1995), and FILATOTCHEV/TOMS (2006).

226 See for the following ROBBINS/PEARCE (1992, p. 290).

overlapping stage, includes restructuring actions that stimulate financial performance. The objective is to assure long-term profitability and growth.

Figure 7: Restructuring process.

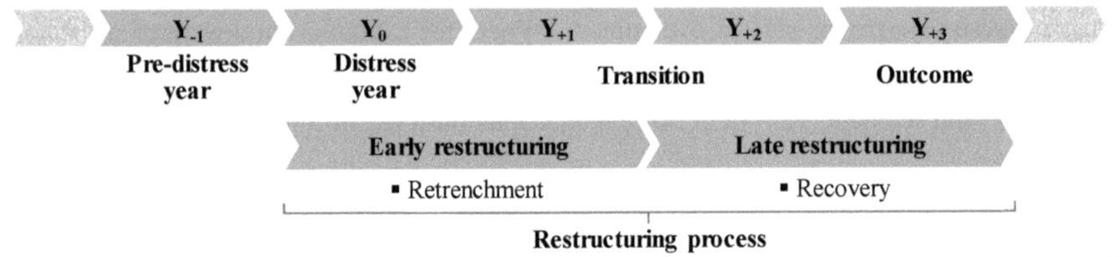

Source: Own illustration based on EICHNER (2008, p. 70).

Following EICHNER (2008), the differentiation between early restructuring (Y_0 and Y_{+1}) and late restructuring (Y_{+2} and Y_{+3}) is introduced (see FIGURE 7).[227] The temporal deployment of each restructuring action within these two phases is analyzed and integrated into the empirical analysis of restructuring effectiveness. Analyzing the time periods of the turnaround process should provide "more insight into the dynamics of corporate revival"[228] and in addition a change in the restructuring activities is expected for Y_{+2} and the following years.[229]

3.2.3 Content

3.2.3.1 Overview

Content is the 'what' of change and includes analysis of actions undertaken to overcome distress situations.[230] The empirical analysis examines the managerial, operational, financial, and asset restructuring carried out after companies become financially distressed. The restructuring actions were chosen for analysis because they are frequently recommended in the literature of corporate turnaround.[231] Selected restructuring actions must be relevant and observable.[232] Relevant means that existing theory and empirical findings consider the activity to influence corporate turnaround. Observable means the research employs secondary sources accessible to an external observer. Based on the literature review, nine key restructuring actions are identified (see FIGURE 8).[233]

---

227 Compare EICHNER (2008, pp. 69-75).

228 FRANCIS/DESAI (2005, pp. 1220-1221).

229 Compare the research of DENIS/KRUSSE (2000), OFEK (1993), and KANG/SHIVDASANI (1997).

230 See PETTIGREW (1987, p. 5) and PANDIT (2000, p. 37).

231 This approach accords with SMITH/GRAVES (2005) and THIÉTART (1988, p. 37).

232 See for the following EICHNER (2008, p. 77).

233 Partially, capital expenditure intensity is considered an operational restructuring activity, compare for example NAUJOKS (2012, p. 14) or EICHNER (2008, p. 53). This research follows the view of SUDARSANAM/LAI (2001, pp. 189) who consider capital expenditures one special form of asset restructuring.

Figure 8: Restructuring content.

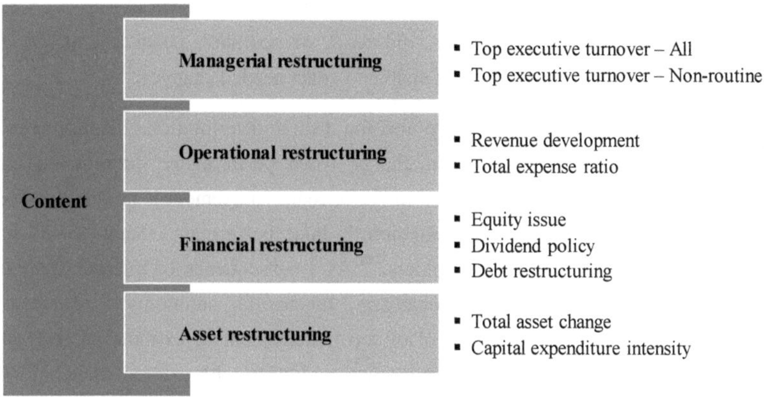

Source: Own illustration.

The central issue in managerial restructuring is replacement of the firm's top manager, in most cases the CEO. Routine and non-routine replacements are differentiated. Operational restructuring includes revenue growth and cost-cutting. Debt restructuring, equity issuance, and dividend cuts are the main financial restructuring actions of interest. Asset restructuring includes both expanding and reducing total assets and changes in capital expenditures. The remainder of this section discusses each of these variables, the rationale for their effectiveness in turnarounds, and existing empirical evidence. Key hypotheses are derived for the theorized impact of restructuring actions within the two phases of the turnaround process.

3.2.3.2 Managerial restructuring

Managerial restructuring—changing top management—is widely cited as a precondition for successful turnarounds and is considered a "first level action"[234]. Management changes can be distinguished as routine (unforced) and non-routine (forced), hence whether the change is part of the turnaround efforts or just part of the normal course of business. Distressed companies often invoke the former—i.e., they replace their top executive[235] for reasons other than retirement, illness, or death.

Top management affects the decisions that influence organizational performance and is therefore directly associated with the company's distressed situation.[236] Management inaction

---

234 SCHENDEL ET AL. (1976, p. 11). See also SUDARSANAM/LAI (2001, pp. 184-185) who quote BIBEAULT (1982), HOFER (1980), SLATTER (1984), and LAI/SUDARSANAM (1997, pp. 197-198).

235 In general, the CEO is considered the firm's top executive. If the position of CEO is not formally established, as is customary for Asian firms, the president or chairman is considered the top executive. Compare BRUTON (1989, p. 526).

236 See BARKER/BARR (2002, p. 963).

is said to be responsible for many distressed organizations because managers persist with a course of action, being unable to adapt to change and create a culture for change.[237] A distress situation can be seen as one in which "old ways of operating need to undergo drastic change"[238] and incumbent management is unable to enact needed changes.[239]

If management can be held responsible for the firm's deterioration, dismissing current management seems logical, as those in charge when performance deteriorated are not considered capable of correcting the situation.[240] Current management is assumed to lack the knowledge and insight to rectify the situation.[241] Poor performance leads to the loss of management's credibility among stakeholders.[242] As a consequence of internal and external corporate controls and monitoring mechanisms, managerial autonomy is reduced as a disciplinary pressure, leading to dismissal of top management in extreme cases.[243] During distress, top management is stigmatized and loses credibility with external stakeholders and employees.[244] Boards of directors believe managerial restructuring will restore investor confidence in their ability to act decisively in times of trouble, and debt holders expect to deal with a new, credible management in the case of a debt restructuring.[245]

Although empirical evidence documents that distress leads to replacing the incumbent senior management,[246] the effectiveness of managerial restructuring on corporate turnaround is not conclusively established.[247] The impact on financial performance of replacing top management is only indirect.[248] Three arguments show the importance of new management for successful turnarounds and why management turnover might be significant for corporate turnaround. First, the company's internal climate and decision processes are important for the

---

237 See WEITZEL/JONSSON (1989, p. 100), SCHENDEL ET AL. (1976, p. 11), and PRETORIUS (2010, p. 223). CHOWDHURY/LANG (1993, p. 8) use the threat-rigidity theory that management faces a sudden crisis and freezes into inaction—i.e., experiences cognitive rigidity. Although this dissertation examines sudden crises (plus-minus pattern of distress), the same logic applies when management fails to detect or react to a creeping crisis; compare PRETORIUS (2010, p. 223).

238 SUDARSANAM/LAI (2001, pp. 184-185).

239 See SUDARSANAM/LAI (2001, pp. 184-185).

240 Compare PRETORIUS (2010, p. 223) for further references.

241 See WEITZEL/JONSSON (1989, p. 100).

242 See CASTROGIOVANNI/BRUTON (2000, pp. 26-27).

243 See DENIS/KRUSE (2000, pp. 392-395). Internal and external corporate controls include, but are not limited to, monitoring by the board of directors, large blockholders, the takeover market, and other managers within the firm; see DENIS/KRUSE (2000, p. 395).
YAWSON (2009, p. 224) examines the role of the board that removes the incumbent CEO, which has received support in the empirical literature.

244 See AROGYASWAMY ET AL. (1995, p. 506).

245 See YAWSON (2009, p. 224) and SUDARSANAM/LAI (2001, p. 205).

246 Compare for example GILSON (1989, pp. 246-247), BARKER/DUHAIME (1997, p. 33), or DENIS/KRUSE (2000, p. 411). For an overview see YAWSON (2009, p. 224). Some empirical evidence shows that the incidence of CEO turnover does not significantly differ for distressed and non-distressed firms; compare SMITH/GRAVES (2005, pp. 315-316).

247 See SUDARSANAM/LAI (2001, p. 184).

248 See SUDARSANAM/LAI (2001, p. 192).

turnaround process, and top management influences those significantly.[249] Second, a new top management heightens the level of strategic change by instilling a sense of fresh direction throughout the firm.[250] In addition, the new management lacks personal commitments to previous policies, and former managements' pet projects frequently are divested. Third, even if the causes for poor performance are beyond top management's control, financially distressed situations need support from multiple stakeholders, and replacing top management suggests to bankers, investors, and employees that something positive will be done to improve performance.[251]

As for the effectiveness of managerial restructuring in the turnaround process, research shows that the successor management has a long-term influence on performance with a one-to–two-year time-lag for observation of results.[252] This effect can be due to two reasons. First, evidence suggests that incoming executives manage earnings early in their tenure and that reported earnings therefore are lower immediately following replacement of the top executive.[253] Second, anecdotal evidence shows that a new top executive's first priority is to establish a long-term plan before operational measures are implemented. [254] Despite the persuasive argument for replacing top management in distress situations, negative consequences can be expected if top management has valuable connections and replacement is difficult.[255]

Regarding the timing of the top executive change, if it is "deferred too long by hesitant corporate boards, the crisis might have evolved too far for bringing about a near term turnaround."[256] After two years the incumbent CEO is expected to have initiated turnaround actions and that late replacement causes disruptions in the organization.[257]

Although the focus for distressed companies is on forced top executive changes, prior research also shows that a general replacement of the top executive increases the level of change within the company and is positively related to turnaround.[258] To account for the

---

249 See SMITH/GRAVES (2005, p. 311).

250 See for the following YAWSON (2009, pp. 224, 229) and BARKER/DUHAIME (1997, pp. 18-20).

251 See SUDARSANAM/LAI (2001, pp. 184-185).

252 See YAWSON (2009, pp. 226-228).

253 For a detailed discussion of earnings management during financial distress, compare LEE (2000, pp. 25-27). See also DENIS/KRUSE (2000, p. 401), who do not find empirical evidence for this effect in their sample by testing differences in performance in the year of top management turnover with a sample of companies with no turnover. By using EBITDA, this effect should be minimized in this sample.

254 See YAWSON (2009, p. 227).

255 This discussion is related to the importance of social capital of top management; compare BRUTON (1989, p. 526) for further references and the differentiation between Western firms and East Asian firms.

256 EICHNER (2009, p. 95).

257 See EICHNER (2008, p. 95), who quotes HOFER (1980), BIBEAULT (1982) or FILATOTCHEV/TOMS (2006)

258 Compare for example SCHENDEL ET AL. (1976, pp. 8-9) and BARKER/DUHAIME (1997, p. 33). BRUTON ET AL. (2003) also analyze top executive turnover in general, but find no significant impact on corporate turnaround.

differences of routine and non-routine turnarounds, the research framework includes top executive changes in general and forced changes specifically.

Hypothesis 1.1a

Top executive changes during the early restructuring phase are positively related to the probability of a successful turnaround for financially distressed automotive suppliers.

Hypothesis 1.1b

Top executive changes during the late restructuring phase are negatively related to the probability of a successful turnaround for financially distressed automotive suppliers.

Hypothesis 1.2a

Forced (non-routine) top executive changes during the early restructuring phase are positively related to the probability of a successful turnaround for financially distressed automotive suppliers.

Hypothesis 1.2b

Forced (non-routine) top executive changes during the late restructuring phase are negatively related to probability of a successful turnaround for financially distressed automotive suppliers.

3.2.3.3 Operational restructuring

Operational restructuring strategies comprise a number of actions to generate short-term cash flow and profit improvement.[259] Operational restructuring often is considered essential to improve efficiency, control costs, and cope with the changing business environment.[260] But existing empirical research found mixed conclusions if operational restructuring establishes firms in a more efficient and competitive position or if it disrupts organizations, unsettles a business, and creates uncertainty about a firm's prospects. The focus here is on revenue generation and cost-reduction.[261]

Revenue growth

The first operational restructuring activity is revenue growth. Revenue growth is considered essential for the recovery of distressed firms and partially even as the single-most important

259 See SUDARSANAM/LAI (2001, pp. 185-186).

260 See for the following LIN ET AL. (2008, p. 540).

261 Revenue growth and cost reduction are more the results of management actions than discrete management actions themselves. Still, their use as a proxy is common within turnaround research; compare SUDARSANAM/LAI (2001, p. 185) and the discussion of observability in SUB-SECTION 3.2.3.1.

activity in corporate turnaround.[262] Since the first empirical studies of turnarounds, actions to increase sales have been cited as important aspects of corporate turnaround.[263]

Internal and external revenue growth can be differentiated. Internal revenue growth derives from the firm's extant resources, and external growth primarily comes from acquisitions.[264] Internal revenue growth is the issue for operational restructuring because growth from acquisitions is linked to asset restructuring. Internal revenue generation strategies can have a short-term operational character—for instance, sales promotions, price changes, and advertising—or a more strategic character, such as new products and services, delivery approaches, and territories.[265] Revenue growth seems feasible for companies whose product portfolio remains competitive and demand is sufficient. [266] Another argument for the beneficial effect of revenue growth is its impact on the company's efficiency.[267] Directors of distressed firms believe "that an aggressive revenue growth strategy" [268] can lead to turnarounds. Higher revenues from the same resource base show an increase in efficiency and are considered a primary contributor to turnarounds in previous studies.[269] Besides finding general support for revenue-generating strategies, some researchers argue that the timing of revenue growth within the turnaround process must be considered. They argue that revenue growth early during restructuring might reduce the likelihood of turnaround because companies must focus on revenue-reducing strategies such as culling their product portfolio or closing facilities.[270] Eliminating unprofitable operations can mean "regain[ing] profitability by selling less"[271]. In addition, price cuts are a means to increase competitiveness that often adversely affects revenue.[272]

---

262 See YAWSON (2009, p. 236) and NOTHARDT (2001, pp. 264-265). BRUTON ET AL. (2003) and THIÉTART (1988) find that revenue growth negatively impacts the probability of turnaround.

263 See for example SCHENDEL/PATTON (1976) and compare SCHLEY (2010, p. 91) for an overview. SCHLEY (2010) notes that empirical evidence for the effectiveness of revenue growth does not show if this restructuring activity is part of a turnaround strategy or part of the general strategy that also applies to non-distressed companies. Because SCHLEY (2010) applies this differentiation only to revenue growth, it seems artificial, but in this dissertation Research question 2 will address whether the chosen restructuring actions are distress-specific.

264 Compare SCHMIDT-GOTHAN (2008, pp. 68-69) for a classification of revenue generation activities.

265 See SUDARSANAM/LAI (2001, p. 185) and HOFER (1980, p. 26).

266 See BRUTON ET AL. (2003, p. 525). Distressed companies are considered to have the resources necessary to pursue actions like revenue growth, whereas bankrupt do not; see BRUTON ET AL. (2003) and SLATTER (1984).

267 Compare BARKER/DUHAIME (1997, p. 177), who draws empirical evidence from AROGYASWAMY (1992) to support this argument. SG&A expense divided by sales ratio is provided as an example.

268 YAWSON (2009, p. 218).

269 Compare FURRER ET AL. (2007, p. 1217).

270 See for the following BUSCHMANN (2006, p. 187). Contrary empirical evidence comes from YAWSON (2009, p. 217).

271 BRUTON ET AL. (2003, p. 533).

272 See BRUTON ET AL. (2003, p. 533).

In line with the retrenchment and recovery phases of the turnaround process, internal revenue growth is expected to decline during early restructuring but to contribute to turnarounds during later restructuring phases.

Hypothesis 2.1a
Internal revenue growth during the early restructuring phase is negatively related to the probability of a successful turnaround for financially distressed automotive suppliers.

Hypothesis 2.1b
Internal revenue growth during the late restructuring phase is positively related to the probability of a successful turnaround for financially distressed automotive suppliers.

The effectiveness of revenue growth strategies is often discussed in relation to the next operational restructuring activity—cost-cutting.

Cost-cutting

Cost-cutting is also considered an essential element of any turnaround and is directed toward improving the firm's efficiency.[273] Comparable to managerial restructuring, cost control is a step in reestablishing a company.[274] The focus here is on operating cost because for example financing costs are influenced by financial restructuring actions.

Overall, a variety of operating costs can be addressed—for example, reducing labor, production, or selling and administrative costs.[275] Cost-cutting actions, independent of the specific industry, can be clustered along the main cost categories.[276] Manufacturing industries often concentrate on material and personal costs. Material cost can be reduced by effective supplier management or by reducing materials used in production. Apart from layoffs, personnel costs are reduced by imposing flextime, trimming overtime, reducing incidental wage costs. LIN ET AL. (2008) give one specific measure as an example of cost retrenchment in manufacturing: outsourcing production processes.[277] Outsourcing entails relocating processes to low-cost countries so manufacturers can concentrate on core competencies. Also, replacing or modernizing antiquated production facilities can reduce costs, even if critical capital outlays are required.[278]

---

273 See SUDARSANAM/LAI (2001, p. 185) and YAWSON (2009, p. 236).
274 See LIN ET AL. (2008, p. 543).
275 See ROBBINS/PEARCE (1992, p. 296), DENIS/KRUSE (2000, p. 394), and LIN ET AL. (2008, p. 547).
276 Compare for the following SCHLEY (2010) with a detailed discussion of cost-reduction measures.
277 See for the following LIN ET AL. (2008, p. 547).
278 See CHOWDHURY/LANG (1996, p. 171).

Cost-cutting improves short-run profitability and allows the company to redirect resources.[279] During financial distress, cost retrenchment is indispensable to conserve cash flow.[280] Still, negative effects arise if implementation costs are underestimated and savings are overestimated.

As part of a general retrenchment strategy, cost reduction is important for successful turnarounds,[281] and empirical evidence shows it is essential and effective.[282] Still, it can be argued that it is "a necessary, but not a sufficient condition for recovery of many firms"[283]. Also, analysis of timing patterns shows that the impact of cost reductions diminishes over time and even might hinder successful turnarounds.[284] This leads to the assumption that companies must cut costs quickly to initiate turnaround, but that later cost-cutting may have a negative impact.

Hypothesis 2.2a

Cost-cutting during the early restructuring phase is positively related to the probability of a successful turnaround for financially distressed automotive suppliers.

Hypothesis 2.2b

Cost-cutting during the late restructuring phase is negatively related to the probability of a successful turnaround for financially distressed automotive suppliers.

3.2.4 Financial restructuring

Financial restructuring can be a short-term solution to performance and liquidity problems and can "constitute the bedrock for a sustainable performance"[285]. Financial restructuring is primarily concerned with reworking the firm's capital structure to relieve the strain of interest and debt repayments and can be broadly categorized into equity-based and debt-based strategies.[286] The role of financial restructuring in corporate turnaround is still ambiguous.[287] Although some researchers identify financial restructuring as an integral part of corporate turnaround,[288] others state there is no significant influence.[289] In the remainder of this section, debt restructuring and the two main equity-based strategies are analyzed. Equity issues and dividend cuts are equity-based restructuring strategies because they affect shareholders.

279 See SMITH/GRAVES (2005, p. 306) and AROGYASWAMY/YASAI-ARDEKANI (1997, p. 3).
280 See for the following LIN ET AL. (2008, p. 547).
281 See FURRER ET AL. (2007, p. 385) and ROBBINS/PEARCE (1992, p. 296).
282 See YAWSON (2009, p. 236), LIN ET AL. (2008, p. 544), and FURRER ET AL. (2007, p. 379).
283 SUDARSANAM/LAI (2001, pp. 185-186). Compare also FRANCIS/DESAI (2005, p. 1219).
284 See SUDARSANAM/LAI (2001, pp. 192-196) and JOHN ET AL. (1992, pp. 907-908).
285 YAWSON (2009, pp. 222, 226) with reference to CHOWDHURY/LANG (1996).
286 See for the following SUDARSANAM/LAI (2001, p. 187) and YAWSON (2009, p. 222).
287 Compare SUDARSANAM/LAI (2001, p. 187) for an overview.
288 E.g., YAWSON (2009, p. 228), ASQUITH ET AL. (1994, p. 656), and JOHN ET AL. (1992, p. 911).
289 E.g., SUDARSANAM/LAI (2001, p. 196).

Equity issues

Equity issues are an attempt to raise funds by issuing shares.[290] Examples include rights issues, public offerings, or institutional placements. When circumstances prevent debt restructuring, equity offerings are a possibility for raising funds.[291] Compared to operational restructuring—for example, cost-cutting—issuing equity requires the involvement of key stakeholders.[292] For example, creditors concerned with the security of their lending might pressure firms to issue equity.[293]

Issuing equity has the benefit of raising cash without raising indebtedness, thereby improving the company's capital structure and creditworthiness.[294] Especially during financial distress, adding equity capital can help to avoid bankruptcy and improves financial flexibility for later restructuring activities.[295] But if investor support is fading, issuing additional equity might be difficult for financially distressed firms.

Empirical evidence regarding the effectiveness of equity issuance in turnarounds is mixed. Although SUDARSANAM/LAI (2001) and YAWSON (2009) find no significant relation between turnarounds and equity issuance, BUSCHMANN (2006) finds a strong positive correlation.[296] The effect of equity issuance on corporate turnarounds is therefore expected to be positive during both restructuring phases, even if frequent equity restructuring actions must be validated.[297]

Hypothesis 3.1a

Equity issues during the early restructuring phase are positively related to the probability of a successful turnaround for financially distressed automotive suppliers.

Hypothesis 3.1b

Equity issues during the late restructuring phase are positively related to the probability of a successful turnaround for financially distressed automotive suppliers.

---

290 See for the following SUDARSANAM/LAI (2001, p. 187).
291 See for the following YAWSON (2009, p. 222).
292 See BUSCHMANN (2006, p. 61).
293 See SUDARSANAM/LAI (2001, p. 187).
294 See BUSCHMANN (2006, p. 61) and EICHNER (2008, p. 107). JOSTARNDT (2007) analyzes distressed equity offerings with respect to wealth transfer, ownership structure, and managerial discretion, all of which exceed the scope of this study; compare for details JOSTARNDT (2007, pp. 127-155).
295 See SCHLEY (2010, pp. 99-100).
296 See SUDARSANAM/LAI (2001, p. 196), YAWSON (2009, p. 227), and BUSCHMANN (2006, pp. 190-191).
297 In comparison, EICHNER (2008, pp. 108-109) expects a negative relation during the early restructuring phase because of the large discounts required.

Dividend policy

Changes in dividend policy, especially cuts or omissions, are frequently applied restructuring strategic actions for distressed firms.[298] Because cash flows to shareholders are affected, changes in dividend policy are equity-based turnaround actions.[299]

Distressed firms are characterized by liquidity constraints, and dividend cuts or omissions allow them to retain cash and preserve scarce internal funds for regular operations.[300] Dividend cuts also can be enforced by existing debt covenants, which force distressed companies to reduce cash outflows.[301] In addition, more strategic considerations like bargaining with trade unions can induce companies to cut dividends and broadcast the seriousness of their financial troubles and management's willingness to address the problem.[302] At the same time, because cutting dividends is a negative signal to the market that may trigger a fall in share prices, management may be reluctant to cut dividends.[303] Management in many cases aims to maintain an existing dividend history.

Empirical evidence regarding dividend cuts is twofold. Various studies show a high frequency of dividend reductions among distressed firms and also that they are "rapid and aggressive[304]. Still, no convincing evidence demonstrates that dividend cuts contribute to turnarounds. Although there is a strong argument for the role of dividend cuts in turnarounds, empirical evidence is missing or even contrary to this argument.[305] SUDARSANAM/LAI (2001) conclude that "a dividend cut [...] may merely contribute to survival. Thus is a necessary but not a sufficient condition for subsequent recovery."[306]

Prior studies show that dividend reductions occur early in the turnaround process.[307] This can be partially explained by managers' anticipating that the distress situation will persist.[308] At the same time, a dividend cut late in the recovery process can be necessary because earlier reductions failed, and in such a case is associated with unsuccessful turnarounds.[309] Therefore, a positive relation to the probability of turnaround is expected for the early restructuring phase, but a negative relation is expected for the late restructuring phase.

---

298 See SUDARSANAM/LAI (2001, p. 217).
299 See OFEK (1993, p. 11).
300 See WHITING/GILKISON (2000, p. 6) and YAWSON (2009, p. 222).
301 DEANGELO/DEANGELO (1990, p. 1430) find that debt covenants affect dividend policies of half the firms in their distressed sample.
302 See DEANGELO/DEANGELO (1990, pp. 1420-1421) and YAWSON (2009, p. 222).
303 This effect can be explained in terms of cash flow signaling, agency costs, overinvestment, and dividend clientele; see WHITING/GILKISON (2000, p. 5) for an overview.
304 SUDARSANAM/LAI (2001, p. 187). Compare also JOHN ET AL. (1992) and DEANGELO/DEANGELO (1990).
305 Compare SUDARSANAM/LAI (2001, p. 196), who found a high frequency of dividend reductions, especially for non-recovering companies.
306 SUDARSANAM/LAI (2001, p. 194). The same argument is made for debt restructuring.
307 See DEANGELO/DEANGELO (1990, p. 1420).
308 See OFEK (1993, p. 12).
309 See SUDARSANAM/LAI (2001, pp. 194-196).

Hypothesis 3.2a
Dividend cuts during the early restructuring phase are positively related to the probability of a successful turnaround for financially distressed automotive suppliers.

Hypothesis 3.2b
Dividend cuts during the late restructuring phase are negatively related to the probability of a successful turnaround for financially distressed automotive suppliers.

Debt restructuring

Debt-based strategies refer to the restructuring of the company's debt as a possible way to resolve financial distress.[310] The general goals of debt restructuring are to reduce cash outflows and to improve profitability by reducing interest cost.[311] This research focuses on changes in leverage as an explicit subset of debt restructuring that is directly related to the financial liability burden.[312]

Debt restructuring can increase or decrease the proportion of debt in the capital structure.[313] An increase in debt can improve liquidity and provide incentives for management to take corrective actions. At the same time, distressed firms have an incentive to reduce debt to improve their financial health.[314] However, financially distressed firms will have difficulties gaining access to new credit and may resort to equity issuance.[315] There is no consensus in existing research if debt restructuring is more effective than equity issuance for corporate turnarounds.[316]

Empirical evidence shows that failure to reduce debt early in the restructuring process increases the probability of non-turnaround, whereas an early reduction in leverage contributes to turnaround.[317] Non-turnaround companies are expected to restructure their debt too late in the turnaround process.[318] Therefore, relation of debt restructuring to corporate turnaround is expected to be positive during the early restructuring phase and a negative for the late restructuring phase.

---

310 See YAWSON (2009, p. 228) and LAI/SUDARSANAM (1997, p. 205).
311 See ASQUITH ET AL. (1994, p. 644).
312 See EICHNER (2008, p. 110).
313 See YAWSON (2009, p. 222).
314 See FAN ET AL. (2011, p. 23).
315 See YAWSON (2009, p. 222).
316 See SUDARSANAM/LAI (2001, p. 187).
317 See LIN ET AL. (2008, p. 549), SUDARSANAM/LAI (2001, pp. 194-196), and JOHN ET AL. (1992, pp. 909-911).
318 See SUDARSANAM/LAI (2001, p. 196).

Hypothesis 3.3a

Debt reduction during the early restructuring phase is positively related to the probability of a successful turnaround for financially distressed automotive suppliers.

Hypothesis 3.3b

Debt reduction during the late restructuring phase is negatively related to the probability of a successful turnaround for financially distressed automotive suppliers.

3.2.4.1 Asset restructuring

Companies can attempt to mitigate financial distress through changes in their asset base.[319] Asset restructuring, also called portfolio or strategic restructuring, is often associated with improved performance for distressed firms. Asset restructuring in general and capital expenditures in particular are differentiated in the remainder of this section.[320]

General asset restructuring

For asset restructuring in general, asset reduction and asset expansion as reflected on the balance sheet are differentiated. Financially distressed companies can attempt to restore profitability and liquidity by expanding their asset base.[321] The goal of *asset expansion* is to increase sales, which should result in improved profit margins and operating cash flows and ultimately enhance probability of turnaround. But asset expansion that results in "diversification or a loss of focus can be detrimental to firm value."[322] Increasing the asset base also might increase the need for additional capital and might even increase the severity of distress.[323]

Asset reduction or downsizing is the other mode of asset restructuring. Financially distressed companies can eliminate unprofitable ventures to generate cash inflow, improve profitability, and reduce required operating capital.[324] Financially distressed firms often lack the cash to continue operations, and selling assets raises cash.[325] Reductions in scope of assets can include such measures as divesting or discontinuing subsidiaries and divisions or disposing of plants, property, and equipment.[326] By disposing of non-core assets, the firm focuses its

---

319 Compare KANE/RICHARDSON (2002, p. 2002), who focus on fixed assets.
320 See JOHN ET AL. (1992) for the same differentiation.
321 See for the following KANE/RICHARDSON (2002, p. 260) and SMITH/GRAVES (2005, p. 317).
322 YAWSON (2009, p. 224).
323 See KANE/RICHARDSON (2002, p. 259).
324 Compare KANE/RICHARDSON (2002, p. 260).
325 DENIS/SHOME (2005, pp. 437).
326 For asset reductions see for example YAWSON (2009), JOHN/OFEK (1995), KAHL (2002), BERGER/OFEK (1999), JOHN/OFEK (1995), LANG ET AL. (1995).

businesses to improve performance and generate cash to improve liquidity and fund ongoing operations.

Although shareholders are interested in divestitures because they are expected to increase shareholder value, corporate managers are interested in larger firms.[327] Also, creditors often demand divesture of assets as a prerequisite for debt restructuring.[328]

Empirical evidence shows that downsizing is capable of overcoming distress situations.[329] Partial asset divestiture is even "deemed imperative for turnaround"[330] of companies in severe distress.[331] Empirical evidence shows that distressed companies initiating asset reductions directly after the initial distress are more likely to turn themselves around than those that do not.[332] By comparison, asset expansion is expected to play a more important role during the later restructuring phase when the emphasis shifts from retrenchment to expansionary restructuring. Therefore, a positive relation of asset reduction and corporate turnaround is expected during the early restructuring phase, and a positive relation of asset expansion and corporate turnaround is expected during late restructuring.

Hypothesis 4.1a

Asset reduction (expansion) during the early restructuring phase is positively (negatively) related to the probability of a successful turnaround for financially distressed automotive suppliers.

Hypothesis 4.1b

Asset expansion (reduction) during the late restructuring phase is positively (negatively) related to the probability of a successful turnaround for financially distressed automotive suppliers.

Capital expenditures

Internal capital expenditures are additions to fixed assets like machinery, property, plant, or equipment. They represent funds used to acquire fixed assets other than those associated with acquisitions.[333] Changes in capital expenditures are therefore a sub-set of general asset restructuring.

327 DENIS/SHOME (2005, pp. 427-428).
328 DENIS/SHOME (2005, p. 437).
329 DENIS/SHOME (2005, p. 429).
330 SUDARSANAM/LAI (2001, p. 186).
331 See also ROBBINS/PEARCE (1993) and HOFER (1980).
332 See DENIS/KRUSE (2000, p. 394).
333 Compare Footnote 403 for the corresponding definition.

Empirical evidence concerning the use of capital expenditures to overcome corporate distress situations is mixed. On the one side, capital expenditures of turnaround firms drop dramatically, and reductions in capital expenditures as part of a retrenchment strategy are common for financially distressed firms.[334] Liquidity is a primary concern for a financially distressed firm, and it may be unable to invest due to cash shortages or creditor constraints. On the other side, some researchers show that financially distressed firms do not reduce their capital expenditures despite their difficulties.[335] Capital expenditures might be used to improve efficiency by upgrading plants and equipment.[336] In this case, an increase in capital expenditures "complements, rather than conflicts with efficiency driven operational restructuring."[337] Also, shareholders and managers might be interested in further investments because the risk associated with new investments increases the option value of equity.[338]

Empirical evidence about the effectiveness of reducing capital expenditures on corporate turnarounds is also mixed. Although many companies reduce capital expenditures to overcome distress situations, companies unable to turn themselves around reduce capital expenditures more intensively than successful turnarounds.[339] Observations from prior research suggest that the impact of capital expenditures changes over time. Although capital expenditure reductions will have a positive effect during the early restructuring phase, a negative effect is expected during the late restructuring phase when capital expenditures are required to support reestablishment of revenue growth.[340]

Hypothesis 4.2a

Capital expenditure reductions during the early restructuring phase are positively related to the probability of a successful turnaround for financially distressed automotive suppliers.

Hypothesis 4.2b

Capital expenditure reductions during the late restructuring phase are negatively related to the probability of a successful turnaround for financially distressed automotive suppliers.

334 Compare for the following ASQUITH ET AL. (1994, p. 650), BARKER/DUHAIME (1997, p. 25). This might also be voluntary because of missing investment opportunities. This aspect is analyzed in Research question 2 in comparison to healthy firms; see SECTION 5.3.2.

335 See SUDARSANAM/LAI (2001, pp. 191-192) and JOHN ET AL. (1992, p. 907).

336 See SUDARSANAM/LAI (2001) and GRINYER ET AL. (1990, p. 121).

337 SUDARSANAM/LAI (2001, p. 186).

338 See ASQUITH ET AL. (1994, p. 650).

339 Compare SUDARSANAM/LAI (2001, pp. 191-192).

340 See FURRER ET AL. (2007, p. 379) and SCHENDEL/PATTON (1976, p. 238).

3.2.5 Context

Although this research focuses on restructuring content, the appropriateness and success of any restructuring action are likely to depend on the context of the corporation.[341] Therefore, eight context variables are included in the research framework to avoid distortions from different pre-distress characteristics. This includes financial pre-distress characteristics and general firm characteristics (see FIGURE 9).

Figure 9: Restructuring context.

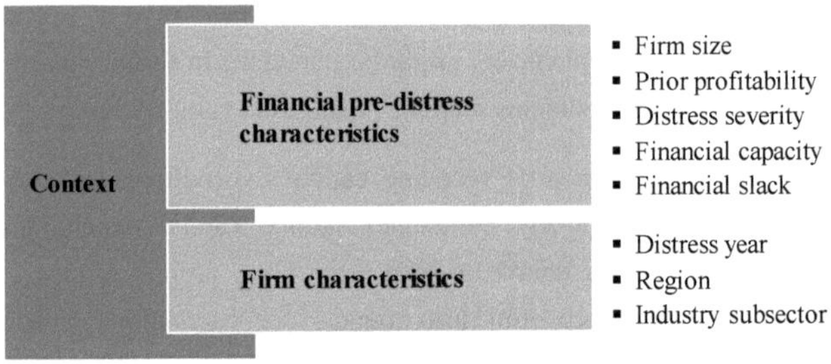

Source: Own illustration.

The main financial pre-distress characteristics included in existing research are firm size, prior profitability, distress severity, financial slack, and financial capacity. As already outlined in the sampling procedure, company *size* might affect the restructuring actions chosen. Therefore, a size limit was introduced to exclude small firms.[342] Although most studies use some proxy of firm size to control for size effects in dealing with distress situations, empirical evidence concerning these effects is mixed.[343] In general, there is a tendency to expect that larger firms will turn around more quickly, as potential losses for stakeholders are greater and they "have a higher profile and therefore more likely to be kept alive."[344] Based on the assumption that size is a tangible resource for the firm, a positive role for size in the turnaround process is expected.[345] Firm size also can impact market power, access to capital, and flexibility with creditors, so that larger firms might be better able to turn themselves around.[346] But it also must be noted that other studies found no significant influence or a negative influence for organizational size on turnarounds.[347] Overall, larger firms in distress

341 See CHOWDHURY/LANG (1994, p. 206).

342 Compare SUDARSANAM/LAI (2001, p. 189) and see CHAPTER 4.1 for details.

343 See FURRER ET AL. (2007, p. 1207) for a detailed discussion, including the arguments of the resource-based view.

344 SMITH/GRAVES (2005, p. 306). See also YAWSON (2009, p. 226) for the relationship between speed of turnaround and firm size.

345 See FURRER ET AL. (2007, p. 1207).

346 See KANE/RICHARDSON (2002, p. 262) and BARKER/DUHAIME (1997, p. 33).

347 See for example FRANCIS/DESAI (2005, p. 1219) for no significant impact and BRUTON ET AL. (2003, p. 530) or PANT (1991, p. 638) for a negative impact on firm performance in turnarounds.

situations are expected to have greater resources and more alternatives for counteractions and that these benefits outweigh potential negatives such as size-related inertia.[348]

Because no profitability threshold is introduced in the definition of distress, prior profitability is included as a context variable.[349] In general, it is assumed that superior *profitability prior to distress* gives a company a higher probability to turn around.[350] But empirical evidence shows only a slightly positive and statistically insignificant effect.[351]

Closely related to profitability in the pre-distress year is the *distress severity*. The severity of distress influences "the ability of the firm to enact a recovery"[352]. With a severe erosion of profitability, firms are expected to have greater difficulty executing successful turnarounds.[353] Firms in severe distress are likely to encounter skeptical stakeholders and to suffer a dysfunctional internal climate, making turnaround more difficult.[354]

Financial resources are also expected to influence distressed firms.[355] *Financial capacity* is the firm's long-term ability to obtain capital.[356] Higher financial capacity is associated with a lower breakeven point and should elevate probability of a turnaround.[357] *Financial slack* is the firm's short-term ability to meet needs.[358] Slack in the form of unabsorbed and uncommitted resources can take any form, including cash, inventory, or access to credit.[359] Empirical evidence that unabsorbed slack reduces the firm's sensitivity to decline and therefore its turnaround is limited. A higher level of slack is therefore expected to increase firms' prospects for overcoming financial distress.[360]

---

348 Compare the detailed discussion by FRANCIS/DESAI (2005, p. 1207).
349 Compare LIN ET AL. (2008), SMITH/GRAVES (2005), or BARKER/DUHAIME (1997).
350 See KANE/RICHARDSON (2002, p. 262).
351 Compare ASQUITH ET AL. (1994, p. 654).
352 SMITH/GRAVES (2005, p. 307).
353 See FRANCIS/DESAI (2005, p. 1218).
354 See AROGYASWAMY ET AL. (1995, p. 504).
355 See for the following MORROW ET AL. (2007, p. 277).
356 See MORROW ET AL. (2007, p. 277). Financial capacity is also an indicator of the company's leverage; see KANE/RICHARDSON (2002, p. 262).
357 See KANE/RICHARDSON (2002, p. 262).
358 Slack also indicates the firm's liquidity; see KANE/RICHARDSON (2002, p. 262).
359 See for the following FURRER ET AL. (2007, p. 1207).
360 See KANE/RICHARDSON (2002, pp. 262: 262) and SMITH/GRAVES (2005, p. 317).

Hypothesis 5.1
Firm size is positively related to the probability of a successful turnaround for financially distressed automotive suppliers.
Hypothesis 5.2
Prior profitability is positively related to the probability of a successful turnaround for financially distressed automotive suppliers.
Hypothesis 5.3
Distress severity is negatively related to the probability of a successful turnaround for financially distressed automotive suppliers.
Hypothesis 5.4
Financial capacity is positively related to the probability of a successful turnaround for financially distressed automotive suppliers.
Hypothesis 5.5
Financial slack is positively related to the probability of a successful turnaround for financially distressed automotive suppliers.

In addition, the research framework controls for the distress year, the regional origin of the firm, and the two industry subsectors in the sample.

Time-specific industry and macro-economic effects are considered important influences on the probability of turnaround in most research settings.[361] Because this research includes only one industry segment, time-specific industry and macroeconomic effects can be analyzed by including the *distress year* as context variable.

Prior research into turnarounds shows only small differences between Western European and North American companies,[362] but US turnaround models of firm turnaround must be adjusted when applied to Asian firms.[363] To control for potential differences, *regional origin* is included as a context variable. Because the automotive supplier industry is global,[364] this aspect is expected to have no significant impact compared to studies covering multiple diverse industry segments.

The final context variable is membership in one of the two *industry subsectors* 'Auto Parts' or 'Tires'. Because no previous research has analyzed turnarounds so specifically, industry membership is expected to demonstrate no impact on corporate turnaround.

361 See for the following YAWSON (2009, p. 226).
362 Compare EICHNER (2008, p. 221) for the analysis of firms from Germany, the UK and the US.
363 Compare BRUTON ET AL. (2003) for the analysis of East Asian firms.
364 Compare SECTION 1.2.1 for the detailed discussion of globalization within the automotive industry.

Hypothesis 6.1

Distress year is not related to the probability of a successful turnaround for financially distressed automotive suppliers.

Hypothesis 6.2

Regional origin is not related to the probability of a successful turnaround for financially distressed automotive suppliers.

Hypothesis 6.3

Industry membership in one of the two industry subsectors is not related to the probability of a successful turnaround for financially distressed automotive suppliers.

The context variables complement the theoretical framework for the analysis of financial distress and corporate turnaround among automotive suppliers. The process, content, and context dimension are included within the holistic research model for the later empirical analysis. Before a summary of the key hypothesis is provided in CHAPTER 3.3, the following section introduces combinations of restructuring actions categorized as turnaround archetypes.

3.2.6 Turnaround archetypes

During the early era of turnaround research, HOFER (1980) introduced so called turnaround archetypes or turnaround gestalts that anticipated the later search for generic turnaround strategies.[365] HAMBRICK/SCHECTER (1983) followed by asking if any combinations of strategic moves are common in achieving turnarounds.[366] This section concentrates on "holistic patterns, that is, genuine strategies, rather than isolated moves."[367] Later, LAFRENZ (2004) and EICHNER (2008) examined the occurrence of these generic turnaround archetypes in their respective samples (see FIGURE 10).

Figure 10: Turnaround archetypes.

Study	HOFER (1980)	HAMBRICK/SCHECTER (1983)	LAFRENZ (2004)	EICHNER (2008)
Turnaround gestalts	▪ Revenue generation ▪ Product/ market refocusing ▪ Cost-cutting ▪ Asset reduction ▪ Combination strategies	▪ Asset and cost surgery ▪ Selective product/ market pruning ▪ Piecemeal productivity	▪ Profitable growth for challengers ▪ Gradual efficiency improvement for medium sized firms ▪ Refocusing of giants ▪ Redimensioning of stars	▪ Radical growth strategy ▪ Strategic reorientation ▪ Cash flow optimization ▪ Asset retrenchment ▪ Operational reorientation ▪ Right sizing

Source: Own illustration.

The four generic strategies identified by HOFER (1980) are basis for any discussion of turnaround archetypes. Two strategies—revenue generation and product/market refocusing—are more entrepreneurial, whereas cost-cutting and asset reduction have more to do with efficiency.[368] Combinations of these four generic strategies are identified as combination strategies in Hofer's fifth turnaround gestalt. The four generic turnaround gestalts are introduced briefly below.

Revenue-generation is a strategy that attempts to achieve turnaround by increasing sales.[369] Sales increases result from some combination of, for instance, product introductions, increased advertising, increased sales efforts, and lower prices. Revenue generation is associated with an increase in organic sales, but also with substantial increases in capital expenditures and total assets. *Product/market refocusing* involves shifting the emphasis to defensible or lucrative niches. Although product innovations play a central role,

365 See HOFER (1980).
366 See for the following HAMBRICK/SCHECTER (1983, pp. 231-233).
367 HAMBRICK/SCHECTER (1983, p. 233).
368 Compare HAMBRICK/SCHECTER (1983, pp. 233-234).
369 See for the following HOFER (1980, pp. 26-28), HAMBRICK/SCHECTER (1983, pp. 233-236), and EICHNER (2008, pp. 130-132).

product/market refocusing often involves the forced exchange of the top executive. Relative direct costs are partially expected to increase during the early phase due to the expansionary nature of the strategy. A *cost-cutting strategy* typically involves cutbacks in administrative, R&D, marketing, and other seemingly discretionary expenses. Improved management of receivables and inventories also can be considered as cost-cutting. Cost-cutting strategies relate to significant reductions in operating expenses and to cuts in capital expenditures. Sales growth is not expected due to the retrenchment nature of activities. An *asset reduction strategy* involves the disposal of assets, primarily fixed assets. Asset reduction will be reflected in a decrease in total assets, but also in a decrease in capital expenditures.

HAMBRICK/SCHECTER (1983) reconfirm the *selective product/market pruning* strategy, but they find only a combination of asset reduction and cost-cutting called *asset/cost surgery.*[370] The third cluster, not directly related to the generic strategies in HOFER (1980), is *piecemeal productivity.* This strategy is characterized by increased capacity utilization and improved employee productivity.

In addition to identifying generic turnaround strategies, LAFRENZ (2004) analyzes related pre-distress characteristics and process aspects.[371] He shows that smaller companies are able to implement operational restructuring strategies and simultaneously strive to increase revenues, even during the initial consolidation (*profitable growth for challengers*). Medium-sized companies instead focus on continuous efficiency improvements (*gradual efficiency improvement for medium sized firms*), and extreme retrenchment or recovery actions do not exist. The largest companies in the sample of LAFRENZ (2004) refocus their activities, accompanied by divestiture of assets but also continuous efforts to boost revenue (*refocusing of giants*). The last turnaround gestalt (*redimensioning of stars*) especially fits smaller companies, where a strong initial consolidation precedes a reversal of the prior growth strategy.

EICHNER (2008) itemizes six turnaround gestalts that closely match the generic turnaround strategies identified by HOFER (1980).[372] Although EICHNER (2008) also includes the pre-distress characteristics of turnaround firms, the process dimension is excluded. The *radical growth strategy* matches Hofer's revenue growth strategy and is applied by small companies with low distress levels. A high distress level leads to *strategic reorientation,* which matches the generic product/market refocusing strategy. This archetype is characterized by a high frequency of forced top executive turnover accompanied by product innovations and acquisitions. Divestiture of non-core assets also is part of the strategic reorientation. Cost-

---

370 See for the following HAMBRICK/SCHECTER (1983, pp. 242-243).
371 See for the following LAFRENZ (2004, pp. 231-241).
372 See for the following EICHNER (2008, pp. 254-257).

cutting strategies are labeled *cash flow optimization* in EICHNER (2008) and are associated with slightly distressed companies which only selectively apply restructuring actions and concentrate on controlling capital expenditures and limiting growth. *Asset retrenchment* is applied by large firms with low initial leverage and especially includes operational and asset-side capacity reductions through layoffs and plant closures. The last two turnaround archetypes—*operational reorientation* and *right sizing*—are specifications of HOFER'S (1980) combination strategies. Both strategies include intensive asset and cost retrenchment, but the former is applied by small, highly distressed firms and the latter by larger, highly distressed firms.

Due to the explorative research setting and the taxonomic approach, no hypotheses are derived for the identification of turnaround archetypes.[373] The goal for the third research question is to identify combinations of turnaround actions typically found within distressed automotive suppliers and to discuss them based on existing theory. The research question concerning turnaround archetypes is to be considered a supplement to the main question about the effectiveness of restructuring actions by distressed automotive suppliers.

3.3 Summary of research hypotheses

This chapter briefly summarizes the research hypotheses outlined in the previous research framework (see FIGURE 11). For each restructuring action identified in previous research, a hypothesis for its influence on the probability of turnaround is derived from existing theory and empirical evidence, differentiated according to whether the action is applied during the early or late restructuring phase. Also included are hypotheses concerning impact of financial pre-distress and firm characteristics.

[373] Compare for the following LAFRENZ (2004, p. 193). Details on the research approach are provided in CHAPTER 1.3.

Figure 11: Overview research hypotheses.

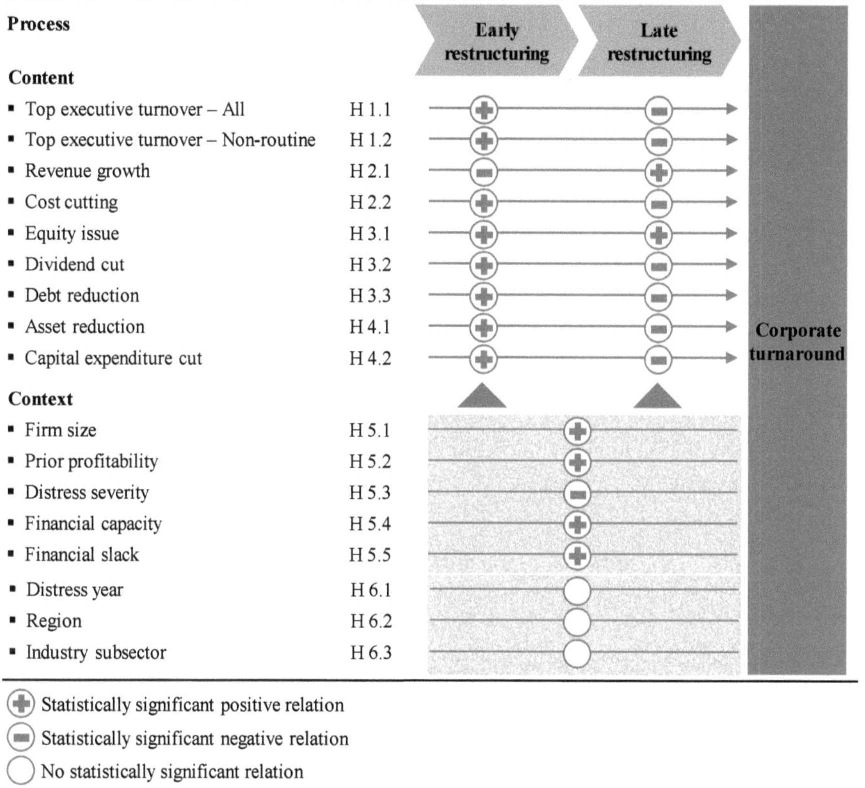

Source: Own illustration.

The third research question concerning the comparison of distressed and non-distressed firms and the second research question concerning turnaround archetypes are explorative in nature, hence no hypotheses based on existing theory can be drawn. For the second research question, the effective restructuring actions identified are compared to a matched sample of non-distressed companies. For the third research question, archetypes for successful turnarounds are discussed.

4. SAMPLE SELECTION AND ANALYTICAL METHODS

This part gives an overview of the methodological background of the study. CHAPTER 4.1 describes the sampling process of distressed and non-distressed automotive suppliers. This includes a discussion of the initial population and several selection criteria such as size and data requirements before the distress criterion is applied. In addition, a control group of non-distressed companies is selected. Variables introduced in the theoretical framework are operationalized in CHAPTER 4.2. This includes the independent variables related to managerial, financial, operational, and asset restructuring and the chosen context variables. Finally, CHAPTER 4.3 reviews the statistical methods applied and discusses the rationale for their selection.

4.1 Sample selection process

The sample is based on the population of 661 publicly listed automotive suppliers between 1999 and 2008 (see FIGURE 12). The population is drawn from the ONE Banker database[374] and includes inactive companies to avoid survivorship bias.[375] Publicly listed equity is a necessary requirement for access to full financial data and is a common constraint in turnaround research.[376] The industry selection is based on the Industry Classification Benchmark (ICB) provided by FTSE and Dow Jones. The sample comprises the ICB subsectors '3355 Auto Parts' and '3357 Tires' which are part of the '3000 Consumer Goods' industry and the '3300 Automobile & Parts' supersector.[377]

Figure 12: Sample selection process.

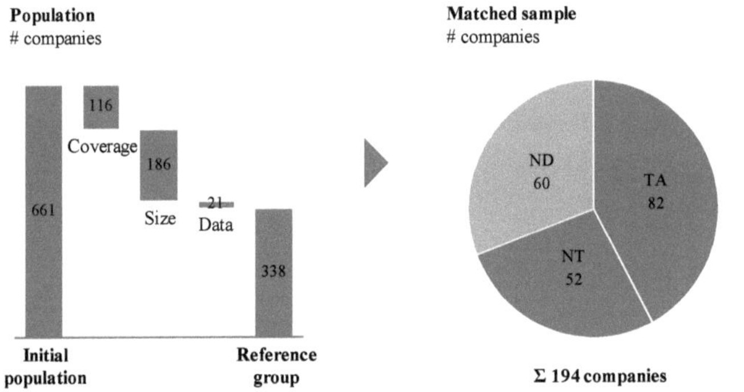

Abbr.: TA Turnaround, NT Non-turnaround, ND Non-distress

Source: Own illustration.

[374] The Thomson ONE Banker database uses Thomson Financial, a composite database combining the most popular accounting and market data items provided by a variety of fundamental data providers. Worldscope is the primary data source within Thomson Financial in this research.

[375] For the discussion of survivorship bias in the context of databases see ALVES ET AL. (2007, p. 8). The Thomson ONE Banker database targets worldwide coverage of publicly quoted companies and establishes consistency on an item-by-item basis for international datasets; see THOMSON REUTERS (2010). For a discussion of various databases, related advantages and disadvantages, and for international normalization in financial databases compare TRIMBATH (2006, p. 412). Consult ULBRICHT/WEINER (2005) for the advantages of Worldscope compared to Compustat when using data after 1998.

[376] ASQUITH ET AL. (1994, p. 629) provides the rationale for selecting publicly listed companies. Among the reviewed studies, ACHARYA ET AL. (2007) is the only study to include private firms, but they focus on debt restructuring only. At the same time, the focus on exchange listing is a self-selecting-process that could introduce bias, but it is consistent with the research focus of this dissertation; see TRIMBATH (2006, p. 413) for details.

[377] ICB 3353 is defined as manufacturers and distributors of new and replacement parts for motorcycles and automobiles, such as engines, carburetors, and batteries and excludes producers of tires, which are classified under Tires. ICB 3357 is defined as manufacturers, distributors, and retraders of automobile, truck, and motorcycle tires. Consult http://www.icbenchmark.com for further information.

In addition, three filters are applied in the sampling process to assure a homogenous reference group: continuous coverage, minimum size requirement, and data availability.[378] First, five years of *continuous coverage* in the Thomson ONE Banker database are required to analyze the pre-distress, distress, transition, and turnaround phases.[379] This excludes companies which were covered four or fewer years during the sample period. Reasons for discontinued coverage include delisting due to mergers, takeovers, liquidation, or going private. Excluding delisted firms is required because details of turnaround actions for those companies generally are not available publicly.[380] This filter relates to the goal of the selection process of identifying companies that were under financial distress while avoiding takeovers or liquidation.[381] This filter eliminates 116 companies.

Second, a *minimum size requirement* of USD 50 million for total assets and for revenues each year is applied.[382] The size requirement satisfies two needs: data availability and a homogeneous sample. Data availability means that sufficient financial data are available for the companies analyzed, which is often not the case for very small firms, even those publicly listed.[383] In addition, prior literature has established that turnarounds of small companies significantly differ from those of larger companies.[384] The company's size influences the turnaround process and the choice of turnaround actions; without the minimum size criterion, a homogeneous sample cannot be assured.[385] Its application eliminates 186 companies.[386]

Third, companies with *missing data* were excluded from the potential sample.[387] Eleven companies were eliminated because data were insufficient to determine if they were

378 See BARKER/DUHAIME (1997, p. 15), who outline the need for a homogeneous sample to increase validity of results.

379 A common timeframe for all companies is required for the sensitivity stage of the analysis; compare SMITH/GRAVES (2005, p. 312).

380 This approach accords with prior research from e.g. JOHN ET AL. (1992, p. 894), SUDARSANAM/LAI (2001, p. 190), or BRUTON ET AL. (2003, p. 529).

381 This target for the sampling approach is based on JOHN ET AL. (1992, p. 894). In the case of non-turnarounds, LIN ET AL. (2008, p. 540) point out that being merged or taken private cannot be interpreted as failure.

382 Turnaround of small companies can be considered a separate research stream; see e.g. ROBBINS/PEARCE (1993), CHOWDHURY/LANG (1996), or RASHEED (2005). Selection of the threshold is based on existing literature; compare CHOWDHURY/LANG (1996, p. 172) for a discussion of various threshold values. For the selection of the USD 50 million threshold see EICHNER (2008, p. 188) and BUSCHMANN (2006, p. 160). Market capitalization as used by SUDARSANAM/LAI (2001) is rejected because of problems with market-based data; see the corresponding discussion in SECTION 3.1.1.

383 See SUDARSANAM/LAI (2001, p. 190) and DENIS/SHOME (2005, p. 432).

384 See for example CHOWDHURY/LANG (1996) and DENIS/KRUSE (2000, p. 399).

385 CHOWDHURY/LANG (1994, p. 206) point out that "certain strategic actions are unrealistic for smaller firms," and YAWSON (2009, p. 226) concludes that "large firms are more likely to achieve a quick turnaround".

386 Besides the clear rationale for the size limit, certain aspects—for example, the stronger role of institutional investors for larger companies—might be overstated and must be considered in interpreting results where applicable; see DENIS/KRUSE (2000, p. 399).

387 For the same approach compare for example BARKER/DUHAIME (1997, p. 22), CASTROGIOVANNI/BRUTON (2000, p. 28), or MORROW ET AL. (2007, p. 275).

financially distressed, and 10 more companies were eliminated because there was insufficient data to observe their chosen turnaround actions following the onset of distress. This case-wise deletion is the most conservative approach to avoid distortions.[388] In all, 21 companies are excluded from the sample for insufficient data.

The 338 companies remaining in the reference group represent 1,684 five-year timeframes between 1999 and 2008 to which the distress criterion of negative interest coverage is applied. Overall, 150 companies suffering a shortfall in interest coverage are identified. Of these, 16 are excluded from the final sample because they suffer financial distress in more than one five-year timeframe.[389] The exclusion of multiple distress situations leaves a sample of 134 companies. Of these, 82 (61%) recover, have positive interest coverage after three years, and are labeled turnaround (TA). The remaining 52 companies (39%) are unable to establish positive interest coverage three years after the onset of distress and are labeled non-turnaround (NT). These 134 companies are labeled 'distressed sample' in the remainder of this research.

The last step in sampling is related to the second research target: selecting a control sample of non-distressed companies. The selection is necessary in order to compare the restructuring actions of healthy, non-distressed companies with those in the distressed sample. To be included in the non-distressed sample, firms must meet the same size and data requirements as the distressed sample and in addition must stay out of distress, showing continuous positive interest coverage for the entire sample period.[390] A total of 60 non-distressed control firms (ND) are identified. Because the non-distressed firms have multiple five-year timeframes with continuous positive interest coverage, a matching procedure is included in the sampling process.[391] The matching is based on two criteria: year and size. First, the five-year timeframes of the non-distressed companies are selected to show a distribution similar to the distress years of the turnaround firms. Second, firm size, measured as total assets in the first year of the five-year timeframe, is chosen to approximate that of the turnaround firms in the pre-distress year.[392] Accordingly, timing and size effects have been controlled for at the sample construction stage.[393]

388 Compare EICHNER (2008, pp. 147-148) and TSIKRIKTSIS (2005, p. 60).

389 Compare for the same approach KANG/SHIVDASANI (1997, p. 33). For a general discussion of multiple restructurings compare ATIASE ET AL. (2004, pp. 504-505). Bias for multiple distress situations might result from the higher possibility of not turning around after the initial period of distress; see LIN ET AL. (2006, p. 547), and also from mismatching actions in the turnaround process when they were triggered by earlier distress situations; compare SUDARSANAM/LAI (2001, p. 194).

390 The same prerequisite is used by FAN ET AL. (2011, p. 15). "The entire sampling period" means for any available five-year timeframe, not merely a single five-year timeframe.

391 Subsample sizes need not be equal because the matching is based on minimizing the difference in sample means for firm size, not on matched pair design; compare KANG/SHIVDASANI (1997, p. 35).

392 The same criteria are used by ROSSER/CANIL (2011, p. 8). A common timeframe is needed for sensitivity

The distressed sample of 134 companies falls within the boundaries of the first research question concerning the effectiveness of restructuring actions. The entire matched sample of 194 firms, including the 60 non-distressed companies, is the basis for the third research question concerning the comparison of distressed and healthy firms and is labeled 'matched sample' in the remainder of this study.[394] The final research question focuses on the 82 successful turnarounds and the identification of successful turnaround gestalts within them.

4.2 Variables and measures

The operationalization of variables is based on the predictive-validity framework by RUNKEL/MCGRATH (1972) (see FIGURE 13).[395] At the conceptual level, theory is formalized within a structural equation.[396] Hypotheses concerning restructuring actions and their impact on corporate turnaround are derived within the conceptual framework. Explanatory (X_p) and explained variables (Y) are then operationalized through observable variables, and their relationship is examined within the operational framework. To minimize endogeneity problems in testing the theory, control variables (X_q) assumed to have a potential influence on the selection of restructuring actions are introduced at the operational level.[397]

---

analysis of the different subsamples; see SMITH/GRAVES (2005, p. 312). A matching of the industry is not required here because the research is already based on one single industry sector.
Although control firms are selected to minimize deviations in timeframes and firm size, the control sample still differs in terms of these two measures, but not with statistical significance. See CHAPTER 5.1 for the corresponding analysis. But even if this control is necessarily imperfect, a non-random, matched sampling is preferred over a random sampling for the control group because it provides a closer comparator; see SUDARSANAM ET AL. (2011, p. 244).

393 Compare ROSSER/CANIL (2011, p. 8).

394 Sample size in general can be considered a trade-off. Although larger samples yield more precise and hence more valid statistical results, smaller samples in most cases are more homogenous, allowing for better explanation of differences between turnarounds and non-turnarounds; see BRYMAN/BELL (2007, pp. 195-197). In this research, an industry-specific sample is preferred over a larger sample encompassing various industries; compare SECTION 1.1.3 for a discussion.

395 Compare RUNKEL/MCGRATH (1972) in general and CHENHALL/MOERS (2007) for theory-based, quantitative management research in particular.

396 See for the following CHENHALL/MOERS (2007).

397 Endogeneity formally is present when an explanatory variable is correlated with the error term and exists in virtually all studies using accounting, finance, and economic variables; compare CHENHALL/MOERS (2007, p. 192). Compare SECTION 4.3.2 for details concerning the test for endogeneity.

Figure 13: Predictive-validity framework.

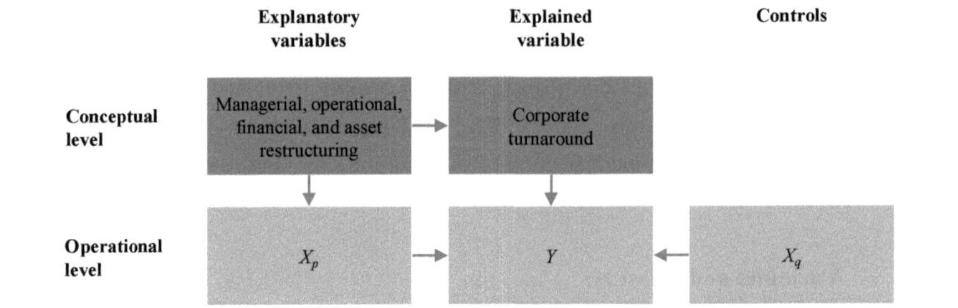

Source: Own illustration based on CHENHALL/MOERS (2007, p. 176).

As customary with research on corporate turnaround, this research primarily adopts an accounting perspective with the collection and analysis of financial data.[398] Because publicly available reporting information has been found useful in researching corporate turnaround,[399] the proxies used for restructuring actions are based on financial information from the annual accounts of companies within the sample.

Most managerial actions are measured at three points in time: at the pre-distress level (Y_{-1}), after the end of the early restructuring phase (Y_{+1}), and after the end of the late restructuring phase (Y_{+3}) when the outcome of turnaround or non-turnaround is determined.[400] The control variables, when applicable, are measured at the pre-distress level (Y_0) to capture potential differences between turnaround and non-turnaround firms. As far as possible, metric scaling of variables is retained to avoid loss of information in the following statistical analysis.[401]

In the remainder of this chapter, the dependent variable and the independent and control variables are operationalized (see FIGURE 14 for an overview).

Corporate turnaround

Based on the definition of financial distress in SECTION 3.1.1 and the definition of corporate turnaround in SECTION 3.1.2, corporate turnaround is defined as the reestablishment of positive interest coverage in Y_{+3}. Positive interest coverage is operationalized as EBITDA[402]

---

398 See LIN ET AL. (2008, p. 540). A consideration in using accounting data as proxy for managerial actions is that some variables might influence other restructuring actions as well. CHOWDHURY/LANG (1996, p. 173) consider this a "minor problem" and still recommend the use of accounting data. Compare SECTION 4.3.2 for the analysis of inherent multicollinearity.

399 See KANE/RICHARDSON (2002, p. 271).

400 Compare SECTION 3.2.2 for details.

401 Compare for this argument BORTZ (2005, p. 570). In addition, the introduction of thresholds always must be considered arbitrary, and results might be sensitive to the threshold applied.

402 Item 18198: EARNINGS BEFORE INTEREST, TAXES, DEPRECIATION & AMORTIZATION represent the earnings of a company before interest expense, income taxes, and depreciation. It is calculated by taking pre-tax income and adding back interest expense on debt plus depreciation, depletion

being sufficient to cover capital expenditures (CAPEX)[403] and interest expense on debt (INT)[404].

Managerial restructuring

Management turnover is a change in the firm's top executive, generally the CEO. If the position of CEO is not formally established, which is often the case for Asian firms, the president or the chairman is defined as the top executive.[405] Following convention,[406] routine and non-routine turnover of the top executive are differentiated. Change due to death, illness, or normal retirement is classified as *routine turnover*. Any other change, including retirement under age 65, is treated as a forced or *non-routine turnover*. Routine and non-routine turnover are analyzed both in the years of the early and late restructuring phases.[407]

Operational restructuring

Operational revenue-generating actions are hard to operationalize when organic revenue growth is the variable of interest because "the effect of asset restructuring such as acquisitions, obscures operational-revenue generating efforts."[408] Especially if change in sales is used as a proxy for revenue growth, this limitation occurs. In this research, growth in net revenue (REV) [409] is adjusted for growth in fixed assets (FAS)[410] to proxy for organic revenue growth and to at least partially avoid distortions from expansion of the asset base.[411] This adjusted growth ratio is closely related to fixed asset turnover and shows the ability of the firm to generate revenue from its fixed asset base. Hence it can also be interpreted as a productivity measure.[412] A positive growth ratio indicates more effective use of the asset base

---

and amortization and subtracting interest capitalized.

403 Item 04601: CAPITAL EXPENDITURE represents funds used to acquire fixed assets other than those associated with acquisitions. It includes but is not restricted to additions to property, plant, and equipment and investments in machinery and equipment.

404 Item Field 01251: INTEREST EXPENSE ON DEBT represents the service charge for the use of capital before the reduction for interest capitalized.

405 See BRUTON (1989, p. 526).

406 E.g., DENIS/KRUSE (2000, p. 407), SUDARSANAM/LAI (2001, p. 189), or YAWSON (2009, p. 225).

407 For analysis of managerial restructuring additional sources such as annual reports, corporate websites, and analyst reports are used. In addition, a press research in FACTIVA and LexisNexis is conducted when necessary.

408 SUDARSANAM/LAI (2001, p. 185).

409 Item 01001: NET SALES OR REVENUES represent gross sales and other operating revenue less discounts, returns, and allowances.

410 Item 02501 (Fixed assets): PROPERTY, PLANT AND EQUIPMENT (NET) represents gross property, plant, and equipment less accumulated reserves for depreciation, depletion and amortization.

411 This scaling introduces the problem, that an increase in the proxy for revenue generation cannot be fully separated from efficiency improvements and leaves room for judgment; compare CHOWDHURY/LANG (1996, p. 173) for a discussion of the general problem related to the asset reduction/revenue-generating typology. Still, CHOWDHURY/LANG (1996) recommend this typology for the analysis of managerial actions in corporate turnaround.

412 Compare also FRANCIS/DESAI (2005, p. 1212), who use revenue divided by property, plant, and equipment.

and is especially suitable for manufacturing industries where asset purchases often are linked to increased output and can distort results.

For *cost-cutting* efforts, change in total operating expenses (EXP)[413] compared to the pre-distress level is analyzed. This is the most comprehensive cost measure and is considered a good proxy for retrenchment actions.[414] Operating expenses are scaled by net sales, the primary driver of operating costs, to allow comparison of different companies.[415]

Financial restructuring

The first financial restructuring action, *equity issue* (EQU), is a dummy variable coded 1 if the company issued equity within the turnaround process.[416] An equity issue is defined as any proceeds from the sale of common or preferred stock.[417] Common dividends (DIV)[418] are used as a proxy for the *dividend policy* of the company. An alternative proxy, the dividend per share, is rejected due to distortions if the number of shares outstanding changes.[419] The absolute change compared to the pre-distress level is analyzed. *Debt restructuring* is analyzed by change in total debt (DBT)[420] relative to total assets (TAS)[421] compared to the pre-distress level. The impact of debt restructuring is measured as a change in the proportion of debt in the capital structure.[422] Prior research showed that a change in long-term debt instead of total debt does not change the results.[423]

---

413 Item 1249: OPERATING EXPENSES - TOTAL represents the sum of all expenses related to operations. This includes cost of goods sold, depreciation, depletion and amortization, and sales, general, and administrative expenses.

414 See FRANCIS/DESAI (2005, p. 1212).

415 Compare LIN ET AL. (2008, p. 544) or FURRER ET AL. (2007, p. 382).

416 Equity issue is defined as any amount a company received from the sale of common and/or preferred stock. It includes amounts received from the conversion of debentures or preferred stock into common stock, sale of treasury shares, and shares issued for acquisitions (Item 04302: OTHER PROCEEDS FROM SALE/ISSUANCE OF STOCK).

417 Compare YAWSON (2009, p. 224) or SUDARSANAM/LAI (2001, p. 189).

418 Item 05376: COMMON DIVIDENDS (CASH) represent the total cash common dividends paid on the company's common stock during the fiscal year, including extra and special dividends.

419 See YAWSON (2009, p. 222). For the use of total dividend see also OFEK (1993, p. 11). For the use of dividend per share see SUDARSANAM/LAI (2001, p. 188). JOHN ET AL. (1992, pp. 909-910) do not indicate which proxy they use for dividend policy.

420 Item 03255: TOTAL DEBT represents all interest-bearing and capitalized lease obligations. It is the sum of long- and short-term debt.

421 Item 02999: TOTAL ASSETS represent the sum of total current assets, long-term receivables, investment in unconsolidated subsidiaries, other investments, net property plant, and equipment, and other assets.

422 See YAWSON (2009, p. 222) and JOHN ET AL. (1992, pp. 909-910). Alternatively, the debt-to-equity ratio can be used; see LIN ET AL. (2008, p. 542). In addition, prior research showed that distressed companies do not issue new debt and therefore a broad proxy for debt restructuring is recommended; compare YAWSON (2009, p. 222). Book values are recommended because it is "virtually impossible to measure market value of most debt for a distressed firm"; ASQUITH ET AL. (1994, p. 646).

423 See YAWSON (2009, p. 226).

Asset restructuring

Change in total assets (TAS) is used as a proxy for *general asset restructuring*. Change in total assets compared to the pre-distress level captures general asset retrenchment actions of the company as well as expansionary moves expected during the late restructuring phase.[424] More specifically, the level of *capital expenditures* (CAPEX), hence additions to fixed assets other than those from acquisitions, in relation to fixed assets is analyzed.[425]

Context variables

The most common firm characteristic used as a control variable is firm size. The proxy for *firm size* is the natural log of total assets.[426] The natural log transformation is required to overcome problems with skewness.[427] Two specific context variables to control for performance differences are prior performance and severity of distress. *Prior performance* is measured by a relative operating performance measure, EBITDA divided by total assets in the pre-distress year. This is used to avoid distortions from different profitability levels prior to distress. *Severity of distress* is the absolute change in EBITDA divided by total assets between the pre-distress year and the year of onset. This is necessary because the probability of non-turnaround is expected to be influenced by the severity of distress.[428] In addition, differences in financial resources prior to onset of distress can affect the probability of turnaround.[429] *Slack* is operationalized as working capital (WC)[430] over total assets and *financial capacity* as the debt-to-equity[431] ratio (DBT/CE).

Any time-specific impact is controlled for by using yearly dummies for the *distress year*. *Regional specifics* are controlled by introducing the Asia-Pacific origin as a binary variable. Asia-Pacific is selected because it is the dominant group among the three regions included in the sample, and specific corporate actions might occur.[432] The last control variable is membership in one of the two *industry subsectors* included in the sample, either ICB subsector "3355 Auto Parts" or "3357 Tires."

---

424 See FRANCIS/DESAI (2005, p. 1212). This proxy is also used by LIN ET AL. (2008, p. 544) and JOHN ET AL. (1992, pp. 905-906). Partially, fixed assets are focused on; see BRUTON ET AL. (2003, p. 540). Using total assets largely avoids including firms that eliminate assets but retain the proceeds within the firm, DENIS/SHOME (2005, p. 431).

425 See JOHN ET AL. (1992, pp. 907-908), ASQUITH ET AL. (1994, p. 650), SUDARSANAM/LAI (2001, p. 189), or FURRER ET AL. (2007, p. 382).

426 USD values are used for the proxy of firm size to allow comparisons within the international sample. For all other variables national currency values are applied to avoid distortions from exchange rates over time.

427 See SMITH/GRAVES (2005, p. 315).

428 The change in EBITDA also controls for time series properties in accounting earnings; see YAWSON (2009, p. 226).

429 See for the following MORROW ET AL. (2007, p. 277).

430 Item 03151: WORKING CAPITAL represents the difference between current assets and current liabilities.

431 Item 03501: COMMON EQUITY represents common shareholders' investment in a company.

432 Compare BRUTON ET AL. (2003) for East Asia and KANG/SHIVDASANI (1997) for Japan.

Figure 14: Variable definitions.

Variable	Process	Definition	Abbr.
Corporate turnaround			
Status	Y_{+3}	[1] Turnaround : $EBITDA_{+3} - INT_{+3} - CAPEX_{+3} \geq 0$ [0] Non-turnaround: $EBITDA_{+3} - INT_{+3} - CAPEX_{+3} < 0$	TA NT
	Y_{-1}-Y_{+3}	[3] Non-distressed : $EBITDA_t - INT_t - CAPEX_t > 0$	ND
Managerial restructuring			
Top executive change – All	ER	[1] for any top executive change in Y_0 and/or Y_{+1}, [0] otherwise	MRA-ER
	LR	[1] for any top executive change in Y_{+2} and/or Y_{+3}, [0] otherwise	MRA-LR
Top executive change – Non-routine	ER	[1] for non-routine top executive change in Y_0 and/or Y_{+1}, [0] otherwise	MRN-ER
	LR	[1] for non-routine top executive change in Y_{+2} and/or Y_{+3}, [0] otherwise	MRN-LR
Operational restructuring			
Revenue development	ER	$((REV_{+1} - REV_{-1}) / REV_{-1}) - (FAS_{+1} - FAS_{-1}) / FAS_{-1})$	REV-ER
	LR	$((REV_{+3} - REV_{+1}) / REV_{-1}) - (FAS_{+2} - FAS_{+1}) / FAS_{-1})$	REV-LR
Operating expense ratio	ER	$((EXP_{+1}/REV_{+1}) - (EXP_{-1}/REV_{-1})) / (EXP_{-1}/REV_{-1})$	EXP-ER
	LR	$((EXP_{+3}/REV_{+3}) - (EXP_{+1}/REV_{+1})) / (EXP_{-1}/REV_{-1})$	EXP-LR
Financial restructuring			
Equity issue	ER	[1] for equity issue in Y_0 and/or Y_{+1}, [0] otherwise	EQU-ER
	LR	[1] for equity issue in Y_{+2} and/or Y_{+3}, [0] otherwise	EQU-LR
Dividend policy	ER	$(DIV_{+1} - DIV\text{-}_1) / DIV_{-1}$	DIV-ER
	LR	$(DIV_{+3} - DIV_{+1}) / DIV_{-1}$	DIV-LR
Debt restructuring	ER	$((DBT_{+1}/TA_{+1}) - (DBT_{-1}/TA_{-1})) / (DBT_{-1}/TAS_{-1})$	DBT-ER
	LR	$((DBT_{+3}/TA_{+3}) - (DBT_{+1}/TA_{+1})) / (DBT_{-1}/TAS_{-1})$	DBT-LR
Asset restructuring			
Total assets change	ER	$(TAS_{+1} - TAS\text{-}_1) / TAS_{-1}$	TAS-ER
	LR	$(TAS_{+3} - TAS{+}1) / TAS_{-1}$	TAS-LR
Capital expenditure intensity	ER	$((CAPEX_{+1}/FAS_{+1}) - (CAPEX_{-1}/FAS_{-1})) / (CAPEX_{-1}/FAS_{-1})$	CAP-ER
	LR	$((CAPEX_{+3}/FAS_{+3}) - (CAPEX_{+1}/FAS_{+1})) / (CAPEX_{-1}/FAS_{-1})$	CAP-LR
Context			
Firm size	CTX	$\ln (TAS_{-1})$	TA-CTX
Prior performance	CTX	$EBITDA_{-1}/TAS_{-1}$	PP-CTX
Distress severity	CTX	$(EBITDA_0/TAS_0)$ - $(EBITDA_{-1}/TAS_{-1})$	DS-CTX
Financial capacity	CTX	DBT_{-1}/CE_{-1}	FC-CTX
Financial slack	CTX	WC_{-1}/TAS_{-1}	FS-CTX
Distress year	CTX	YEAR Y_0: [2000, 2001, 2002, 2003, 2004, 2005]	DY-CTX
Region	CTX	[1] for Asia-Pacific [0] for Europe & Africa and Americas	RG-CTX
Industry subsector	CTX	[1] for ICB '3357 Tires' [0] for ICB '3355 Auto Parts'	IN-CTX

Process: ER early restructuring, LR late restructuring, CTX context factor

Source: Own illustration.

4.3 Statistical methods

4.3.1 Preliminaries

CHAPTER 4.3 provides a short introduction to the statistical methods applied in PART 5. Because each of the three research questions addresses a different aspect of corporate turnaround, different statistical methods are applied (see FIGURE 15).

Figure 15: Overview statistical methods.

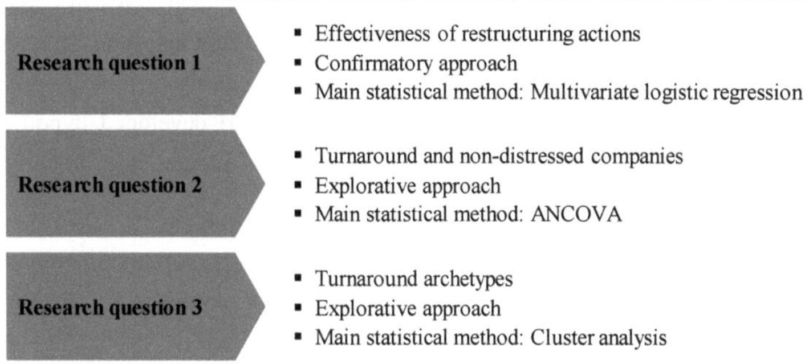

Source: Own illustration.

The first research question addresses the effectiveness of various restructuring actions in corporate turnaround in the automotive supplier industry. Because the selection of restructuring actions is theory-based and existing empirical research is incorporated, a confirmatory approach is chosen. Due to the binary character of the dependent variable corporate turnaround, a multivariate logistic regression is used. The rationale for the selection of the logistic regression and a detailed introduction are provided in SECTION 4.3.2.

The second research question differentiates turnaround strategies from strategies of non-distressed, healthy firms. Because this research question is comparably novel, no theory-based hypotheses are available, and an explorative research method is selected. With the 'analysis of covariance' (ANCOVA), the relation of the company status (turnaround, non-turnaround, and non-distressed) to the selected single restructuring strategies is examined. An synopsis of the concept of ANCOVA follows in SECTION 4.3.3.

The third research question aims to identify patterns of restructuring actions within successful turnarounds. As with the second research question, no hypotheses for restructuring patterns in the context of the automotive supplier industry are derived, and cluster analysis as an explorative research method is selected. Further details are provided in SECTION 4.3.4.

4.3.2 Logistic regression

In this section, a short summary of multivariate statistical methods available for the analysis of the effectiveness of restructuring actions in corporate turnaround is given before providing the rationale for selection of the logistic regression. This section concludes by introducing the methodology of logistic regression required for interpretation of results in CHAPTER 5.2.

Selection of statistical method for the first research question

Within multivariate analysis methods there is a general differentiation between explorative and confirmatory statistical methods.[433] Because the first research question refers to the testing of hypotheses about the effectiveness of various restructuring actions for corporate turnaround, a confirmatory statistical method to test the a-priori developed hypotheses is required in this explanative research setting. The goal is to estimate the probability of turnaround given the restructuring actions chosen.

Along with the complementary binary dependent variable[434] 'corporate turnaround' and independent variables with metric and nominal scales, four confirmatory, multivariate statistical methods are available for this research setting: linear probability model, multivariate discriminant analysis, binary logistic regression, and binary probit regression.[435] Each will be introduced, and a rationale for the selection of logistic regression is provided.

The *linear probability model* is a regular linear regression model applied to a binary dependent variable (see EQUATION 2).[436] For case *i*, there are *P* independent variables, x_{pi}, and β_p are the corresponding parameters, and ε_i is the residual for this single case.

Equation 2: Linear probability model.

$$y_i = \beta_o + \sum_{p=1}^{P} \beta_p x_{pi} + \varepsilon_i$$

Source: BACKHAUS ET AL. (2008, p. 248) and LONG (1997, p. 35).

Estimation of model parameters in the context of linear regression models most often is based on ordinary least squares (OLS). Hence the estimation of parameters β_p is based on the minimization of the squared residuals ε_i^2. The problem is that the linear probability model is set up to estimate the empirical observations directly, although in fact the probability of the

433 Compare BACKHAUS ET AL. (2008, pp. 12-14) for an overview of multivariate statistical methods.

434 P(y=1) + P(y=0) = 1; see BACKHAUS ET AL. (2008, p. 244).

435 See BACKHAUS ET AL. (2008, pp. 12-14) and LONG (1997, p. 34). Although 'independent variables' is the wording used here, this term is interchangeable with predictor and explanatory variables or covariates. For discussion of alternative statistical methods, including tobit regression, panel regression models with fixed or random effects, cox regression, structured equation models, and reasons for their de-selection, compare EICHNER (2008, p. 154).

436 Compare for the following LONG (1997, pp. 35-40) with a detailed description of the linear probability model.

observation is required for this research setting. The linearity of the model leads to two major problems. First, the model can result in values larger than 1 or negative values, both nonsensical estimates for the phenomenon of interest. Second, a one-unit increase in an independent variable x_{pi} always results in the constant change β_p in the dependent variable y_i. This also is unrealistic in the context of corporate turnaround. The linear probability model is therefore unsuitable in this research setting.[437]

Discriminant analysis and logistic regression are comparable multivariate approaches to analyzing similarities and differences between groups.[438] Linear discriminant analysis is a statistical technique for classifying an observation into one of two or more mutually exclusive groups based on linear combinations of values of predictor variables and for determining which variables contribute to the separation. The disadvantage of discriminant analysis is that it requires data to be drawn from a multivariate normal distribution with equal variances and covariances for all variables. Therefore, it is more restrictive than logistic regression in modeling binary outcomes.[439] Accounting values and ratios as they are used in this research are expected to exhibit skewness and kurtosis and therefore violate the required normality assumption.[440] Parameter estimates in multidiscriminant analysis in the context of corporate turnaround are accordingly often not considered as robust as in logistic regression.[441]

Binary logit and probit models are closely related non-linear probability models and are often considered interchangeable. Because logistic regression offers minor practical advantages compared to probit regression, a logistic regression model is chosen for the statistical analysis of the first research question.[442] In general, logistic regression is the most popular regression technique for modeling binary dependent variables.[443] But for research on corporate turnaround in particular, many researchers consider logistic regression the primary choice. It was applied in more than 40% of the studies included in the literature review.[444]

---

437 Compare LONG (1997, pp. 38-39) for discussion of the two further problems: non-normal distribution of the residuals and heteroscedasticity.

438 See for the following BACKHAUS ET AL. (2008, p. 182).

439 Compare PENG/SO (2002) and the listed references.

440 See TAIMER (2007, p. 2631).

441 Compare LO (1986) and PRESS/WILSON (1978) for a detailed discussion of logistic regression and discriminant analysis.

442 Compare EICHNER (2008, p. 151) for the corresponding discussion. A supplemental probit regression analysis is provided to assure the robustness of results; compare APPENDIX 9 for details.

443 Compare HOETKER (2007) for the importance of logistic regression models in strategic management research. Among the reviewed empirical studies on corporate turnaround in CHAPTER 2.2, only ASQUITH ET AL. (1994) used probit regression.

444 Nine of the 22 studies reviewed used logistic regression, in addition several related articles like DENIS/SHOME (2005), ROUTLEDGE/GARDENNE (2004), KANE/RICHARDSON (2002) , or WHITING/GILKISON (2000) apply the same statistical method.

Introduction to logistic regression

Logistic regression has two major characteristics favorable for analysis of corporate turnaround: First, the dependent variable is limited to the interval [0; 1]. Second, its distribution is intuitively attractive because the impact of changes in the independent variables depends on the initial probability.[445] Logistic regression is developed in terms of the regression of a latent, unobservable variable *z*, which is related to the observed binary variable *y* (see EQUATION 3).[446] Whereas there is a linear relationship between the latent variable *z* and the independent variables x_p, there is a non-linear, logistic relationship between the latent variable *z* and the probability of event *P(y)*.[447] If the latent variable *z* is larger than the threshold or cutoff point τ, then the dependent variable *y* is classified as y=1.

Equation 3: Logistic regression model and curve.

Logistic regression model

$$P_i(y=1) = \frac{1}{1+e^{-z_i}}$$

with:

$$z_i = \beta_0 + \sum_{p=1}^{P} \beta_p x_{pi} + \varepsilon_i$$

$$y_i = \begin{cases} 1 \text{ if } z_i > \tau \\ 0 \text{ if } z_i \leq \tau \end{cases}$$

Logistic regression curve

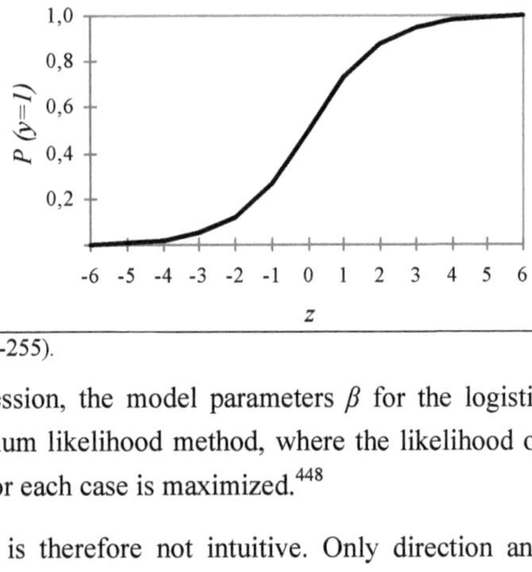

Source: Based on BACKHAUS ET AL. (2008, pp. 253-255).

Contrary to the OLS method in linear regression, the model parameters β for the logistic regression are estimated based on the maximum likelihood method, where the likelihood of deriving the observed outcome $y_i=1$ or $y_i=0$ for each case is maximized.[448]

Interpretation of the regression coefficients is therefore not intuitive. Only direction and significance can be interpreted directly. No direct interpretation of the magnitude of the effect is possible because the effect of a change in one variable depends on values of the other variables.[449] The discussion of results provides the effect on the probability of turnaround of a

---

445 See HOETKER (2007, pp. 332-333).

446 See for the following LONG (1997, p. 35).

447 P(y) is simplifying for P(Y|x), hence the probability of the outcome y given the values of x.

448 Compare BACKHAUS ET AL. (2008, p. 253) for details concerning the maximum likelihood method in the context of logistic regression. Maximization of the likelihood function L can be simplified by using the log of the likelihood function, the log-likelihood function LL. Parameter maximizing the log-likelihood function also maximize the likelihood function. The maximization process itself is based on the iterative Newton Raphson algorithm. The resulting parameters that maximize the log-likelihood function are called maximum likelihood estimators.

449 See for the following HOETKER (2007, p. 334) and his recommendations. The often-recommended odds ratios are not presented because they "seem to have little to offer either readers or researchers." Compare

change in one variable if other variables are at their average values. Significance levels for all variables are based on the Likelihood-Ratio-Test because it is expected to be the most accurate.[450]

The evaluation of the logistic regression model is based on the overall model evaluation, the inferential and descriptive goodness-of-fit evaluation, and the validation of predicted probabilities through measures of association. The overall model evaluation is based on the *Likelihood-Ratio*-Test hence the null hypothesis that all population coefficients are 0.[451] The Likelihood-Ratio-Test shows that the model is an improvement of the intercept-only model.

To evaluate the model's goodness-of-fit of the model, and hence the fit of a model against the data, the inferential *Hosmer-Lemeshow (H-L) statistic* is provided. This statistic tests whether the observed values differ significantly from the predicted values within the model. It should be non-significant.[452] As a descriptive goodness-of-fit measure, two Pseudo-R^2 measures are provided. The Pseudo R^2 is not directly comparable to an R^2 metric from linear regression and typically will yield much smaller values for logistic regressions. The advantages of the chosen *Nagelkerke* R^2 are that it still has a maximum value of 1, and it can be interpreted as the variation in outcome explained by the logistic regression model.[453] As an alternative to the Nagelkerke R^2, *McFadden's* R^2 is also provided, as it is preferred by some scholars.

Three supplementary measures for the assessment of model fit and the model discrimination in particular are provided. The *c-statistic* indicates the degree to which predictions from the model agree with the data.[454] It is a measure of association and is the proportion of pairs of cases with different outcomes which are classified correctly by the model. It ranges from 0.5 to 1, while 0.5 would be same the probability as by chance.[455] The *percentage of correct classification* or *Count* R^2 shows the proportion of correct predictions by the model.[456] As

---

HOETKER (2007, p. 335) and the related discussion of frequent misinterpretation among researchers.

450 See MENARD (1995, p. 38).

451 Compare NORUSIS (2009, pp. 331-332) and PENG/SO (2002, p. 42).

452 The Pearson χ^2 and the deviance-based goodness-of-fit statistic are not used because of problems with data basis used by SPSS; compare PENG/SO (2002, p. 44).

453 Some scholars even recommend not including Pseudo-R^2 measures in logistic regression; compare HOSMER/LEMESHOW (2000, p. 167). HOETKER (2007, p. 342) recommends clearly indicating which R^2 measure is used, if one is reported.

454 See for the following PENG/SO (2002, pp. 47-48) and NORUSIS (2009, pp. 346-347). The c-statistic is related to the receiver operating characteristics (ROC) cure and the concept of sensitivity (proportion of cases with the event correctly predicted to have the event) and specificity (proportion of cases without the event correctly predicted to not have the event).

455 Because SPSS does not directly calculate the c-statistic, Somer's D is divided by 2, and 0.5 is added; compare PENG/SO (2002, p. 46).

456 See for the following HOETKER (2007, pp. 340-342), who also discusses problems related to this measure. Classification tables should be used with caution and cannot be considered a goodness-of-fit measure. They ignore actual predicted probabilities and use dichotomized predictions based on a cutoff values instead (0.5 in most cases). This means predicting a 0 (non-turnaround) or 1 (turnaround) dependent, but the classification table does not show how close to 1 the correct predictions are (nor how close to 0 the

recommended, this measure is adjusted to account for the proportion of the most frequent outcome in the sample and therefore the *Adjusted Count R^2* is also provided. The Adjusted Count R^2 is the percentage of correct predictions beyond the number that would be correctly guessed by choosing the largest marginal.

Modeling approach

The modeling strategy recommended by PENG/SO (2002) is followed in developing the logistic regression model.[457] The preliminary first step is the descriptive analysis of each variable. The initial step in model-building for the multivariate logistic regression is a series of univariate logistic regressions, each based on a single independent variable. An alternative to the univariate logistic regression analysis is calculation of the χ^2 ratio test for binary variables and a two-sample t-test for metric variables.[458] This is required for a pre-selection of variables to determine which have at least some influence on the probability of turnaround. Based on the univariate analysis, variables with a p-value below 0.25 should be considered for inclusion in the multivariate logistic regression analysis.[459] The higher significance level is recommended because more traditional levels like 0.05 fail to identify variables which are not strongly significant in the univariate analysis but might be important in the multivariate context. The inclusion of variables with an overall questionable importance is already avoided due to the theory-based deviation of variables.[460]

First, all variables are included in a preliminary multivariate regression. Based on the analysis of the preliminary multivariate model, a fitted model is developed. This model-building approach accords with the objective of HOSMER/LEMESHOW (2000) to seek "the most parsimonious model that still explains the data well."[461] A backward variable selection process based on the Likelihood-Ratio-Test is used.[462] This process will avoid the problem of overfitting if too many variables, even though theoretically justified, are included in the model. Backward selection is preferred over a forward selection because it reduces the risk of not identifying important relations due to "suppressor effects"[463]. An entry probability of 0.25 and an exit probability of 0.15 are applied.

---

errors are). Thus, models in which the predictions are mostly close to the cutoff does not have as good a fit as a model where the predicted scores cluster near 1 or 0.

457 Compare PENG/SO (2002, pp. 53-55).

458 See HOSMER/LEMESHOW (2000, pp. 92-93).

459 Compare for the following HOSMER/LEMESHOW (2000, p. 95) and the corresponding references.

460 Because the differentiation of early and late restructuring phases is comparatively new in empirical research, variables for both phases are included in the multivariate model if the univariate analysis shows significance in only one phase. This approach accords with PENG/SO (2002), who recommend including additional variables of theoretical interest; see PENG/SO (2002, p. 54).

461 HOSMER/LEMESHOW (2000, p. 92).

462 See NORUSIS (2009, p. 339) for recommendations of the Likelihood-Ratio.

463 Forward selection starts without any variables, whereas backward elimination starts with all variables in

The final step is the evaluation of the model based on the criteria outlined along with model and outlier diagnostics. These diagnostics address the issues of linearity, multicollinearity, endogeneity, and the impact of single outliers. First, the *Box-Tidwell transformation test* is used to test the requirement that the relationship between the latent variable z and each of the independent variables is linear.[464] To identify problems related to nonlinearity, the interaction term of any dependent variable with its logarithmized value is included in the multivariate logistic regression. The method's advantage is that it is not sensitive to minor degrees of nonlinearity. Significant interaction terms are proof of nonlinearity and indicate that transformation of variables might be required.

Second, the analysis of potential problems due to multicollinearity is required.[465] Here the level of correlation among the independent variables is analyzed and should be below 0.5.[466] In addition, two popular multicollinearity diagnostic statistics, Tolerance (T_i) and Variance Inflation Factor (VIF_i) for each independent variable, are provided. Tolerance is 1 minus the coefficient of determination for the regression of one independent variable on all remaining independent variables. VIF is 1 divided by the Tolerance value. VIF larger than 2.5 indicates the presence of collinearity might be a concern in logistic regression.

Third, potential issues of endogeneity must be controlled for. Endogeneity means that one of the independent variables is correlated with the error term and therefore the estimators will be biased and inconsistent. The endogeneity problem is especially relevant for variables during the late restructuring phase, whereas variables during the early restructuring phase occur two years before the definition of the company status and can therefore be considered exogenous due to the timing.[467] Per EICHNER (2008) and JOSTARNDT (2007), an augmented regression test (Durbin-Wu-Hausman test) is conducted to identify potential endogeneity errors.[468] This is a two-step approach that regresses the residuals of each potentially endogenous independent variable against all exogenous variables in a regression of the original model. The Durbin-Wu-Hausman then tests if those residuals affect the final model significantly. A significant test statistic would indicate that the exogeneity assumption must be rejected.

---

the model; compare NORUSIS (2009, p. 344). The chosen approach accords with EICHNER (2008, p. 162).

464 Compared to OLS regression, which requires a linear relationship between the independent variables and the dependent variable, logistic regression assumes a linear relationship among the independent variables and logit of the dependent variable.

465 See for the following FIELD (2005, pp. 259-263) and the quoted references.

466 See also EICHNER (2008, p. 171), who proposes 0.7.

467 Compare EICHNER (2008, p. 172) and JOSTARNDT (2007, p. 103).

468 Most empirical strategy research does not explicitly test for endogeneity. Compare the analysis of HAMILTON/NICKERSON (2003) for details. Therefore, the approach outlined by JOSTARNDT (2007, p. 121) and EICHNER (2008, p. 172) is followed.

In the last step, logistic regression diagnostics, potential outliers are identified and their impact on the regression results is evaluated.[469] Although not necessarily undesirable, influential observations can make relatively large contributions to values of the estimates—that is, observations whose inclusion or exclusion may yield substantial changes in the fitted model. Outlier diagnostics include *Cook's distance measure* (CD), leverage (ht), and the analysis of residuals. Cook's distance is a measure for the influence of an individual case, hence the change in the regression coefficients if a case is deleted from the model. The CD should always be below 1. *Leverage*, which is also called a hat statistic, takes values between 0 and 1 and is a measure of the influence of a single case on the total model. In general, data points with a leverage value between 0.2 and 0.5 are considered moderately influential, whereas values above 0.5 are indicators for concern. *Standardized residuals (e*)* can be analyzed to detect large errors in a model. Standardized residuals should follow a normal distribution: 95% of all cases should lie between ±1.96, and 99% of all cases should lie between ±2.58. Therefore, any case outside ±3 should be examined closely. If outliers are found in the data, they should not be eliminated merely to increase model fit; instead, the reason for the unusual pattern should be identified.

In addition to the logistic regression diagnostics, several boundary conditions are in place to avoid overfitting of the model.[470] The total sample size for the logistic regression should exceed the threshold of 100 cases, and the number of cases within subsamples should exceed 25.[471] Regarding the number of independent variables, a guideline of at least 10 observations per variable is provided, and as an alternative four events per variable, hence the number of cases in the less frequent outcome of the independent variable.

4.3.3 Analysis of covariance

The second research question relates to the identification of 'true' turnaround strategies—i.e., how the restructuring actions of turnaround companies differ from the actions of non-distressed, healthy companies. This rationale expands to the question of whether non-turnaround firms fail to adjust their strategies to the distress situation and retain the conventional strategies of non-distressed firms. The research approach for this research questions is, like the cluster analysis, explorative in nature and no theory-based a priori predictions can be tested.

To analyze whether the choice of restructuring activity is influenced by the status of the company as turnaround, non-turnaround, or non-distressed, analysis of covariance (ANCOVA) is applied. Compared to the regular analysis of variance (ANOVA), which

---

469 See for the following FIELD (2005, pp. 246-248).
470 Compare EICHNER (2008, p. 171) and ROHRLACK (2007, p. 199) for an overview.
471 See LONG (1997, p. 54) and BACKHAUS ET AL. (2008, p. 480).

analyzes how independent variables interact with each other and what effects these interactions have on the dependent variable, ANCOVA additionally includes covariates.[472] Covariates are variables that are, besides the variable of primary interest, expected to influence the dependent variables. In this research, the theory-based context variables are included as covariates in the analysis, and it will be possible to examine the potential relation of company status and the selected restructuring actions, adjusted for effects of covariates.[473]

Compared to logistic regression, ANCOVA is not a standard statistical method in research on corporate turnaround. Although ANOVA was used by ROBBINS/PEARCE (1992) and FURRER ET AL. (2007), the approach proposed by FIELD (2005) and applied by LACEY ET AL. (2007) is followed.[474] To test the overall model, a preliminary multivariate analysis of covariance (MANCOVA) is conducted, including all relevant restructuring actions (dependent variables) while controlling for context factors (covariates). In this traditional approach the following ANCOVA analyses are to be protected by the preliminary MANCOVA.[475] To better understand the effect of the company's status on each restructuring actions, separate ANCOVA analyses are then conducted on single dependent variables while still controlling for the context factors.

The ANCOVA is based on the assumptions that observations are independent and normally distributed and that equal variances in all groups exist.[476] Besides these three assumptions that are also required for ANOVA, for ANCOVA homogeneity of the regression slopes is also required.[477] Although the independence of variables is assured through the sampling process described in CHAPTER 4.1, statistical tests and plots are provided to test the other assumptions and to assure the robustness of results. *Levene's test of equality* is provided to test the assumption of equal variances between the three subsamples of turnarounds, non-turnarounds and non-distressed companies. *Normality plots* to control the normal distribution of dependent variable residuals and scatterplots to control the *homogeneity of regression slopes* are also provided.[478]

The interpretation of separate ANCOVA results for each restructuring action selected as dependent variable is based on the significance level of the *F-statistic*.[479] Significant values

---

472 Compare FIELD (2005, pp. 309-311) for an introduction to ANOVA and FIELD (2005, pp. 363-364) for an introduction to ANCOVA.

473 With the effects of covariates controlled, within-group error variance is reduced and confounds are eliminated; see FIELD (2005, p. 365).

474 Compare for the following LACEY ET AL. (2007, p. 248) and FIELD (2005, p. 594).

475 The idea is that the overall multivariate test protects against inflated Type I error rates because if this initial test is not significant then any subsequent tests are ignored; see FIELD (2005, p. 594).

476 See NORUSIS (2009, pp. 147-150).

477 See FIELD (2005, pp. 380-383), who recommends a visual check for smaller sample sizes.

478 The graphical analysis is recommended for small sample sizes; see NORUSIS (2009, p. 570).

479 See for the following FIELD (2005, pp. 371-373).

indicate that the independent variable—in this context the company's status—is significantly related statistically to the selection of the restructuring strategy adjusted for the impact of control variables. The next step is the analysis of differences between the subsamples. The *b-values* represent the difference between subsamples adjusted for the impact of the covariates and the corresponding *t-test* indicates if these differences are significant. Because the research setting is explorative in nature, the more conservative Sidak corrected post hoc comparison is used to determine the significance level.[480] The corrected significance levels are therefore adjusted for multiple comparisons.[481] The b-value is also the basis for analysis of the covariate and can be interpreted as, other things being equal, a relative increase in the dependent variable if the variable is increased by one unit.

4.3.4 Cluster analysis

The third research question relates to the identification of archetypes in successful turnarounds, hence the identification of turnaround gestalts. Cluster analysis is a heuristic, explorative method to classify objects systematically within a group of objects.[482] In a taxonomic approach, archetypes for successful turnarounds are identified based on 'real' data and within a statistical approach.[483] The goal is to identify "sets of firms that share a common profile along conceptually distinct variables"[484]. The classification itself is based on a determined set of variables with the goal of creating internally homogenous and externally heterogeneous clusters. The focus is on the sample of turnaround companies to avoid distortion of results by including non-turnarounds.[485] In the remainder of this section, the four main steps and the rationale for selecting the statistical methods are introduced briefly.

The *selection of variables* for clustering the objects is considered "the most fundamental step in the application of cluster analysis, and thus, perhaps the most important."[486] Although a large number of variables is generally preferred, a deductive, theory-based variable selection is recommended to assure the exclusion of irrelevant variables that might bias results.[487] The theory-based selection of variables also assures a close link to the first research question. All

---

480 The Sidak correction is also recommended when an initial MANCOVA analysis is used as 'protection' for the following ANCOVA analyses; see FIELD (2005, p. 594).

481 Compare NORUSIS (2009, pp. 154-155) for details concerning the issue of comparing multiple means.

482 For an introduction to cluster analysis, see BORTZ (2005, pp. 565-584), BACKHAUS ET AL. (2008, pp. 389-449), or NORUSIS (2009, pp. 359-388).

483 The taxonomic approach is in comparison to the typological approach, which identifies archetypes based on prior theoretical reasoning LAFRENZ (2004, pp. 193-194) for details.

484 KETCHEN/SHOOK (1996, p. 441).

485 This approach accords with HAMBRICK/SCHECTER (1983) and EICHNER (2008). The alternative approach is to define clusters based on the full sample of distressed companies with the advantage of identifying strategic archetypes independent of later success. Compare LAFRENZ (2004, pp. 197-198), who chooses this approach primarily because of the low sample size in his study.

486 KETCHEN/SHOOK (1996, p. 443).

487 See KETCHEN/SHOOK (1996, pp. 443-444) and HARRIGAN (1985, p. 61).

variables identified in CHAPTER 3.2 are used for clustering the turnaround companies.[488] Because the variables are on different scales, variables on an interval scale are dichotomized.[489] In the context of variable selection, *multicollinearity* among variables can be problematic in the clustering process, and correlations of >±0.9 should be eliminated.[490]

Selection of the appropriate cluster algorithm is the next step in cluster analysis. In this research, a hierarchical, agglomerative algorithm is proposed.[491] Ward's algorithm is popular and has proven reliable in finding very good partitions and assigning the right objects to single cluster groups.[492] Because Ward's algorithm is very sensitive to outliers, a preliminary single-link algorithm is applied to identify possible outliers in the data.[493] Both algorithms use the squared Euclidian distance as a distance measure because it is expected to produce more interpretable clusters.[494]

The next step—determining the *number of clusters*—adopts a three-way approach.[495] First, a visual check of the dendogram is applied. Second, the change in the agglomeration coefficient (fusion coefficient) is graphically analyzed in an elbow chart. Third, a priori theory is used to validate the statistical derivation of the number of clusters.

The last step in cluster analysis is the *validation* of the results based on analysis of the single clusters and a comparison with the initial population for the cluster analysis. This is based on F-ratio and t-ratio.[496] The F-ratio is calculated for each variable within each cluster and is used to assess the homogeneity of the clusters. It divides the cluster variance by the population variance of the population. The smaller the F-ratio, the more homogeneous the cluster. The t-ratio is the difference between the cluster mean and the population mean divided by the standard deviation of the population. It is a measure of the goodness of the

488 This approach accords with LAFRENZ (2004, p. 193), who points out that a sufficiently large number of variables should be included. For the cluster analysis, only ‚Top executive turnover – Non-routine‘ is excluded because of the conceptual overlap with ‚Top executive turnover – All‘. ‚Top executive turnover – All‘ is included in the clustering process because of its higher relevance; see CHAPTER 5.2.

489 See the recommendation of BORTZ (2005, p. 570). Given that 0 is a natural breakpoint for all restructuring actions considered, and thus differentiates between retrenchment and expansion, it is used as a cut point.

490 See BACKHAUS ET AL. (2008, p. 443). A standardization of variables is often recommended to harmonize different weights of variables with large ranges and with small ranges. Because the variables in this research are relative changes compared to a similar pre-distress level, standardization is unnecessary; compare HARRIGAN (1985, p. 61).

491 Hierarchical methods are required if the number of clusters is unknown, and divisive methods are not commonly applied in social sciences; see KETCHEN/SHOOK (1996, pp. 444-445).

492 See PUNJI/STEWART (1983, p. 138) and BACKHAUS ET AL. (2008, pp. 424-425). Ward's algorithm minimizes within-cluster variance; see PUNJI/STEWART (1983, p. 139).

493 This two-step approach is recommend and applied by HAUSCHILDT ET AL. (2006, p. 23), LAFRENZ (2004, p. 226), and EICHNER (2008, p. 176). The single-linkage algorithm, also called the nearest-neighbor method, adds an object to clusters if it displays a specified level of similarity with at least one other object in the cluster; see PUNJI/STEWART (1983, p. 139).

494 See HARRIGAN (1985, p. 60).

495 See for the following KETCHEN/SHOOK (1996, p. 448).

496 See for the following BACKHAUS ET AL. (2008, pp. 439-440).

cluster solution and is also used for interpretation of the cluster results. Positive t-ratios indicate overrepresentation of the variable in the cluster compared to the sample, and negative t-ratios indicate underrepresentation.[497]

497 For interpretation of the cluster analysis results, compare also LAFRENZ (2004, pp. 231-232).

5. EMPIRICAL RESULTS: DISCUSSION AND ANALYSIS

PART 5 includes the main empirical analysis of the restructuring strategies in the automotive supplier industry. CHAPTER 5.1 provides a brief overview of the main descriptives of the matched sample. CHAPTER 5.2 addresses the first research question concerning the effectiveness of restructuring actions. This includes the univariate analysis in the first section and the multivariate logistic regression in the second section. CHAPTER 5.3 compares the strategies of distressed and non-distressed companies based on multiple univariate ANCOVA analyses. The third research question is addressed in CHAPTER 5.4. Successful turnaround archetypes within the automotive supplier industry are identified within an explorative cluster analysis.

5.1 Sample descriptives

This chapter describes the matched sample of 194 publicly listed automotive suppliers (see TABLE 1). An overview of the three firm characteristics—distress year, region, and industry—is provided for all three subsamples along with descriptives for firm size and firm profitability.

Table 1: Matched sample – Firm characteristics.

	TA	N=82	NT	N=52	ND	N=60	Σ	N=194
Variable	n	%	n	%	n	%	n	%
Distress year Y_0								
2000	11	13.4%	5	9.6%	11	18.3%	27	13.9%
2001	22	26.8%	9	17.3%	16	26.7%	47	24.2%
2002	15	18.3%	3	5.8%	10	16.7%	28	14.4%
2003	11	13.4%	10	19.2%	7	11.7%	28	14.4%
2004	13	15.9%	9	17.3%	6	10.0%	28	14.4%
2005	10	12.2%	16	30.8%	10	16.7%	36	18.6%
Region								
Americas	12	14.6%	12	23.1%	12	20.0%	36	18.6%
Asia-Pacific	62	75.6%	36	69.2%	37	61.7%	135	69.6%
Europe & Africa	8	9.8%	4	7.7%	11	18.3%	23	11.9%
Industry subsector								
ICB '3355 Auto Parts'	68	82.9%	43	82.7%	52	86.7%	163	84.0%
ICB '3357 Tires'	14	17.1%	9	17.3%	8	13.3%	31	16.0%

Abbr.: TA Turnaround, NT Non-turnaround, ND Non-distressed

Source: Own illustration.

The distribution of distress years[498] for the matched sample varies from 27 companies (13.9%) in 2000 to 47 companies (24.2%) in 2001. The annual distribution shows that distress years do not cluster in any particular year. Based on the Pearson χ^2 test, the distribution of distress years among the three subsamples also does not differ significantly.[499] Most companies became distressed in 2001 (31 companies), the majority of which (22 companies) were able to turn around. Only nine companies did not recover. The high share of distress situations coincides with the industry downturn in 2001, when global light vehicle production declined 3.3% compared to 2000.[500] An average annual growth rate of 4.3% for the industry between 2002 and 2004 contributed to the high share of successful turnarounds. In 2005, 26 companies became distressed, but only 10 turned around. The high share of distressed

498 For simplification, the timeframe of the non-distressed firms is also positioned along the distress year, which for this subsample simply indicates the second year of the five-year timeframe.

499 Pearson χ^2 test value of 15.228 with a significance level of 0.124.

500 Compare SECTION 1.2.1for information concerning industry growth trends.

companies might be attributable to the industry slowdown of 2.8% compared to 5.4% growth the previous year. At the same time, the high share of unsuccessful turnarounds might be attributable to the industry downturn in 2008.

As outlined in SECTION 1.1.3, the sample is international. Most companies are from the Asia-Pacific region (69.6%), with 18.6% from the Americas and 11.9% from Europe-Africa. Again, the Pearson χ^2 test shows no significant differences in the regional split among subsamples.[501]

The last firm characteristic is the *industry subsector*. As introduced in SECTION 1.1.3, a restricted industry focus forms the basis for the sample. Still, two subsectors within the automotive supplier industry are included in the sample: automotive parts suppliers and tire companies. Most companies (84%) fall under ICB '3355 Auto Parts', whereas 16% are classified as ICB '3357 Tires'. The Pearson χ^2 test for the industry membership also indicates no significant differences among subsamples.[502]

The three firm characteristics—distress years, region, and industry subsector—are included in the following analyses to determine if they significantly influence the choice of restructuring actions and their effectiveness.

Regarding the size of sampled companies, total assets and net revenue figures are provided (see TABLE 2).

Table 2: Matched sample – Pre-distress firm size.

	TA	N=82	NT	N=52	ND	N=60	Σ	N=194
In USD million	mean	s.d.	mean	s.d.	mean	s.d.	mean	s.d.
Total assets Y_{-1}	1,295.8	2,627.5	1,553.7	3,398.4	1,447.4	3,371.0	1,411.8	3,071.6
Net revenue Y_{-1}	1,322.6	2,645.8	2,009.7	5,332.3	1,777.8	4,080.2	1,647.5	3,953.0

Abbr.: TA Turnaround, NT Non-turnaround, ND Non-distressed, s.d. standard deviation

Source: Own illustration.

Average total assets in the pre-distress year are USD 1,411.8 million, and average net revenues are USD 1,647.5 million. The smallest company in the sample is Armour Group PLC, with total assets of USD 52.3 million and net revenues of USD 56.1 million in 2004. The largest company by total assets is Denso Corp., with USD 17.4 billion in 2002. By net revenues, the largest company is Delphi Corp., with USD 29.1 billion in 2000. Although Delpi is a non-turnaround company, both Armour and Denso are non-distressed companies. The average firm size accords with recent research on publicly listed manufacturing

501 Pearson χ^2 test value of 5.478 with a significance level of 0.242.
502 Pearson χ^2 test value of 0.454 with a significance level of 0.797.

companies like for example LIN ET AL. (2008, p. 544) or EICHNER (2008, p. 192).[503] Based on One-Way ANOVA analysis and the non-parametric Kruskal-Wallis test, average total assets and net revenues for the three subsamples can be assumed to be equal.[504]

For pre-distress profitability of sampled companies, the common metrics Return-on-assets (ROA)[505], Return-on-investment (ROI)[506], and Return-on-equity (ROE)[507] are provided (see TABLE 3).

Table 3: Matched sample – Pre-distress profitability.

	TA	N=62	NT	N=52	ND	N=60	Σ	N=194
In %	mean[a]	s.d.	mean[a]	s.d.	mean[a]	s.d.	mean[a]	s.d.
ROA Y_{-1}	3.94	3.41	6.24	3.62	6.26	3.48	5.27	3.66
ROI Y_{-1}	5.60	4.88	9.13	5.34	9.24	5.18	7.66	5.37
ROE Y_{-1}	7.80	7.80	13.53	8.94	12.75	7.92	10.83	8.52

a. All observations that lie ± 3 standard deviations from the mean are winsorized.
Abbr.: TA Turnaround, NT Non-turnaround, ND Non-distressed, s.d. standard deviation

Source: Own illustration.

Pre-distress ROA for the matched sample is 5.27%. The average turnaround company has a significantly lower pre-distress ROA of 3.94% compared to non-turnaround companies with 6.24% and non-distressed companies with 6.26%. The same pattern applies for ROI and ROE. Turnaround companies show below-average values (ROI 5.60% and ROE 7.80%) compared to the sample average of 7.66% and 10.83%, respectively. Non-turnaround and non-distressed companies exhibit similar profitability of 9.13% and 9.24% for ROI and 13.53% and 12.75% for ROE, respectively.

The profitability development of the three subsamples within the five-year timeframe clearly reflects the sample selection process with a one-year pre-distress phase, the following distress state, and the definition of turnaround and non-turnaround in the third year after the initial distress (see FIGURE 16).

---

503 Other samples showed lower firm size averages because the sampling period is earlier than the 1999-2008 timeframe or no size limit is introduced, e.g. MORROW ET AL. (2007, p. 278) or SMITH/GRAVES (2005, p. 315).

504 One-way ANOVA yields an F-statistic of 0.117 and 0.525 and a significance level of 0.890 and 0.592 for total assets and net revenues, respectively. The Kruskal-Wallis χ^2 test statistic is 2.377 for total assets and 3.290 for net revenues and has significance levels of 0.305 and 0.193, respectively. The hypothesis of equal mean values cannot be rejected within both tests.

505 Item 08326: (Net Income + ((Interest Expense on Debt - Interest Capitalized) * (1-Tax Rate))) / Average of Last Year's and Current Year's Total Assets * 100.

506 Item 08376: (Net Income before Preferred Dividends + ((Interest Expense on Debt - Interest Capitalized) * (1-Tax Rate))) / Average of Last Year's and Current Year's (Total Capital + Last Year's Short Term Debt & Current Portion of Long Term Debt) * 100.

507 Item 08375: (Net Income before Preferred Dividends - Preferred Dividend Requirement) / Average of Last Year's and Current Year's Common Equity * 100.

Figure 16: Matched sample - Profitability development.

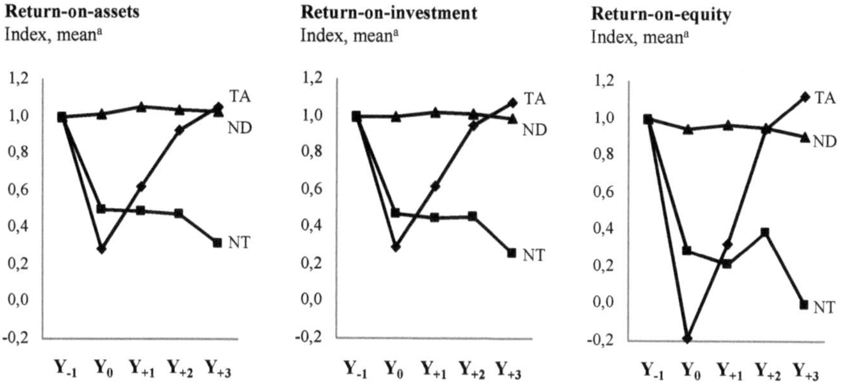

a. All observations that lie ± 3 standard deviations from the mean are winsorized.
Note: Index is the unweighted average of the single company index values based on the initial pre-distress year
Abbr.: TA Turnaround, NT Non-turnaround, ND Non-distressed

Source: Own illustration.

The distressed companies (turnaround and non-turnaround) show a sharp drop in profitability for all three return metrics in the distress year compared to the pre-distress year. The drop in ROA and ROI is approximately the same for turnaround (-71.6% for ROA and -70.4% for ROI) and non-turnaround firms (-50.6% for ROA and -52.4% for ROI). However, the drop in ROE shows the performance decline more sharply. At the end of the turnaround period in Y_{+3}, turnaround companies have established profitability levels slightly above the initial pre-distress level, whereas profitability levels for non-turnaround companies are lower than in the distress year. The profitability development shows that the distress indicator—negative interest coverage in the distress years—cannot be solely attributed to increased interest expense or to overexpansion by increasing capital expenditures. Rather, it is also directly associated with a decrease in profitability. Because profitability remains positive during the distress years, economic distress is not prevalent.[508] The development pattern of firm profitability within the five-year timeframe accords with prior research.[509]

As expected and in line with the sampling criterion of continuous positive interest coverage, non-distressed companies show a constant profitability level for all five years within the sampling timeframe. Although ROA and ROI increase slightly by +5% and +7% respectively, ROE declines slightly by -10% until Y_{+3}.

This chapter provides only a brief overview of the main sample descriptives. Detailed analysis including further descriptives for the relevant subsamples is provided in the following

508 Compare HOTCHKISS (1995, p. 25).
509 Compare BARKER/DUHAIME (1997, p. 23) for ROA and ROI and EICHNER (2008, p. 201) for ROA.

chapters. CHAPTER 5.2 analyzes differences in restructuring actions within the distressed sample. After the discussion of differences between the subsamples of distressed and non-distressed companies in CHAPTER 5.3, turnaround archetypes within successful turnarounds are analyzed in CHAPTER 5.4.

5.2 Effectiveness of restructuring activities

5.2.1 Preliminaries

CHAPTER 5.2 addresses Research question 1: the effectiveness of restructuring actions in the automotive supplier industry.

Research question 1: Effectiveness of restructuring actions

- How effective are frequently recommended restructuring strategies in resolving financial distress among automotive suppliers?
  - Which of the known restructuring actions are applied in this industry segment?
  - How effective are the four categories of restructuring (managerial, operational, financial, and asset restructuring), and what is their relative contribution to turnarounds?

The initial part of the research question is the univariate analysis of the frequency of restructuring actions applied by the automotive suppliers in the distressed sample (SECTION 5.2.2). The analysis includes comparing actions by distressed automotive companies with existing research to determine which actions are applied by turnaround and non-turnaround companies. To analyze differences between the subsamples of turnaround and non-turnaround firms, the parametric two independent samples t-test is performed. In addition, for binary and categorical variables the non-parametric Likelihood-Ratio χ^2 Test and for metric variables the non-parametric Mann-Whitney U-Test are provided.[510]

The second part of the research question is the multivariate logistic regression analysis (SECTION 5.2.3). Only in a multivariate setting can the overall effectiveness of restructuring activities in achieving corporate turnaround be determined. Per the approach recommended by PENG/SO (2002), the univariate analysis at the same time serves as a pre-selection of relevant variables for later inclusion in the multivariate logistic regression.

---

510 Compare BORTZ (2005, pp. 135-174) for details concerning the selection of the appropriate test statistic for analysis of differences in means. For binary and categorical variables, the χ^2 test is the main test; the t-test is only provided as a supplement. In addition, univariate logistic regressions for each independent and control variable are provided as an alternative method in APPENDIX 4. The univariate logistic regression yields the same results as those provided in the next section and allow direct interpretation of the direction of the coefficient and the significance level.

5.2.2 Univariate analysis

Descriptives for the application of various restructuring actions of distressed automotive suppliers and the corresponding test of differences appear below (see TABLE 4).

Table 4: Distressed sample – Descriptives and test of differences.

		TA		NT		Test of difference		
		mean	s.d.	mean	s.d.	t-test sig.	Mann Whitney U sig.	LR χ^2 sig.
Managerial restructuring								
Top executive change –	MRA-ER	0.244	0.432	0.154	0.364	0.197^{+}		0.204^{+}
All	MRA-LR	0.110	0.315	0.173	0.382	0.320		0.300
Top executive change –	MRN-ER	0.110	0.315	0.115	0.323	0.921		0.920
Non-routine	MRN-LR	0.073	0.262	0.115	0.323	0.408		0.410
Operational restructuring								
Revenue development	REV-ER	-0.010	0.239	-0.177	0.323	0.002***	0.001***	
	REV-LR	0.154	0.270	-0.036	0.337	0.001***	0.001***	
Operating expense ratio	EXP-ER	0.010	0.030	0.030	0.037	0.002***	0.001***	
	EXP-LR	-0.009	0.025	0.003	0.031	0.015**	0.053*	
Financial restructuring								
Equity issue	EQU-ER	0.366	0.485	0.288	0.457	0.359		0.353
	EQU-LR	0.305	0.463	0.308	0.466	0.973		0.973
Dividend policy	DIV-ER	0.117	0.814	0.461	1.269	0.058*	0.414	
	DIV-LR	0.266	0.583	0.224	0.995	0.759	0.166^{+}	
Debt restructuring	DBT-ER	0.135	0.375	0.226	0.371	0.170^{+}	0.016**	
	DBT-LR	-0.079	0.304	0.123	0.345	0.001***	0.001***	
Asset restructuring								
Total assets change	TAS-ER	0.112	0.232	0.221	0.299	0.020**	0.060*	
	TAS-LR	0.161	0.270	0.345	0.429	0.003***	0.044**	
Capital expenditure intensity	CAP-ER	0.119	0.473	0.288	0.527	0.063*	0.049**	
	CAP-LR	0.009	0.474	-0.057	0.481	0.437	0.442	
Context								
Firm size	TA-CTX	6.169	1.310	5.938	1.508	0.351	0.117^{+}	
Prior performance	PP-CTX	0.119	4.546	0.138	4.188	0.017**	0.008***	
Distress severity	DS-CTX	-0.044	4.326	-0.045	4.154	0.890	0.954	
Financial capacity	FC-CTX	0.930	0.828	0.910	0.757	0.888	0.887	
Financial slack	FS-CTX	0.101	0.146	0.057	0.147	0.095*	0.082*	
Distress year	DY-CTX	2002.3	1.620	2003.1	1.752	0.007***		0.034**
Region	RG-CTX	0.756	0.432	0.692	0.466	0.421		0.419
Industry	IN-CTX	0.171	0.379	0.173	0.382	0.972		0.972

Abbr.: TA Turnaround, NT Non-turnaround, ND Non-distressed,
s.d. standard deviation, LR Likelihood-Ratio, sig. significance level
$^{+}$, *, **, *** indicate significance at the 25%, 10%, 5%, and 1% levels, respectively

Source: Own illustration.

The following discussion is structured along the theoretical framework of corporate turnaround with the four generic restructuring categories and the selected context variables.

Managerial restructuring

Within the distressed sample, 21% of top executives are replaced within the early restructuring phase and 13% during the late phase.[511] During early restructuring, successful turnaround companies exhibit a higher intensity of top executive replacements with 24% compared to 15% for the non-turnarounds. Although the higher frequency of top executive changes for turnaround companies was expected, the difference is not significant. During the late restructuring phase, the frequency of overall top executive changes decreases slightly to 11% for turnaround companies, but it increases slightly to 17% for non-turnarounds. The frequency of general top executive turnover is slightly higher than the results of BRUTON ET AL. (2003)—19% for a three year timeframe for distressed firms—and slightly lower than the results of BARKER/DUHAIME (1997), who document a 40% turnover of general management during a four-year timeframe for turnaround firms.[512]

As for *forced top executive changes*, approximately 11% of companies change their top executive in the distress year and the year after in both subsamples. Hence, 45% of the changes are forced at turnaround companies compared to 75% at non-turnaround companies. For the late restructuring phase, the frequency of forced top executive changes decreases to 7% for turnaround companies and remains constant at 11% for non-turnaround companies. This means that for both subsamples 67% of top executive changes during the late restructuring phase are forced. Contrary to expectations, non-turnarounds have more forced management changes during the early restructuring phase, but the difference is again not statistically significant. The frequency of forced top executive turnover among distressed companies is comparable to the recent research of YAWSON (2009), where 5.2% of all distressed companies showed a forced turnover the first year after onset of distress.[513] The frequency of forced top executive replacements also is in line with KANG/SHIVDASANI (1997), who report that approximately 40% of top executive changes are forced for distressed Japanese and US firms, leading to forced top executive turnover of 14% and 8%, respectively.[514] DENIS/KRUSE (2000) report a non-routine turnover of 27% for their firms with poor performance. Still, prior research partially also showed higher turnover ratios for non-routine turnover.[515] For example, SMITH/GRAVES (2005) report forced turnovers of 38% among turnaround and 37% among non-turnaround companies in the distress year, and

---

511 None of the companies replaced its top executive twice during either early or late restructuring, but six companies (four Turnaround and two Non-turnaround) replaced their top executives twice during the four-year restructuring period.

512 See BRUTON ET AL. (2003, p. 531), who find a change in top executive for 19% of all companies during the distress phase and the first year of the recovery phase, and BARKER/DUHAIME (1997, p. 31), who find a 40% top executive turnover among turnaround firms during the three-year period after the onset of distress.

513 See YAWSON (2009, p. 225).

514 See KANG/SHIVDASANI (1997, p. 42).

515 See DENIS/KRUSE (2000, p. 408).

LAI/SUDARSANAM (1997) report 67.2% accumulated over the initial onset of distress and the following two years.[516] Although this frequency of forced management changes is clearly higher than for the sample of distressed automotive companies, no differences are found between turnaround and non-turnaround companies during the early restructuring phase. SUDARSANAM/LAI (2001) instead report a frequency of 22% for turnaround and 30% for non-turnaround firms in the distress year, indicating that non-turnarounds force their top executives to leave more often.[517] SUDARSANAM/LAI (2001) also show that the frequency of forced top executive changes remains constant over three years during the turnaround period, showing that non-turnaround companies change their top executives more often during the restructuring process than turnaround companies.

Overall, the frequency of general and forced top executive turnover is approximately in line with prior studies, but at the lower end. Distressed automotive suppliers tend to have less frequent top executive changes but also less frequent forced changes. In line with this overall low frequency of top executive changes, no significant differences appear between turnaround and non-turnaround companies.

Operational restructuring

Within the operational restructuring activities, *revenue development*, adjusted for a stable fixed asset base,[518] remains approximately constant for turnaround companies during the early restructuring phase. Non-turnaround companies exhibit a large 18% decline. This indicates that although turnaround companies are able to generate the same revenues from their fixed asset base as in the pre-distress phase, non-turnaround companies make less effective use of their assets. During the late restructuring phase, non-turnaround companies are able to avoid a further large decrease with a minus of only 4%. Turnaround companies at the same time strongly increase effective use of their assets, resulting in a 15% increase in adjusted revenue during late restructuring. Differences between turnaround and non-turnaround companies indicate a significant positive relation between adjusted revenue growth and corporate turnaround for both restructuring phases. Although an early decrease in revenues from implementing a retrenchment strategy and a later increase from implementing a recovery strategy are expected, a very strong, significant, positive relation is found for both restructuring phases.

EICHNER (2008) finds the same result: organic growth is not common during the early restructuring phase, with only 9% of turnaround and 7 % of non-turnaround companies achieving more than 10% internal revenue growth. However, in his findings differences

---

516 See SMITH/GRAVES (2005, p. 315) and LAI/SUDARSANAM (1997, p. 216).
517 See for the following SUDARSANAM/LAI (2001, p. 192).
518 Compare CHAPTER 4.2 for the operationalization of revenue development.

between turnaround and non-turnaround are not statistically different.[519] EICHNER (2008) also notes a higher frequency of organic revenue growth during the late restructuring phase, but again the relation to corporate turnaround is not significant. The improvement of capital productivity in the form of increasing organic revenues is therefore more important for distressed automotive companies compared to manufacturing companies in general. At the same time, organic revenue growth seems infeasible during the initial distress state where companies are more concerned with stopping further efficiency losses.

On the cost side, turnaround companies experience a slight 1% increase in the ratio of operating expenses to revenues during the early restructuring phase, whereas the figure is 3% for non-turnarounds. During the late restructuring phase, turnaround companies reverse this increase and cut operating costs 1%, whereas the ratio remains approximately constant for non-turnaround companies. With these differences being small at first glance, a one percentage point change in the cost ratio implies an equal change in the operating profitability, all else being equal. The hypotheses for cost-reduction strategies are also closely related to the two phases of retrenchment and recovery, where a cut in expenses contributes to turnaround during the early phase but hinders it during the later expansionary phase.

As for revenue growth, the relation of cost-cutting strategies and corporate turnaround is strongly significant during both phases of the restructuring process. Reductions in operating expenses are positively associated with turnarounds during the early and late restructuring phases. Changes in operating expenses are comparable to results obtained by YAWSON (2009): operating costs of distressed firms on average increase 3%, but a positive relation of cost reductions and turnarounds is also found.[520] FRANCIS/DESAI (2005) find no empirical evidence for cost retrenchment in their sample of turnaround firms, but they expect some positive impact from cost retrenchment.[521] In comparison, LIN ET AL. (2008) find "real" cost-cutting efforts compared to the slight increases in this sample.[522] Overall, although distressed automotive suppliers are unable to implement cost-cutting measures to the same expected extent, the positive relation of cost reductions to corporate turnaround is confirmed.

Both operational restructuring strategies—productivity improvement through internal sales growth and cost reduction—are found to be significantly and positively associated with corporate turnaround for both phases of the restructuring process.

---

519 See for the following EICHNER (2008, p. 211).
520 See YAWSON (2009, p. 223).
521 See FRANCIS/DESAI (2005, pp. 1213-1215).
522 See LIN ET AL. (2008, p. 544).

Financial restructuring

Within the restructuring category of financial restructuring, equity issues, changes in the dividend policy, and debt restructuring are differentiated. *Equity issues* are one of the two equity-related financial restructuring actions and is expected to affect corporate turnarounds affirmatively. During the early restructuring phase, 34% of distressed companies issued equity, and 31% did so during the late restructuring phase. During the first two years of the restructuring process, turnaround companies had more issues, 37% compared to 29% for non-turnaround companies, as the initial hypothesis expected. During the late phase of restructuring, within both groups 31% of companies are able to issue equity, a decrease for turnaround companies but an increase for non-turnaround companies. The increase in equity issuance for non-turnaround companies during late restructuring is surprising, as it was expected that investors lack enthusiasm to support a failing firm in this late phase.[523] Differences between subsamples are not statistically different during both phases, and the corresponding hypotheses are not supported.

The frequency of equity issuance accords with the results of YAWSON (2009), who finds 15% of all companies issuing equity in the year after the onset of distress, and with the results of LAI/SUDARSANAM (1997), who find 31% for both years of the early restructuring phase.[524] Results for the frequency of equity issuance confirm prior research, but the expected significant differences between turnaround and non-turnaround firms are not found for distressed automotive suppliers. The positive relation of equity issuance during early and late restructuring cannot be confirmed. SUDARSANAM/LAI (2001) find similar results for the early phase: no significant differences for turnaround and non-turnaround companies, with 38% of the former and 51% of the latter issuing shares, and no effect on the probability of turnaround.[525] Overall, equity issuance is not significantly associated with successful turnarounds of distressed automotive suppliers, confirming the results for broader industry samples found by SUDARSANAM/LAI (2001) and YAWSON (2009).

The second equity-based restructuring activity relates to changes in dividend policy. Contrary to the expectation that dividend cuts are common during the restructuring process, dividend payments of distressed companies increase by 25% in each of the two phases. Although the 12% increase during the early restructuring phase was moderate for turnaround companies, non-turnarounds increased their dividend payments 46%. During the late restructuring phase, both subsamples had further increases of 25% each. This means an increase in dividends for turnaround firms, but a decrease in growth for non-turnaround firms. A positive relationship between reducing dividends and the probability of turnaround is found for the early

523 See SUDARSANAM/LAI (2001, p. 194).
524 See YAWSON (2009, p. 223) and LAI (1997, p. 216).
525 Compare SUDARSANAM/LAI (2001, pp. 192-196).

restructuring phase, supporting the initial hypothesis. The expected positive effect of later dividend increases is not found to be statistically significant.

The comparison with prior research shows that distressed automotive suppliers do not cut dividends, but they avoid future increases. YAWSON (2009, p. 223) finds a dividend decrease of 6% in the initial year for his sample of distressed companies, and SUDARSANAM/LAI (2001) report that about 30% of turnaround companies reduce or omit dividends during each of the three years of the restructuring process.[526] OFEK (1993) finds that 47% of distressed companies reduced dividends.[527] The significant increase in dividends for distressed automotive suppliers indicates at least a preference for stable dividends during distress situations. This finding partially supports that of JOHN ET AL. (1992), who state that firms are willing to cut dividends during performance declines, but they also find that 41% of firms raise dividends during the restructuring process.[528]

The third financial restructuring activity is debt-based and considers the change in the debt-to-assets ratio over the restructuring process. Turnaround companies exhibit a strong 14% increase in debt-to-asset ratios during the early restructuring phase, while non-turnarounds exhibit an even stronger 23% increase. While turnaround companies decrease leverage 8% during the late restructuring phase, non-turnarounds take on additional debt, increasing their debt-to-assets ratios 12%. For the debt-based financial restructuring strategy of leverage reduction, a significant positive relationship between reducing leverage and turnaround was found during both restructuring phases. Although this relationship is in line with the hypothesis for the early restructuring phase, an unexpected strongly significant positive relationship also is found for the late restructuring phase. Continuous reduction in leverage throughout the restructuring process contributes to turnarounds.

Compared to the results of LIN ET AL. (2008) and JOHN ET AL. (1992), which indicate quick reductions in leverage for their sample firms, turnaround companies in the automotive supplier industry are only able to reduce the increase in leverage during the early restructuring phase.[529] Although this result confirms those of SUDARSANAM/LAI (2001) and YAWSON (2009) for the importance of debt restructuring, there is a shift in temporal preferences where automotive suppliers reduce leverage significantly only during the late restructuring phase.[530]

For the financial restructuring category, the univariate analysis shows that dividend cuts and debt reduction are effective strategies for corporate turnaround during the early restructuring

---

526 See YAWSON (2009, p. 223) and SUDARSANAM/LAI (2001, p. 192).
527 See OFEK (1993, p. 8).
528 See JOHN ET AL. (1992, p. 910).
529 See LIN ET AL. (2008, p. 549) and JOHN ET AL. (1992, pp. 909-910). KANG/SHIVDASANI (1997, p. 50) also find a 3.2% increase in leverage in the first year of the turnaround process among their sample of US firms.
530 See SUDARSANAM/LAI (2001, p. 196) and YAWSON (2009, p. 227).

phase. In addition, continuous leverage reduction during the late restructuring phase is also related to corporate turnaround. Equity issuance is not identified as a distinctive characteristic of successful turnarounds.

Asset restructuring

For changes in total assets, turnaround and non-turnaround companies grow during both phases of restructuring. Whereas turnaround companies grow their assets 11% during the early and 16% during the late restructuring phase, non-turnarounds exhibit significantly higher growth rates of 22% and 35%. Lower growth rates for turnaround companies support the a priori expected negative relationship between asset increases and corporate turnaround and is found to be statistically significant. Contrary to the derived hypothesis for the late restructuring phase, the positive relation of an expansionary strategy with corporate turnaround is not found. Instead, as for the early phase, a significant, negative relation between asset increases and turnarounds is found.

Therefore, distressed automotive suppliers focus on reducing asset growth rather than on real asset reductions. This result is comparable to that of FRANCIS/DESAI (2005), whose sample of turnaround companies grew their asset bases 12%.[531] Still, they find a positive impact of asset retrenchment on firm performance. Also, JOHN ET AL. (1992) find annual asset growth rates of 0.5%, 7.1%, and 6.7% for each year after the onset of distress for their sample of turnaround firms. The strong reduction of assets found by LIN ET AL. (2008) is atypical for this sample of distressed automotive suppliers.

Growth in total assets is also reflected in the ratio of capital expenditures to fixed assets. Capital expenditure intensity for turnaround companies increased 12% during the first two years but stayed nearly constant in the next two years with only slight growth of 1%. During early restructuring, non-turnaround companies increased their capital expenditure intensity 29%, even more than turnaround companies. Although this increase might already signify overexpansion, the ratio decreased by 6% during the late restructuring phase. This supports the hypothesis that strong growth in capital expenditures during the early restructuring phase is negatively related to corporate turnaround. This difference is not found statistically significant and therefore does not support the initial hypothesis for the late restructuring phase. The growth rate of capital expenditures is lower than the annual 13% to 20% found by SUDARSANAM/LAI (2001). The expected reduction in capital expenditures, especially during the early restructuring phase, is not apparent among distressed automotive suppliers.

---

531 See for the following FRANCIS/DESAI (2005, p. 1214).

Context

The context variables of firm size, distress year, region, industry subsector, and profitability were already described for the matched sample in the prior section; severity of distress, financial capacity, and financial slack are discussed in the remainder. *Distress severity* is the decrease in firm profitability from the pre-distress to the distress year and averages 4.4% for the distressed sample. The decrease in profitability is the same for turnaround and non-turnaround companies, indicating they occupy the same distress level across the subsamples. *Financial capacity*, measured as the ratio of total debt to common equity in the pre-distress year, varies only slightly: 0.93 for turnaround companies and 0.91 for non-turnaround companies. Accordingly, no statistically significant differences are found. The final context variable is *financial slack*, measured as working capital divided by total assets in the pre-distress year. Financial slack for turnaround companies is with 0.10 considerably higher for turnaround companies compared to 0.05 for non-turnaround companies.

The univariate analysis in this section investigates the relation of the restructuring actions and context factors to corporate turnaround in an isolated perspective to initially identify significant variables but does not take possible interrelations into account. Because prior research showed that the chosen restructuring actions impact each other, the following multivariate analysis provides a more holistic view on the effectiveness of these actions in overcoming financial distress in the automotive supplier industry.

5.2.3 Multivariate logistic regression analysis

The primary objective of the multivariate logistic regression compared to the previous univariate analysis is to statistically adjust the estimated effects of each single independent variable for differences in the distributions and associations with the other independent variables.[532]

The multivariate logistic regression follows a two-step approach. First, all relevant variables are included in the preliminary full model before a stepwise backward procedure is used to develop the fitted model. Although all variables at a significance level of 0.25 are included in the multivariate analysis, variables for both phases of the restructuring process are included even if only one was statistically significant in the univariate analysis.[533] This approach addresses the issue that the differentiation of early and late restructuring phases is comparatively new in empirical research and accords with PENG/SO (2002), who recommend including additional variables of theoretical interest.[534]

---

532 Compare NOTHARDT (2001, p. 196).
533 Therefore MRA-LR, DIV-LR, and CAP-LR are included in Model 1.
534 Compare PENG/SO (2002, p. 54).

Before the discussion of results, the model evaluation including goodness-of-fit measures and the model diagnostics for issues of linearity, multicollinearity, endogeneity, and impact of single outliers are discussed. The following discussion is then structured along the main restructuring dimensions of content, process, and context. In addition, a sensitivity analysis for the probability of turnaround based on changes in single restructuring actions is provided.

Table 5: Multivariate logistic regression – Models 1 and 2.

		Model 1 - Preliminary			Model 2 - Final[a]		
		β	s.e.	sig.[b]	β	s.e.	sig.[b]
Constant		0.18	1.50	0.903	0.91	0.29	0.001***
Top executive change	MRA-ER	0.31	0.69	0.652			
– All	MRA-LR	-0.73	0.71	0.303			
Revenue development	REV-ER	2.94	1.16	0.007***	2.16	0.85	0.008***
	REV-LR	2.04	0.98	0.029**	2.21	0.85	0.006***
Operating expense ratio	EXP-ER	-23.38	9.54	0.009***	-29.18	7.81	0.001***
	EXP-LR	-15.42	11.12	0.160	-14.58	9.34	0.110
Dividend policy	DIV-ER	-0.08	0.32	0.813			
	DIV-LR	0.11	0.41	0.787			
Debt restructuring	DBT-ER	-0.46	0.75	0.544			
	DBT-LR	-1.39	0.89	0.114	-1.32	0.72	0.064*
Total asset change	TAS-ER	3.05	1.63	0.051*			
	TAS-LR	-1.39	1.09	0.200			
Capital expenditure intensity	CAP-ER	-1.27	0.58	0.022**	-1.17	0.52	0.018**
	CAP-LR	-1.34	0.63	0.028**	-1.07	0.53	0.038**
Firm size	TA-CTX	0.10	0.21	0.633			
Prior profitability	PP-CTX	-6.02	6.88	0.381			
Financial slack	FS-CTX	4.90	1.80	0.004*	4.18	1.63	0.008***
Distress year: 2000	DY-CTX	0.91	1.07				
2001		0.63	0.81				
2002		1.99	0.99	0.378[c]			
2003		0.63	0.87				
2004		1.26	0.89				
2005		c					
Model evaluation		χ2	df	sig.	χ2	df	sig.
Likelihood-Ratio-Test		64.169	22	0.001***	53.773	8.0	0.001***
Hosmer-Lemeshow Test		21.398	8	0.006***	5.267	8.0	0.729
Nagelkerke R^2		0.52			0.45		
McFadden R^2		0.36			0.30		
c-statistic		0.88			0.86		
Count R^2		80.6%			81.3%		
Adj. Count R^2		50.0%			51.9%		

a. Backward variable selection process based on the Likelihood-Ratio with entry probability of 0.25 and exit probability of 0.15.
b. Based on Likelihood-Ratio-Test.
c. Likelihood-Ratio-Test for variable DY-CTX, only one significance level since entered as block.
Note: Reference category Non-turnaround
Abbr.: s.e. standard error, df degrees of freedom, sig. significance level
*, **, *** indicate significance at the 10%, 5%, and 1% levels, respectively.

Source: Own illustration.

Model evaluation

The evaluation of the logistic regression model as outlined in SECTION 4.3.2 is based on the overall model evaluation, the inferential and descriptive goodness-of-fit evaluation, and the validation of predicted probabilities through measures of association (see TABLE 5).

For the overall model evaluation, the significant *Likelihood-Ratio-Test* for Model 1 and Model 2 shows that all coefficients together are significantly different from zero and both models therefore have explanatory power. The significant *Hosmer-Lemeshow Test* as an inferential goodness-of-fit measure instead indicates that Model 1 does not fit the data well. This problem might arise because of overfitting of the model. For Model 2, the observed significance level 0.729 indicates that the model appears to fit the data reasonably well. In addition, as descriptive goodness-of-fit measures Nagelkerke and McFadden R^2 are provided. Although typically smaller than in regular OLS regression, the *Nagelkerke* R^2 indicates the variation in outcome explained by the model: it is 0.52 for Model 1 and 0.45 for Model 2, consistent with prior research. *McFadden* R^2 is 0.36 for Model 1 and 0.30 for Model 2, in line with the expected range of 0.2 to 0.4 for both models. Nagelkerke and McFadden R^2 decrease only slightly from the full model to the fitted model, indicating the model fit is still assured with the limited set of independent variables. The results indicate better results than the models employed, for example, by SUDARSANAM/LAI (2001), with a McFadden R^2 of 0.17.[535]

Three supplementary measures are provided for model evaluation: the c-statistic, the Count R^2 and the Adjusted Count R^2. The *c-statistic* of 0.88 indicates that for 88% of all pairs of companies, one turnaround the other non-turnaround, the model correctly assigns the higher turnaround probability to the turnaround case. The *Count* R^2 indicates that approximately 81% of all cases are classified correctly by Model 1 and approximately the same amount by Model 2. This is a better ratio then for example the model developed by FRANCIS/DESAI (2005) with 70%.[536] The *Adjusted Count* R^2 takes the largest marginal of the dependent variable into account and is 55.8% for Model 1 and 51.9% for Model 2. The analysis of these two measures again shows that the predictive ability of the model increases only slightly even if the number of independent variables is reduced from 17 to eight.

Due to similar descriptive measures but a better model fit, Model 2 forms the basis for further analysis, including model and outlier diagnostics. In the following, linearity, multicollinearity, endogeneity, and the impact of single outliers are analyzed. Logistic regression requires that the relationship between the latent variable z and each of the independent is linear. Proof of *nonlinearity* is not found, as none of the Likelihood-Ratio-Tests for single interactions terms

---

535 See SUDARSANAM/LAI (2001, p. 196). A direct comparison of R^2 measures between different studies is not possible.

536 See FRANCIS/DESAI (2005, p. 1218).

is significant in the Box-Tidwell transformation test (average p-value of all interaction terms of 0.633 and minimum of 0.285 for REV-ER).[537] The overall effect of the interaction effects was also not statistically significant (change in Likelihood-Ratio χ^2 of 5.96 with 8 degrees of freedom and a p-value of 0.652). Therefore nonlinearity between the independent and latent variable is not an issue and no transformation of variables is required.

The next step is the test for potential problems of *multicollinearity* between the independent variables.[538] Here the average value for the Pearson correlation coefficient is 0.13 with a maximum of 0.33 and therefore well below the established threshold of 0.5. Variance Inflation Factors (VIF) for all independent variables are on average 1.17 with a maximum value of 1.27. Because all VIF are again well below the maximum threshold of 2.5, multicollinearity is of no concern for Model 2.

The four variables of the late restructuring phase are tested for potential endogeneity problems. The Durbin-Wu-Hausman test is not significant at the 10% level, hence the assumption of exogeneity cannot be rejected and no problems related to endogeneity are assumed for Model 2.[539]

The last step in the model evaluation is the identification of single *outliers* that might have an impact on the results.[540] Outlier diagnostics also show no unusual impact of single cases with an average *leverage value (hat)* of 0.07 and only 4 cases with a value between 0.2 and 0.5. All *Cook's distance measures* are well below 1 with an average of 0.09 and a maximum of 0.78. *Standardized residuals* e^* stayed within the boundaries of normal distribution with 5% of all values larger than ±1.96 (7 cases) and no values outside ±2.58 standard deviations.

Also all *boundary conditions* are met for Model 2. The final model has 16.8 observations per variable and 6.5 events per variable, well above the thresholds of ten and four respectively.[541]

Discussion of restructuring content

The final model includes seven restructuring actions and one context variable which are related to corporate turnaround. A graphical analysis of the relation between these restructuring actions and corporate turnaround is provided below (see FIGURE 17).

Both *operational restructuring* actions are included in the final model and support the important role of operational restructuring measures in the corporate turnaround of distressed

---

537 See APPENDIX 5 for details.

538 See APPENDIX 6 for details.

539 See APPENDIX 7 for the test of model coefficients.

540 See APPENDIX 8 for details.

541 Overfitting for Model 1 is also indicated here because both boundary conditions are not met with 7.9 observations per variable and 3.1 events per variable.

automotive suppliers. Revenue growth in both restructuring phases and cost-cutting during the early restructuring phase are strongly significant operational restructuring strategies. If companies are able to generate *internal revenue growth* – during the early and late restructuring phases – the probability of turnaround increases significantly. Although this result is expected for the late phase, the expected retrenchment actions for the early phase cannot be observed.[542] This result supports recent research of YAWSON (2009) who also finds a positive impact of revenue growth on turnarounds during the early restructuring phase.[543] The positive relation can be explained if the product portfolio of the supplier that turns around successfully is still competitive and demand for its products is sufficient.[544] The close relation of automotive suppliers and their customers, the automotive OEMs, is one indicator for the stable demand level even if the supplier is in a distress situation.[545] The positive impact of internal revenue growth also during the early restructuring phase confirms the research results by FRANCIS/DESAI (2005) who find that a strong focus on more effective use of firm resources is critical for recovery.[546] Turnaround companies are able to continuously increase their revenues adjusted for a fixed asset base and distressed firms ignoring productivity do so at their peril.[547]

542 Compare for example the empirical evidence by BRUTON ET AL. (2003, p. 533).
543 See YAWSON (2009, p. 227).
544 See BRUTON ET AL. (2003, p. 525). This also differentiates distressed from bankrupt companies, where the latter typically do not have the resources to pursue revenue growth strategies.
545 See BRUTON ET AL. (2003, p. 525).
546 See FURRER ET AL. (2007, pp. 1218-1219).
547 See WINN (1997, p. 595).

Figure 17: **Model 2 – Sensitivity analysis.**

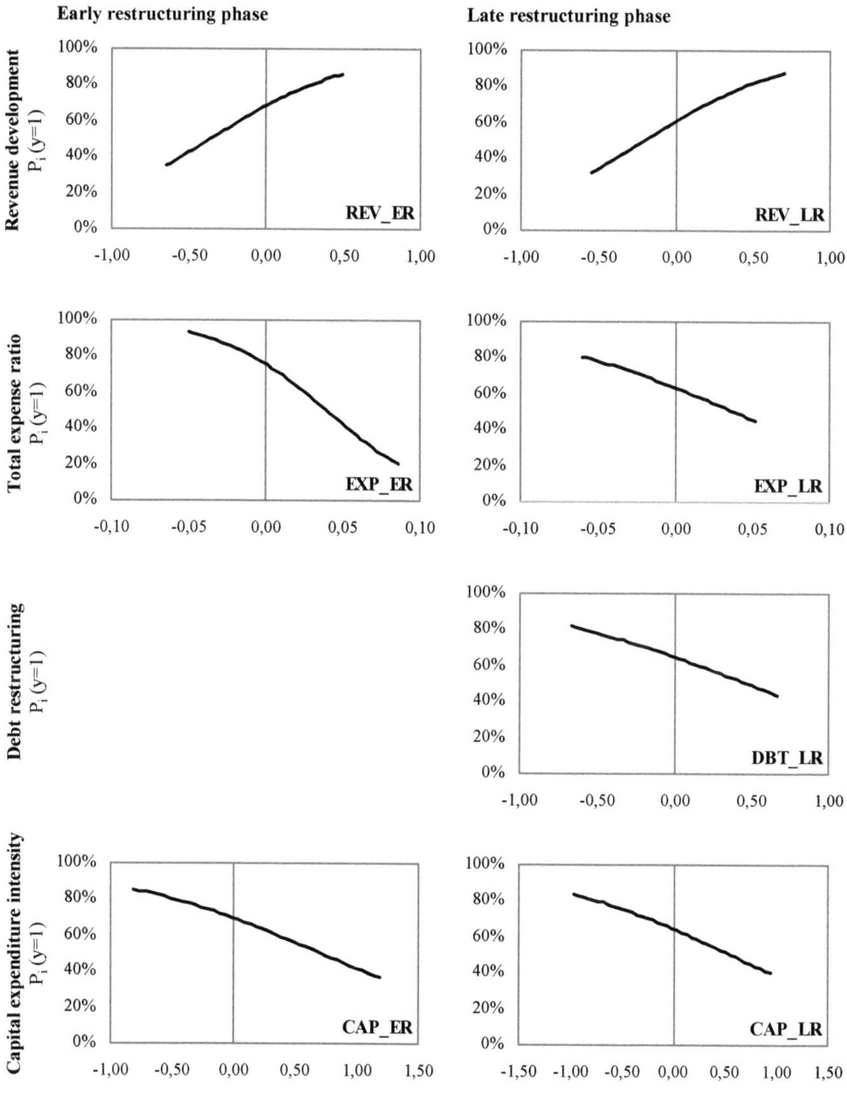

Note: Changes in independent variables are standardized to ± two standard deviations from the mean.

Source: Own illustration.

Cost-cutting during the early restructuring phase is also an efficient means to increase the probability of turnaround. Whereas turnaround companies are able to stop the increase in expenses after the distress year, non-turnarounds exhibit increased cost ratios, which negatively impact their prospects of turnaround. This result is in line with prior research and can be proof of a cost retrenchment strategy. Cost-cutting during the late restructuring phase is also included in the final model, but is not significant. These results are in line with YAWSON (2009) who finds a positive impact of cost-cutting during the early and late restructuring phase, but only reports significant results for the first year after distress. Cost-cutting can be considered an essential element for corporate turnaround in the automotive supplier industry and supports the research recent results of for example LIN ET AL. (2008) and FURRER ET AL. (2007).[548]

Overall, the results for the operational restructuring category support that companies, which pursue growth strategies and at the same time are able to cut down on operating costs, are able to achieve turnaround.[549]

Of the initial six *financial restructuring* actions, only changes in the dividend policy and debt restructuring are found to be related to corporate turnaround and entered the multivariate analysis.[550] In the final model, only debt restructuring, hence reducing leverage during the late restructuring phase is found to be significantly positively related to the probability of turnaround. Whereas turnaround companies are able to reduce their leverage ratio during the late restructuring phase, non-turnarounds exhibit a further increase which reduces the prospects for turnaround. This result accords with prior research who finds that a reduction in borrowings fosters turnaround, but the expected quick debt reduction as proposed by, for example, LIN ET AL. (2008) and SUDARSANAM/LAI (2001) is observed later in the turnaround process.[551] Hence in the sample of automotive suppliers the positive effect of leverage reduction is confirmed only for the late restructuring phase. In summary, the view that financial restructuring plays an ambiguous role for turnarounds is supported for distressed automotive suppliers because only one single activity is significantly related to the turnaround probability in a multivariate setting.[552]

Of the two *asset restructuring* actions, only reductions in *capital expenditures* are significant for both restructuring phases in the final model. Reductions in capital expenditures during the early restructuring phase are part of retrenchment actions and are in line with the initial retrenchment hypothesis as proposed by ASQUITH ET AL. (1994) and BARKER/DUHAIME (1997).[553] Similar results for capital expenditures are found by YAWSON (2009). The positive

548 Compare LIN ET AL. (2008, p. 544), and FURRER ET AL. (2007, p. 379).
549 See YAWSON (2009, p. 226).
550 Equity issuance is not significant in the univariate analysis. This result is in line with YAWSON (2009, p. 227).
551 See LIN ET AL. (2008, p. 549), SUDARSANAM/LAI (2001, pp. 194-196), and JOHN ET AL. (1992, pp. 909-911).
552 Compare SUDARSANAM/LAI (2001, p. 187) for an overview.
553 Compare for the following ASQUITH ET AL. (1994, p. 650), BARKER/DUHAIME (1997, p. 25).

relation of capital expenditures reductions during the late restructuring phase instead is unexpected and also contrary to the results from the univariate analysis. In the context of the multivariate analysis, capital expenditure reductions in both restructuring phases are significantly related to the probability of corporate turnaround for distressed automotive suppliers.

Of the variables included in the preliminary multivariate model, managerial restructuring, dividend cuts, and general asset restructuring are not included in the final model. Each of these variables is discussed briefly in the remainder of this paragraph. Although the forced *replacement of the top executive* was already not significant in the univariate analysis, the general exchange of the top executive is also not included in the final model. Contrary to the expectation that an exchange of the top executive during the early restructuring phase facilitates turnaround, this relationship cannot be established for distressed automotive suppliers. Turnaround companies do not significantly exchange their top executive more or less than non-turnaround companies. In line with BRUTON ET AL. (2003) and SUDARSANAM/LAI (2001), the benefits and drawbacks of top executive changes are expected to cancel each other for distressed automotive companies so that no significant relation to corporate turnaround is found.[554]

The lesser importance of financial restructuring strategies is already reflected in the univariate analysis, where *equity issues* are not identified as significantly different between turnaround and non-turnaround companies. The significant impact of *dividend cuts* during the early restructuring phase in the univariate analysis is then not confirmed in the multivariate analysis. Changes in the dividend policy do not have a strong impact on the probability of turnaround in the context of other restructuring actions. This might be due to the fact that on average turnarounds and non-turnarounds increased their dividend payments during the early and the late restructuring phase. The descriptive analysis already showed that dividend cuts are not very common in automotive supplier sector. This reflects the results of YAWSON (2009) who also finds no significant impact for changes in the dividend payments and also SUDARSANAM/LAI (2001) who state that dividend cuts are "not a sufficient condition for subsequent recovery."[555] Overall, financial restructuring actions are identified having minor importance for successful turnarounds among automotive suppliers and support the view that financial strategies only provide relieve for the short term, not for sustainable recovery.[556]

For *asset restructuring*, *changes in total assets* are strongly significant in the univariate analysis but do not enter the final model. This does not support the initial hypothesis, but is

---

554 See BRUTON ET AL. (2003, p. 526) and SUDARSANAM/LAI (2001, p. 196).

555 SUDARSANAM/LAI (2001, p. 194). The same argument is made for debt restructuring. See also YAWSON (2009, p. 227).

556 See YAWSON (2009, p. 227).

consistent with the overall picture on asset restructuring, where some researchers like KANE/RICHARDSON (2002) find a positive impact due to asset reductions and others like SMITH/GRAVES (2005) find a positive impact due to asset expansion.[557] The ambiguous findings confirm the results of YAWSON (2009) who states that asset expansions are not optimal for firms during distress but also must acknowledge, that reductions in assets might negatively impact corporate turnaround and are accompanied by increasing operating cost and increasing debt levels.[558] With general changes in total assets, capturing all actions including acquisitions and divestitures, not included in the final model, a more important role for internal capital expenditures during the restructuring process of distressed automotive suppliers is indicated.

Discussion of restructuring context

Of the four context variables identified in the univariate analysis, only financial slack entered the final multivariate model. Firm size, prior profitability, and distress year are not included in the final model. For the positive relation of firm size on corporate turnaround, no empirical evidence is found.[559] This supports the research results by FRANCIS/DESAI (2005) who find that "any resulting inertia may offset advantages that size provides to a firm in turnaround situation"[560]. At the same time the role of firm size is often confused with the role of financial slack in prior research. Although financial slack is often indirectly associated with larger firms that have access to more internal resources, it is not the size of the firm itself but the level of financial slack that is important for the probability of corporate turnaround. Financial slack is identified as a strongly significant context variable, hence the availability of excess resources provides firms with an advantage over their counterparts in similar distress situations.[561]

The distress year which is included as a control variable for specific industry and macro-economic effects related to the initial year of distress did also not enter the final model. Because the distress year is not significantly related to the probability of turnaround, the derived restructuring actions can be considered to be valid throughout the whole sampling timeframe.

Discussion of restructuring process

Two additional multivariate logistic regressions are conducted to analyze the contribution of the single restructuring phases to corporate turnaround (see TABLE 6). Model 2-A includes the

---

557 See SMITH/GRAVES (2005, p. 317) and KANE/RICHARDSON (2002, p. 259).

558 See YAWSON (2009, p. 236).

559 Still it must be considered that very small companies are already excluded in the sampling process.

560 FRANCIS/DESAI (2005, p. 1219).

561 See FRANCIS/DESAI (2005, p. 1218).

identified restructuring actions of the early restructuring phase and Model 2-B includes the identified restructuring actions of the late restructuring phase. Both models include financial slack as significant context variable.

Table 6: Multivariate logistic regression – Model 2-A and 2-B.

		Model 2-A Early Restructuring			Model 2-B Late Restructuring		
Variable		β	s.e.	sig.[a]	β	s.e.	sig.[a]
Constant		0.931	0.27	0.001***	0.187	0.22	0.400
Early restructuring							
Revenue development	REV-ER	2.53	0.78	0.001***			
Operating expense ratio	EXP-ER	-20.014	6.36	0.001***			
Capital expenditure intensity	CAP-ER	-0.83	0.41	0.041**			
Late restructuring							
Revenue development	REV-LR				1.563	0.70	0.021**
Operating expense ratio	EXP-LR				-11.179	7.56	0.134
Debt restructuring	DBT-LR				-1.482	0.65	0.019**
Capital expenditure intensity	CAP-LR				-0.093	0.43	0.831
Context							
Financial slack	FS-CTX	3.895	1.47	0.006***	2.081	1.37	0.123
Model evaluation		$\chi2$	df	sig.	$\chi2$	df	sig.
Likelihood-Ratio-Test		31.297	4	0.001***	23.798	5	0.001***
H-L Test		8.338	8	0.401	1.548	8	0.992
Nagelkerke		0.28			0.22		
McFadden		0.18			0.13		
c-statistic		0.78			0.75		
Count R^2		70.1%			70.9%		
Adj. Count R^2		23.1%			25.0%		

a. Based on Likelihood-Ratio-Test.
Abr.: s.e. standard error, df degrees of freedom, sig. significance level
*, **, *** indicate significance at the 10%, 5%, and 1% levels respectively

Source: Own illustration.

Both models have explanatory power as indicated by the strongly significant Likelihood-Ratio-Test and fit the data well as indicated by the insignificant Hosmer-Lemeshow Test. As expected the separate phases explain significantly less of the corporate turnaround phenomenon as the full model with a Nagelkerke R^2 of 0.28 and 0.22 compared to 0.45. The early restructuring phase (Model 2-A) here has more explanatory power than the late restructuring phase (Model 2-B) even if less restructuring actions are included. Overall the analysis confirms, that restructuring actions during both phases are related to corporate turnaround.

For the *early restructuring phase*, the strongly significant impact of cost-cutting and capital expenditure cuts are in line with the retrenchment phase as outlined by ROBBINS/PEARCE (1993). The positive impact of revenue-generating activities is unexpected and provides no empirical evidence for the prior assumption that distressed firms focus on recovery activities only after an initial retrenchment phase during the first years after distress. For the *late restructuring phase*, the positive relation between revenue development and corporate turnaround is empirical evidence for the expansive and entrepreneurial restructuring actions during the recovery phase. At the same time, turnaround is still related to continuous retrenchment—i.e., the reduction in operating costs and the reduction in capital expenditures. This is contrary to the expected recovery phase associated with increasing investments and no further attention to cost reductions. Debt restructuring is also a significant restructuring strategy for the late restructuring phase, indicating the importance of leverage reduction.

Overall, the analysis of the restructuring phases does not yield empirical confidence in the existence of two distinct retrenchment and recovery phases as initially expected. The high significance of revenue growth, cost-cutting, and capital expenditure reductions reflects recent research results that find empirical evidence for successful turnarounds as a simultaneous combination of forward-looking actions and retrenchment.[562] Distinct short- and long-term strategies are not found for this sample. Both periods include retrenchment and entrepreneurial efforts.[563] Successful turnarounds among automotive suppliers are related to a simultaneous combination of entrepreneurial and retrenchment activities.[564]

Summary of multivariate regression results

Overall, the multivariate analysis strongly supports the importance of operational restructuring in turnarounds within the automotive supplier industry, but it provides limited empirical evidence for the effectiveness of financial and managerial restructuring. Specific asset restructuring in the form of capital expenditure reduction is also identified as significantly positive for corporate turnaround.

In this paragraph, the interpretation of research results is facilitated by a sensitivity analysis for the impact of discrete restructuring actions on the probability of turnaround, hence marginal changes are examined (see TABLE 7). As outlined in SECTION 4.3.2, for the interpretation of coefficients in logistic regression, only the direction and the significance level are meaningful. The magnitude of effects is better evaluated based on the variable's marginal effect—i.e., how a change in one restructuring variable changes the probability of

---

562 Compare FRANCIS/DESAI (2005, p. 1220).
563 See SMITH/GRAVES (2005, p. 317).
564 See FRANCIS/DESAI (2005, p. 1220).

corporate turnaround when all other variables are held constant.[565] Consistent with the approach proposed by HOETKER (2007), variables are set at meaningful values, in this case the average values for distressed companies. All changes for the independent variables are selected so that they remain below the restructuring intensity of the average turnaround firm.[566] As an additional limit to increase comparability, the individual change is restricted to one-third of the standard deviation for the selected measure within the group of non-turnaround companies.

Table 7: Multivariate logistic regression – Model 2 Sensitivity analysis.

		Model 2	NT		
Variable		β	mean	Δ mean[a]	Δ P_i (Y+1)
Constant		0.91	-	-	-
Revenue development	REV-ER	2.16	-0.177	+10%	+5.0%
	REV-LR	2.21	-0.036	+10%	+5.1%
Operating expense ratio	EXP-ER	-29.18	0.030	-1%	+6.8%
	EXP-LR	-14.58	0.003	-1%	+3.3%
Debt restructuring	DBT-LR	-1.32	0.123	-5%	+1.5%
Capital expenditure intensity	CAP-ER	-1.17	0.288	-10%	+2.7%
	CAP-LR	-1.07	-0.057	-10%	+2.4%
Financial slack	FS-CTX	4.18	0.057	-	-

a. Absolut percentage changes
P_i (Y+1) is the probability of turnaround
Abbr.: NT Non-turnaround

Source: Own illustration.

The probability of turnaround for the average non-turnaround firm based on the average values for each restructuring action within the subsample is 33.9%. This compares to an 81% turnaround probability for the average turnaround company.

For *revenue development*, an internal growth rate of 10% for each restructuring phase is analyzed. A 10% increase is expected to increase the probability of turnaround by 5.0% during the early and 5.1% during the late restructuring phases. The positive relation of organic revenue growth to turnaround is therefore approximately constant over both restructuring phases.

The effect of *cost reduction* is estimated with a decrease in the ratio of total expenses to revenues of one percentage point. During the early restructuring phase, this improvement leads to a 6.8% increase in the probability of turnaround compared to 3.3% during the late

565 Compare for the following HOETKER (2007, p. 334).

566 Based on the comparison of mean values for both subsamples. For CAP-LR the delta value is based on the values for CAP-ER to allow for comparability.

phase. Therefore, cost-cutting is more valuable during early restructuring, in line with the initial hypothesis for the positive effects of early retrenchment actions.

A reduction in *leverage*, hence the ratio of total debt to total assets during the late restructuring phase, by five percentage points improves the probability of turnaround by 1.5%. This again indicates that financial restructuring has minor importance for the turnaround of distressed automotive suppliers.

For *capital expenditures*, measured as the ratio of capital expenditures to fixed assets, a reduction by ten percentage points increases the probability of turnaround 2.7% during the early and 2.3% during the late restructuring phase. Early capital expenditure reductions are therefore slightly more beneficial, in line with the retrenchment hypothesis.

Overall, the analysis of the marginal effects of changes in restructuring variables on the probability of corporate turnaround emphasizes the importance of operational restructuring strategies. Revenue growth and cost reduction have the largest magnitude of effects compared to debt restructuring as a financial restructuring strategy and capital expenditure reduction as an asset restructuring strategy.

5.3 Strategies of distressed and non-distressed companies

5.3.1 Preliminaries and MANCOVA

The second research question builds upon the effective restructuring actions identified in the previous chapter and analyzes whether these restructuring actions are distinct activities by successful turnarounds or if they match general strategies employed by non-distressed companies. The question is whether distressed companies are simply doing nothing or are changing their strategies substantially.[567] If the financial distress is, for example, predicted to be temporary and available resources are assumed to be sufficient to avoid failure, a firm can choose not to react or to react with minimal or no major changes in strategy. On the other hand, circumstances can force firms to consider substantive changes and apply methods other than business as usual.[568]

Research question 2: Strategies of turnaround and non-distressed companies

- What sets apart successful turnaround strategies from successful strategies of companies not in distress situations?

567 See for the following KANE/RICHARDSON (2002, p. 262).
568 See WEITZEL/JONSSON (1989, p. 102).

- Do restructuring actions in successful turnarounds significantly differ from actions of healthy firms?
- Are there timing differences between strategies of turnaround firms and non-distressed firms?

This research question focuses on the most effective restructuring actions identified in CHAPTER 5.2. Each of the seven restructuring actions, early and late revenue development, early and late expense ratio, late debt restructuring, and early and late capital expenditures is addressed in separate ANCOVA analyses. Based on the theoretical framework and initial univariate analysis in SECTION 5.2.2, the three significant context variables—firm size, prior profitability, and financial slack—are included as context variables. The inclusion of these covariates permits adjusting the relation of the selected turnaround activity and the company status for differences in the context variables.

Before the actual ANCOVA analyses, the three required assumptions of equality of variances, normal distribution, and homogeneity of the regression slopes are tested. For all variables, the significance level of Levene's test of equality is well above 5%, indicating that variances can be assumed to be equal.[569] The Q-Q normality plots indicate that the independent variables follow a normal distribution.[570] For the final assumption regarding the homogeneity of regression slopes, slight deviances can be found in the graphical analysis.[571] Due to the very low R^2, these do not indicate different relationships for the dependent variables within the three subsamples.[572]

To test the overall hypothesis that the status of the company is related to its restructuring activities, an initial MANCOVA analysis is run on the set of dependent variables—the seven restructuring actions—with company status as the independent variable and controlling for the effects of firm size, prior profitability, and financial slack. The MANCOVA results show that company status significantly affects which restructuring actions are chosen (Wilk's lambda = 0.640; F-statistic of 6.493 with a significance level of $p < 0.001$).[573]

To further understand the relation of company status and the choice of restructuring actions, the next section presents the main univariate analyses for each dependent variable. SECTION 5.3.2 includes the descriptive analysis of the restructuring actions for the three subsamples of

569 See APPENDIX 14 for details. The significance level exceeds 0.1 for all variables except REV-ER at 0.098.

570 See APPENDIX 15 for details. Regarding the interpretation, "the points should more or less cluster around the line," and an exact normal distribution cannot be expected; compare NORUSIS (2009, p. 149).

571 See APPENDIX 16 for firm size, APPENDIX 17 for prior profitability, and APPENDIX 18 for financial slack.

572 Compare FIELD (2005, pp. 380-382).

573 The selection of Wilk's Lambda is based on LACEY ET AL. (2007, pp. 248-249). The additional test statistics Pillai's 'Trace, Hotelling's Trace, and Roy's largest Root are all statistically significant at the $p < 0.001$ level; compare FIELD (2005, pp. 593-594) for an overview.

turnaround, non-turnaround and non-distressed companies and the univariate ANCOVA analysis for the relation of company status to each restructuring action.

5.3.2 Univariate ANCOVA

Before the univariate ANCOVA analyses, adjusted mean values are provided for each of the three subsamples (see TABLE 8). By following the approach of FIELD (2005), the mean values are adjusted for the effect of the covariates, hence differences in firm size, prior profitability, and financial slack that are expected to impact the magnitude of the restructuring activity.[574] The original mean values are not related to the group differences reflected in the later ANCOVA analyses and therefore the adjusted means are used for interpretation of group differences.

Table 8: ANCOVA – Descriptives.

	REV-ER	REV-LR	EXP-ER	EXP-LR	DBT-LR	CAP-ER	CAP-LR
Unadjusted mean							
TA	-0.010	0.154	0.010	-0.009	-0.079	0.119	0.009
NT	-0.177	-0.036	0.030	0.003	0.123	0.288	-0.057
ND	0.024	0.115	0.003	0.004	-0.045	0.014	0.098
Adjusted mean [a]							
TA	-0.038	0.152	0.012	-0.008	-0.080	0.131	-0.005
NT	-0.186	-0.042	0.032	0.002	0.134	0.269	-0.043
ND	0.071	0.123	-0.002	0.003	-0.053	0.015	0.104

a. Covariates appearing in the model are evaluated at the following values (estimated marginal means): TA-CTX = 6.07071, PP-CTX = 0.13221, FS-CTX = 0.11868

Source: Own illustration.

The remainder of this section discusses each of the restructuring actions independently, focusing on the differences between distressed and non-distressed companies. The discussion is based on the significance level of the overall ANCOVA analysis, hence if the company status in a test of between-subjects effects is related to the restructuring action at all, and also the significance level of any pairwise comparisons.

574 Compare FIELD (2005, p. 374).

Table 9: ANCOVA – Univariate analysis.

	REV-ER		REV-LR		EXP-ER		EXP-LR	
A. Tests of between-subjects effects								
	F	sig.	F	sig.	F	sig.	F	sig.
Intercept	0.6	0.448	1.7	0.192	3.8	0.053*	0.0	0.960
TA-CTX	2.1	0.145	0.5	0.495	3.7	0.057*	1.4	0.240
PP-CTX	14.7	0.001***	0.0	0.864	5.6	0.019**	2.5	0.114
FS-CTX	7.7	0.006***	0.4	0.524	6.5	0.011**	0.2	0.670
STATUS	13.6	0.001***	7.3	0.001***	13.7	0.001***	3.6	0.029**
B. Pairwise comparison								
	b	sig.[a]	b	sig.[a]	b	sig.[a]	b	sig.[a]
TA vs. ND	-0.108	0.046**	0.029	0.926	0.014	0.047**	-0.011	0.061*
NT vs. ND	-0.257	0.001***	-0.165	0.016**	0.034	0.001***	-0.001	0.996

	DBT-LR		CAP-ER		CAP-LR	
A. Tests of between-subjects effects						
	F	sig.	F	sig.	F	sig.
Intercept	0.1	0.790	0.9	0.357	0.5	0.500
TA-CTX	0.0	0.933	1.0	0.307	0.1	0.809
PP-CTX	0.4	0.516	1.5	0.224	2.6	0.108
FS-CTX	0.9	0.337	0.5	0.474	0.2	0.636
STATUS	7.7	0.001***	3.6	0.031**	1.4	0.241
B. Pairwise comparison						
	b	sig.[a]	b	sig.[a]	b	sig.[a]
TA vs. ND	-0.027	0.948	0.116	0.440	-0.110	0.453
NT vs. ND	0.186	0.010***	0.254	0.025**	-0.147	0.294

a. Adjustment for multiple comparisons: Sidak
Abbr.: sig. significance level
*, **, *** indicate significance at the 10%, 5%, and 1% levels respectively

Source: Own illustration.

Based on the F-statistics of the univariate ANCOVA analyses and the corresponding significance levels (see TABLE 9), the results show that company status is significantly related to all but one restructuring action. The ANCOVA analysis for capital expenditure during the late restructuring phase is not significant. In the broader context of the matched sample including non-distressed firms, the change in capital expenditure intensity during late restructuring is not significantly different among the three groups. The lower significance level for changes in operating expense ratios during the late restructuring phase instead is again in line with the results of the fitted logistic regression in Model 2, where they are not significant.

Discussion of restructuring actions

For the six restructuring actions with significant F-statistics, a further examination via pairwise comparisons for turnaround vs. non-distressed companies and non-turnaround vs. non-distressed companies follows in the remainder of this section.

The adjusted mean values for *revenue development* during the early restructuring phase show that although comparable non-distressed companies are able to increase their adjusted revenues, turnaround companies decreased their adjusted revenues slightly and non-turnaround companies decreased them substantially. Differences for both comparisons are statistically significant. The significant differences for both comparisons support the argument that distressed companies must focus on generating additional revenues based on the existing asset base or, as in this case, avoid further decreases in productivity.[575] During the late restructuring phase, turnaround companies return to their growth track and even exceed the growth rate of non-distressed companies, whereas non-turnaround companies suffer further decline. The difference between turnaround and healthy companies is no longer significant, compared to the still-significant difference between non-turnaround and healthy companies. In addition to the analysis in SECTION 5.2.3, which established a positive relation between internal revenue growth and the probability of turnaround during both phases, this analysis shows that turnaround companies exhibit a growth rate not significantly different from those of non-distressed companies during the recovery phase. Average growth rates of non-distressed companies during the late restructuring phase can therefore be considered sufficient to achieve turnaround, whereas below-average growth rates are related to non-turnaround.

The *operating expense ratio* of non-distressed companies stays approximately constant during both phases of the restructuring process, hence, as expected, healthy companies are not concerned about ongoing improvement of their cost positions. Turnaround companies show a slight increase in their expense ratios during the early restructuring phase and are able to reduce them during the late restructuring phase. Non-turnaround companies by comparison show a stronger increase in expense ratios during the early phase and thereafter are able to keep the ratio constant. During early restructuring, the increase in the cost ratios is significantly higher than for non-distressed companies in both subgroups. For the late restructuring phase, differences are significant only for turnaround companies. The multivariate logistic regression already shows the positive relation of cost-cutting and corporate turnaround, and the significant differences during the early restructuring phase further emphasize that both distressed subsamples must focus on avoiding further cost increases. Cost-cutting during the late restructuring phase is a distinct restructuring action among turnaround companies. Successful turnarounds decrease their operating cost

[575] Compare FRANCIS/DESAI (2005, p. 1217).

significantly more than non-distressed companies, whereas non-turnaround companies act as though they were not in distress and fail to take cost-reduction measures to achieve turnaround. Again, this shows that companies must shift their focus in order to increase the probability of turnaround. Business as usual is no longer appropriate.[576]

The development of the *leverage* ratio shows that during the late restructuring phase both turnaround and non-distressed companies reduce leverage. At the same time, non-distressed companies take on significantly more debt during late restructuring that might hinder a later turnaround. So although leverage reduction is not a distinct characteristic of turnaround companies, an increase in leverage is clearly associated with non-turnarounds.[577]

Turnaround companies increase their *capital expenditure intensity* during the early restructuring phase, and non-turnaround companies increase it even more. The increase for turnaround companies does not differ significantly from non-distressed companies, which keep their level of capital expenditures approximately constant. Overall, reducing capital expenditure intensity is identified as an effective restructuring activity for corporate turnaround, and the comparison with non-distressed companies shows that an expansion exceeding the industry average is especially associated with non-turnarounds.[578]

Summary of univariate ANCOVA analyses

The comparison of the restructuring actions of distressed companies with those of non-distressed companies identifies two sub-sets of turnaround actions: (1) distinct turnaround actions that are not applied by healthy companies, (2) strategies of non-distressed companies that also are related to turnarounds.

(1) The analysis of the effectiveness of restructuring measures in the previous chapter shows that increases in adjusted revenues and cost-cutting are significantly related to corporate turnaround during both phases. The comparison with non-distressed companies additionally finds that only distressed firms are affected by decreasing productivity, especially during the early restructuring phase, and by increasing cost levels during both phases. This result indicates that business-as-usual methods are no longer advisable for distressed companies and that they must focus on generating revenues, hence an improvement in the productivity of their existing asset base during the early restructuring phase, and the continuous improvement of the cost position to achieve turnaround, even throughout the late restructuring phase.

576 Compare LAI/SUDARSANAM (1997, p. 217) and D'AVENI (1989b, p. 580). For the importance of cost-reduction measures during corporate turnaround, see YAWSON (2009, p. 236), LIN ET AL. (2008, p. 544), and FURRER ET AL. (2007, p. 379).

577 For the role of debt restructuring in non-turnarounds, compare LIN ET AL. (2008, p. 549), SUDARSANAM/LAI (2001, pp. 194-196), and JOHN ET AL. (1992, pp. 909-911).

578 Compare YAWSON (2009, p. 224) and KANE/RICHARDSON (2002, p. 259) for the problems related to asset expansion.

(2) Analysis of the effectiveness of restructuring measures in the previous chapter also shows that increases in adjusted revenues during the late restructuring phase, late debt restructuring, and early capital expenditure reductions are positively related to corporate turnaround. For these three measures, turnaround companies show the same level of change as non-distressed firms, indicating these restructuring actions are more general measures rather than measures distinctly associated with distressed companies. First, turnaround companies return to a normal organic *revenue growth* rate—in line with the growth rate of non-distressed companies—during the late restructuring phase. This indicates that a regular industry growth rate in the effective use of the asset base during the late restructuring phase is sufficient to achieve turnaround. Second, turnaround companies do not boost *leverage* during the late restructuring phase and are even able to reduce it slightly, as do healthy companies. Third, although capital expenditures reductions are identified as positively related to corporate turnaround, turnaround companies' changes in capital expenditure intensity do not differ significantly from healthy companies. This leads to the conclusion that although an overall reduction of capital expenditures is required, increases in line with industry averages might also be feasible within successful turnarounds.[579]

Overall, the analysis of the second research question supports the view that there are differences between turnaround strategies and strategies of non-distressed automotive suppliers, but they also share common characteristics. Compared to healthy firms, distressed automotive suppliers must improve their cost position by cutting expenses and improve productivity by generating more revenues from existing assets. These actions are distinctive to turnaround companies, especially during the early restructuring phase, because they are not required for non-distressed firms. At the same time, distressed companies must stick to the same actions as non-distressed companies to achieve turnaround. That is, they must improve leverage, achieve industry-average organic growth in revenues during the late restructuring phase, and reduce capital expenditure growth to industry norms.

579 See ASQUITH ET AL. (1994, p. 650).

5.4 Turnaround archetypes

5.4.1 Preliminaries

The third research question addresses the identification of successful turnaround gestalts, including successful combinations of single restructuring actions. The idea of generic strategies, hence a set of identifiable restructuring actions applicable to distress situations, has been endorsed early on by scholars and practitioners.[580]

Research question 3: Turnaround archetypes

- Are there archetypes of successful turnarounds in the automotive supplier industry?
  - ➢ Which restructuring actions are combined in successful turnarounds?
  - ➢ What is the relevant sequence of these restructuring actions?

As introduced in SECTION 4.3.4, before the discussion of the cluster analysis results, the selection of the clustering variables, the identification of outliers, and the definition of the number of clusters are discussed shortly.

For the cluster analysis, all restructuring activities from the theoretical research framework in CHAPTER 3.2 are used as clustering variables to capture possible interdependencies and interaction effects. To avoid problems arising from different scaling of variables, the variables revenue development, expense ratio, dividend policy, and total asset changes are dichotomized for the clustering process. Given that the average correlation coefficient for all cluster variables is 0.13 and that the maximum value of 0.48 is well below the critical threshold of 0.9, no problem with multicollinearity among clustering variables exists.[581]

In the preliminary single linkage algorithm, one outlier is identified and eliminated for further analysis to increase cluster robustness.[582] One turnaround company, Superior Industries International Inc., is identified as differing considerably from the other turnaround companies and is excluded from the analysis. After exclusion of this outlier, Ward's algorithm is applied to the final sample of 81 turnaround companies.

The number of clusters is then defined based on the graphical analysis of the elbow chart (see FIGURE 18). The elbow chart indicates a four-cluster solution compared to a three- or five-

---

580 See O'NEILL (1986b, p. 166).

581 See APPENDIX 10 for details.

582 See APPENDIX 11 for the corresponding dendogram.

cluster solution. The dendogram for the Wald algorithm supports the choice of the four-cluster solution.[583]

Figure 18: Cluster analysis – Elbow chart.

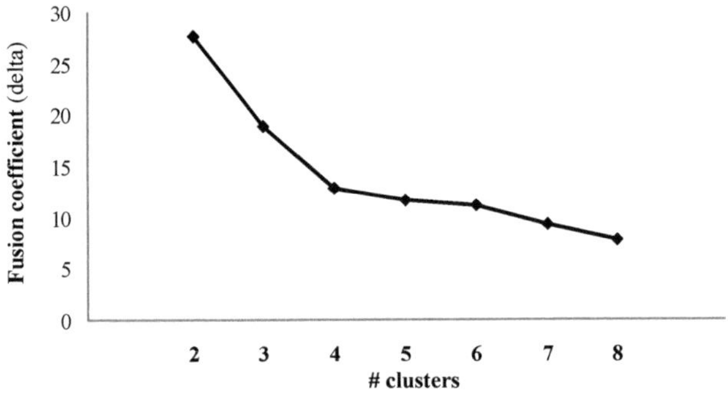

Source: Own illustration.

In addition, prior research shows three- to six-cluster solutions, and the four-cluster solution in this research setting accords with the four generic turnaround gestalts identified by HOFER (1980).[584] The four clusters derived contain 26, 20, 18, and 17 companies, respectively. F-statistics as a measure of cluster homogeneity are well below 1 in all four clusters, for only the selected clustering variables as well as all variables available, including the context variables not used for clustering.[585]

5.4.2 Cluster analysis

The mean values and the t-ratio of the different restructuring and context variables serve as the basis for interpretations of the four clusters. In line with the approach of LAFRENZ (2004), the discussion of the results is structured according to pre-distress firm characteristics and the restructuring actions chosen.[586] The comparison with the outlined turnaround archetypes follows in the last paragraph.

Financial pre-distress and firm characteristics

Of the five financial pre-distress characteristics and two firm characteristics, only firm size, financial capacity, and industry subsector show significant differences among some of the four clusters and the population of successful turnarounds (see TABLE 10).

583 See APPENDIX 12 for details.
584 Compare HOFER (1980), HAMBRICK/SCHECTER (1983), LAFRENZ (2004), and EICHNER (2008).
585 See APPENDIX 13 for details including the F-statistic for non-clustering variables.
586 Compare LAFRENZ (2004, p. 231).

Table 10: Cluster analysis – Context variables.

		TA	Cluster 1			Cluster 2			Cluster 3			Cluster 4		
		N=82[a]	N=26			N=18			N=20			N=17		
		mean	mean	t-ratio	sig.	mean	t-ratio	sig.	mean	t-ratio	sig.	mean	t-ratio	sig.
Context														
Firm size	TA-CTX	6.17	6.12	-0.03		6.48	0.23		5.74	-0.33	*	6.39	0.17	
Prior profitability	PP-CTX	0.12	0.11	-0.19		0.11	-0.14		0.13	0.24		0.13	0.14	
Distress severity	DS-CTX	-0.04	-0.04	0.07		-0.04	0.06		-0.05	-0.12		-0.04	0.05	
Financial capacity	FC-CTX	0.93	0.85	-0.09		1.36	0.52	*	0.65	-0.34	*	0.98	0.06	
Financial slack	FS-CTX	0.10	0.12	0.17		0.06	-0.26		0.09	-0.05		0.10	-0.03	
Region Asia-Pacific	RG-CTX	0.76	0.81	0.12		0.72	-0.09		0.80	0.09		0.71	-0.12	
Industry subsector Tires	IN-CTX	0.17	0.23	0.16		0.22	0.13		0.20	0.08		0.00	-0.45	***

a. One company is eliminated in the outlier analysis.
Abbr.: TA Turnaround, sig. significance level
*, **, *** indicate significance at the 10%, 5%, and 1% levels, respectively

Source: Own illustration.

Cluster 1 is characterized by the highest level of distress. This appears in the combination of lowest pre-distress profitability and highest distress severity. Financial slack is highest among the four clusters, while financial capacity is below average. Based on the analysis of context variables in the previous chapter, the high degree of financial slack is already significantly associated with a higher probability of turnaround. Companies from the Asia-Pacific region and the tire industry are overrepresented in Cluster 1.

The largest companies are represented in *Cluster 2*. The level of distress is also high, with a below-average pre-distress level and an above-average distress severity. The main characteristics of this cluster are significantly higher financial capacity and the least financial slack.

Cluster 3 includes significantly smaller companies with the highest pre-distress profitability and the lowest decline in profitability, hence the lowest level of distress. Cluster 3 exhibits the exact opposite characteristics of Cluster 1, which features the lowest pre-distress profitability and the severest decline in profitability. In addition, companies within Cluster 3 have significantly lower financial capacity and slightly less financial slack than other clusters. As with Cluster 1, Asia-Pacific companies and the tire industry are slightly overrepresented.

Companies in *Cluster 4* are larger than average but exhibit approximately average values for the other financial characteristics. Asia-Pacific companies are underrepresented in this cluster, and no tire companies are included.

Overall, Cluster 1 includes companies with the highest distress level, and Cluster 3 includes companies with the lowest. Only the smaller firm size for Cluster 3 and the highest and lowest financial capacity for Cluster 2 and Cluster 3 are statistically significant. In addition, companies from the Asia-Pacific region are not present in Cluster 4 and therefore are significantly underrepresented statistically.

Discussion of restructuring actions

The discussion of the turnaround actions chosen within each cluster is based on the four restructuring categories within the theoretical framework. The descriptives of each activity are provided below (see TABLE 11).

Table 11: Cluster analysis – Restructuring actions.

		TA	Cluster 1			Cluster 2			Cluster 3			Cluster 4		
		N=82[a]	N=26			N=18			N=20			N=17		
		mean	mean	t-ratio	sig.	mean	t-ratio	sig.	mean	t-ratio	sig.	mean	t-ratio	sig.
Managerial restructuring														
Top executive change –	MRA-ER	0.24	0.15	-0.21		0.39	0.35		0.20	-0.09		0.24	0.00	
All	MRA-LR	0.11	0.00	-0.35	***	0.28	0.54		0.15	0.13		0.06	-0.16	
Top executive change –	MRN-ER	0.11	0.00	-0.35	***	0.28	0.54		0.05	-0.19		0.18	0.22	
Non-routine	MRN-LR	0.07	0.00	-0.27	**	0.17	0.38		0.10	0.11		0.06	-0.04	
Operational restructuring														
Revenue development	REV-ER	-0.01	0.02	0.14		0.13	0.60	**	-0.15	-0.57	**	-0.04	-0.11	
	REV-LR	0.15	0.17	0.04		0.23	0.26		0.19	0.14		0.01	-0.55	
Expense ratio	EXP-ER	0.01	0.00	-0.26		0.00	-0.20		0.02	0.47	*	0.01	-0.10	
	EXP-LR	-0.01	-0.01	-0.09		-0.01	-0.01		-0.01	-0.08		0.00	0.21	
Financial restructuring														
Equity issue	EQU-ER	0.37	0.12	-0.52	***	0.33	-0.08		0.25	-0.25		0.94	1.18	***
	EQU-LR	0.30	0.08	-0.48	***	0.39	0.19		0.05	-0.54	***	0.88	1.25	***
Dividend policy	DIV-ER	0.12	0.03	-0.10		0.15	0.05		0.30	0.23		-0.01	-0.16	
	DIV-LR	0.27	0.12	-0.25		0.92	1.13	***	-0.10	-0.64	***	0.25	-0.04	
Debt restructuring	DBT-ER	0.13	0.03	-0.28		-0.09	-0.59	***	0.29	0.41	*	0.36	0.59	**
	DBT-LR	-0.08	-0.09	-0.04		-0.24	-0.53	**	-0.02	0.18		0.04	0.40	
Asset restructuring														
Total assets change	TAS-ER	0.11	0.12	0.04		-0.05	-0.68	***	0.20	0.36		0.18	0.27	
	TAS-LR	0.16	0.15	-0.03		0.13	-0.10		0.17	0.02		0.21	0.20	
Capital expenditures	CAP-ER	0.12	0.00	-0.25		0.07	-0.10		0.37	0.52	**	0.05	-0.14	
	CAP-LR	0.01	0.23	0.46	**	0.19	0.39		-0.34	-0.73	***	-0.06	-0.15	

a. One company is eliminated in the outlier analysis.
Abbr.: TA Turnaround, sig. significance level
*, **, *** indicate significance at the 10%, 5%, and 1% levels respectively

Source: Own illustration.

Companies in *Cluster 1* retain their managements during their turnaround. They have no forced top executive replacements during the early or late restructuring phases. Existing management implements the turnaround strategy. During the early restructuring phase, these companies maintain approximately constant expense ratios, leverage, dividends, and capital expenditures. Only during the late restructuring phase are these firms able to generate more revenues from their asset bases in combination with improved cost ratios. In line with the expansionary restructuring actions, these companies increase capital expenditures significantly and grow their asset bases during the late phase of the restructuring process. Although these companies issue significantly less equity than other turnaround companies, they are able to reduce leverage during late restructuring. Two of the most effective restructuring actions shown in CHAPTER 5.2 are included in their turnaround strategies: late, internal revenue growth and late debt restructuring.

Cluster 2 is characterized by a higher intensity of routine and forced top executive turnover during both restructuring phases. During early restructuring, the new management is better able to utilize the asset base by significantly increasing revenues. The total asset base is even slightly reduced during the early restructuring phase. Capital expenditures are well below the average for distressed companies during the early phase, and operating expenses are kept stable. During the late restructuring phase, these companies are able to grow revenues further based on their optimized cost positions and expanded asset bases. They complement their expansionary policies by increasing dividends substantially. Also, debt restructuring is relevant to companies within this cluster. They continuously reduce leverage during both phases of the process. Especially, late debt restructuring has been shown to be significantly associated with successful turnarounds. Reducing leverage is in line with one-third of the companies issuing new equity during both phases.

Replacement of top executives among companies in *Cluster 3* is below average during the early restructuring phase but above average during late restructuring. During early restructuring, the asset base grows with a decreasing ability to generate revenues. During the late restructuring phase, these companies cut expenses, dividends, and capital expenditures, although cuts in dividends and capital expenditures are significantly below average. At the same time, the retrenchment actions are combined with expansions of the asset base and better utilization of these assets during the late restructuring phase. Late stage internal revenue growth, debt restructuring, and capital expenditure cuts are significantly associated with the probability of turnaround. For the included companies, the selected restructuring actions indicate that a late retrenchment strategy is implemented.

Companies in *Cluster 4* exhibit strong increases in total assets during both restructuring phases. The strong increase is accompanied by a decrease in fixed asset turnover. The main characteristics of this cluster are a very high share of equity issuance during both phases and an increase in leverage. Expansion of the asset base is financed through new debt and equity. Forced top executive replacements occur early, and dividends and capital expenditures are stable during the early phase. During the late phase, dividends are increased significantly, and capital expenditures are even reduced. Late stage capital expenditure cuts are the only effective restructuring action identified in the previous chapter that are applicable to this cluster.

Discussion of turnaround archetypes

In the remainder of this section the restructuring actions chosen are matched with the generic turnaround archetypes outlined by HOFER (1980).[587]

The restructuring actions chosen by *Cluster 1* companies coincide with a revenue growth strategy, but only during the late restructuring phase. Although restructuring actions during the early phase are not distinctive, existing management starts to expansionary actions during the late phase. Capital expenditures are resumed, and the asset base is growing while fixed asset turnover again increases. The high level of distress might hinder incumbent management from starting an expansionary turnaround during the early phase, when initial stabilization of the company is required. At the same time, the high degree of financial slack makes turnaround possible without substantial dividend or capital expenditure cuts.

Cluster 2 can be compared to HOFER's 'product/ market refocusing' and partially EICHNER's 'strategic reorientation', with the new strategy being implemented by a new top executive.[588] In the first phase, companies divest non-core assets and focus on existing revenue-generating actions. This phase is supplemented by additional capital expenditures on existing fixed assets. The reorientation pays off during the late restructuring phase when companies expand into new business ventures and benefit from a strong increase in revenues in combination with an improved cost position. In addition, the companies are able to reduce leverage significantly during the turnaround. Strategic reorientation fits the group of large companies with the financial capacity to implement the strategic change. The low degree of financial slack requires initial asset sales to enable the turnaround. Cluster 1 fits the research by EICHNER (2008), who states that this turnaround strategy is chosen by companies in above-average distress, and it fits the research by LAFRENZ (2004), who finds that large, distressed companies in particular refocus during their turnaround.[589]

Companies in *Cluster 3* implement a cost-cutting strategy during the late restructuring phase and can be considered late retrenchers. Dividend cuts, cost-cutting, and a robust decrease in capital expenditures are part of the cost-cutting strategy during the late phase, after a period of inactivity with decreasing productivity and worsening cost ratios. The late implementation of turnaround initiatives might be related to having the lowest initial distress level, which

587 Compare HOFER (1980).

588 See HOFER (1980, p. 23) and EICHNER (2008, p. 255). EICHNER (2008) additionally matches CEO turnover with the generic turnaround archetypes, whereas HOFER (1980, pp. 25-26) sees replacing top executives as a "precondition for almost all successful turnarounds."

589 See EICHNER (2008, p. 255) and LAFRENZ (2004, p. 240).

management underestimated. After a higher incidence of late forced turnovers, new management is associated with a retrenchment strategy to enable turnaround. Cluster 3 matches the 'profitable growth' strategy for small companies identified by LAFRENZ (2004).[590]

Cluster 4 cannot be associated clearly with any one of Hofer's four generic turnaround strategies and can be considered a combination strategy. Companies in this cluster expand their asset bases during both restructuring phases, but not by increasing capital expenditures. Expansion is financed through additional leverage and an above-average frequency of equity issuance. To preserve internal cash, dividends are reduced slightly during the early restructuring phase. Neither Asia-Pacific companies nor automotive tire companies appear to apply this strategy. Cluster 4 partially matches the 'cash flow optimization' strategy identified by EICHNER (2008), which features limited internal revenue growth and tough control of capital expenditures.[591]

Overall, the setting for the third research question is explorative in nature, and only three of the generic turnaround gestalts can be identified among successful turnarounds in the automotive industry. The cluster analysis shows that late revenue growth, late retrenchment, and strategic reorientation are successful combinations of restructuring actions. It also indicates which strategies might be appropriate given different firm and financial characteristics in the automotive supplier industry.

590 Compare LAFRENZ (2004, p. 240).
591 Compare EICHNER (2008, p. 255).

6. CONCLUSION

This final part of the dissertation highlights the study's key findings, indicates limitations, and suggests directions for future research. CHAPTER 6.1 summarizes the course of study and major findings regarding the three research questions. CHAPTER 6.2 discusses limitations inherent in this research and, based on the study's design and findings, suggests directions for future research.

6.1 Course of study and main findings

This dissertation investigating financial distress and turnarounds in the automotive supplier industry informs an ongoing debate in corporate turnaround research. It has analyzed three distinct questions concerning the sampled automotive suppliers.

- How effective are frequently recommended restructuring strategies in helping to resolve financial distress in the automotive supplier industry?
- What sets apart successful turnaround strategies from successful strategies of companies not in distress situations?
- Are there archetypes of successful turnarounds in the automotive supplier industry?

The results contribute to research on financial distress and corporate turnaround by providing a long-requested analysis of a narrowly defined industry segment and by including non-distressed companies in the comparative analysis. The remainder of this chapter reviews the course of study briefly before the study's main findings are summarized.

Course of study review

PART 1 introduced the research problem and corresponding research questions. It stated the need for industry specific turnaround research and identified the automotive supplier industry as an industry segment highly relevant for corporate turnaround research. It also articulated the rationale for selecting a pragmatic, normative research target and the empirical, theory-based research strategy.

Based on extensive review of literature concerning corporate crisis in general and corporate turnaround in particular in PART 2, PART 3 integrated existing empirical contributions into a theoretical research framework for financial distress and corporate turnaround. The framework includes the three main dimensions of corporate restructuring: process, content, and context. The focus was on the content dimension—the four restructuring categories of managerial, operational, financial, and asset restructuring. Each identified restructuring action was analyzed during the early and late phases of the restructuring process. The research framework includes hypotheses concerning the effectiveness of single restructuring actions and forms the foundation for the empirical analysis.

PART 4 identified the sample of 134 distressed and 60 non-distressed automotive suppliers among the total population of all publicly listed automotive suppliers. For each of the three research questions, this part identified the appropriate statistical method. Logistic regression was selected as the most appropriate method for identifying effective restructuring actions in a multivariate research setting. The more explorative research questions were addressed within univariate ANCOVA analyses and a cluster analysis. The pluralism of methods applied in this dissertation enhances the validity of its empirical results.

Empirical results for each of the three research questions were presented in PART 5. After a preliminary descriptive analysis of the sample in CHAPTER 5.1, effective restructuring actions for distressed automotive companies were addressed in Chapter 5.2. Distinct turnaround actions different from regular, non-distressed companies were discussed in CHAPTER 5.3, and CHAPTER 5.4 identified four turnaround gestalts.

A summary of the main empirical results and key findings of the dissertation follows.

Summary of primary findings

For the first research question, four effective restructuring actions, each differentiated by early and late phases of the process, were identified as effective in resolving financial distress among automotive suppliers. These four restructuring actions are matched with the strategies of non-distressed firms in the second research question.

- The first operational restructuring action positively related to resolving financial distress is *internal revenue growth* during the early and the late restructuring phase. Companies able to generate higher revenues from their existing asset base significantly increase their probability of turnaround. Although companies emphasize reducing further productivity declines during the early restructuring phase, a return to average growth rates of non-distressed firms during the late restructuring phase already suffices for turnaround.
- Improving the *cost position* is the second restructuring action positively related to probability of a turnaround. Again, companies concentrate on reducing any possible cost increases during the early restructuring phase and pursue "real" cost-cutting during late restructuring. Cost reductions are distinctive turnaround measures not common to healthy companies. Non-turnaround companies are characterized by failure to cut costs, especially during the late restructuring phase. This suggests that business-as-usual measures are inappropriate for distressed automotive suppliers and that cost-cutting is essential in any turnaround strategy.
- *Debt restructuring* stands forth as the only financial restructuring action that significantly contributes to turnarounds. Reducing leverage during the late restructuring phase is positively related to corporate turnaround. Turnaround and non-distressed companies are able to reduce their leverage, whereas non-turnaround companies assume additional debt. This indicates that increasing indebtedness hampers turnarounds, whereas turnaround and non-turnaround companies display similar intensities toward debt restructuring.
- The final effective restructuring action is reducing *capital expenditure intensity* as part of asset restructuring. Especially during early restructuring, growth in capital expenditures must be curtailed to increase the likelihood of turnaround. Turnaround companies are able to keep capital expenditures in line with the average for non-distressed companies, whereas non-turnaround companies show significantly higher increases. Again, capital expenditure

increases are identified with non-turnarounds, whereas turnaround companies maintain capital expenditures at the same level as non-distressed companies.

Pre-distress financial slack emerges as the key context factor related to turnarounds. Results indicate that the degree of slack is the differentiating criterion for turnarounds, not a firm's size, as often stated in previous research. A high level of working capital in relation to total assets is positively related to corporate turnaround. Prior profitability, distress severity, and financial capacity have minor importance for the prospects of turnaround.

Overall, findings suggest that operational restructuring is essential for successful turnarounds in the automotive supplier industry. Indeed, it differentiates turnaround from non-turnaround companies. Contrary to expectations, managerial and financial restructuring are not identified as key contributors to corporate turnaround. Their lack of significant influence should not be interpreted to mean they are not part of turnaround strategies, but that they might not alter whether a firm successfully turns around.[592] Below is a short summary of these two restructuring categories.

Managerial restructuring is commonly employed by both turnaround and non-turnaround automotive suppliers, but it is not strongly related to the probability of successful turnaround. Consistent with prior research, neither forced nor routine replacement of the top executive correlates significantly with turnarounds among automotive suppliers.[593] For distressed automotive suppliers, the benefits and drawbacks of top executive changes seem to cancel each other.

Despite the effectiveness of debt restructuring during the late restructuring phase, other financial restructuring actions, including altering dividend policy and equity issuance, are not identified as significantly related to corporate turnaround. This suggests that financial restructuring can relieve short-term liquidity problems, but it is not a differentiating factor in sustainable recovery.[594]

Regarding the *restructuring process*, results produce no empirical evidence for the two distinct phases of retrenchment and recovery by ROBBINS/PEARCE (1992).[595] Both restructuring phases are found to include actions related to corporate turnaround, but successful turnarounds for distressed automotive suppliers are a simultaneous combination of forward-looking and retrenchment activities.[596]

---

592 Compare FURRER (2007, pp. 385-386).

593 Compare SUDARSANAM (2001, p. 196) and BRUTON ET AL. (2003, p. 530).

594 Compare YAWSON (2009, p. 227).

595 Compare ROBBINS/PEARCE (1992) and the findings of MORROW ET AL. (2004), FRANCIS/PETT (2004), or PAJUNEN (2005).

596 This is in line with more recent contributions by, for example, FRANCIS/DESAI (2005, p. 1220), and

For the final research question, cluster analysis identified four combinations of turnaround actions for distressed automotive suppliers. Three of the *turnaround archetypes* among automotive suppliers resemble the generic turnaround gestalts identified by Hofer (1980).

- The first cluster identified includes companies that pursue an expansionary strategy during the late restructuring phase. Late revenue growth is accompanied by capital expenditure increases, but also by cost-cutting. Existing management implements this strategy, which proves suitable for distressed companies with above-average financial slack—i.e., they have the ability to implement this growth strategy.
- Strategic reorientation is the second identified cluster. It includes automotive suppliers that first undertake asset reductions through significant divestitures and then expand by increasing their asset bases and by growing revenues organically. Replacement of the top executive is another characteristic of firms in the strategic reorientation cluster.
- The third cluster is characterized by a clear retrenchment strategy. Cost-cutting is accompanied by reductions in dividends and capital expenditures, especially during late restructuring. This strategy is especially suitable for smaller companies.

The last cluster cannot be related to any of the previously identified generic turnaround archetypes, so it is considered a combination strategy. Its main characteristics are expansion of the asset base during both restructuring phases and reliance on financial restructuring strategies.

With respect to all three research questions, the dissertation's empirical findings shed light on the corporate turnaround of financially distressed automotive suppliers. This research enlarges understanding of the application of commonly prescribed restructuring actions within a specific industry. Its results emphasize the importance of operational restructuring in the turnaround process and also identify specific financial and asset restructuring actions that contribute to corporate turnaround.

Francis/Desai (2005) quote Carlos Ghosn, then CEO of Nissan, who described successful turnarounds in the automotive industry as a matter of braking and accelerating at the same time. Ghosn is quoted as saying it is impossible to claim "[t]here will be a time for cost reduction and then a time for growth"[597] but that they had to do both at once.[598] This statement exemplifies the main results of this study. Over time, complimentary industry-specific studies are expected to emerge and challenge the findings this study.

Smith/Graves (2005, p. 317).

597 Carlos Ghosn quoted in Francis/Desai (2005, p. 1220).

598 Francis/Desai (2005, p. 1220).

6.2 Limitations and directions for future research

The main limitation of this research, which afflicts any empirical large-sample study, is that although theoretical considerations and methodological rigor improve the robustness of results, only correlations and not causal relationships can be shown based on the research design chosen. This study's results should therefore be considered tentative rather than conclusive. Based on the research design and primary findings, three limitations warrant further consideration and offer attractive opportunities for future research.

The first limitation is related to the research object, the selection of sampled companies, and the chosen timeframe. The sample studied includes only large publicly-listed automotive companies, and the transferability of results to small and privately held companies is limited. Among the 10 largest automotive suppliers worldwide, two large private suppliers are included: Robert Bosch GmbH and ZF Friedrichshafen AG.[599] Even if extant research currently focuses on public companies,[600] an explorative extension of the sample to include large private automotive companies seems promising based on the structure of the automotive industry. The other aspect with respect to the research object is the sampling timeframe. With the US subprime mortgage crisis in the second half of 2007 and the following global financial and economic crisis by the end of 2008, financial distress and insolvency again became common for many corporations.[601] The automobile industry had been hit severely by the recession, and car sales collapsed in 2009.[602] Repeated analyses of financial distress and turnarounds among automotive suppliers after 2009 might yield interesting insights if the same restructuring actions were applied and if the same actions remained effective in overcoming the extreme distress.[603] After 2012, it will be interesting to see which automotive suppliers achieve sustained recovery from this crisis and which restructuring actions were effective in achieving their recoveries.

The second limitation relates to the model. As with any empirical study, the selection and operationalization of variables is a trade-off between representativeness and detail. Given the holistic approach of this research model, one of the results suggests that detailed examination might yield further insights. Managerial restructuring is found to be applied frequently among distressed automotive companies, but it is not identified as a key contributor to turnarounds. Research on non-distressed companies shows that replacing the CEO is important for firm

---

599 Compare AUTOMOTIVE NEWS (2011).

600 ACHARYA ET AL. (2007) is the only study to include private firms.

601 Compare CHAUDHURY (2011, p. 2).

602 Compare HAUGH ET AL. (2010) and WAD (2009).

603 At the same time it is worth noting that crises like the industry crisis in 2009 present problems in empirical research related to non-stationarity and data instability, yielding temporarily distorted data and inconsistent coefficient estimates; compare BALCAEN/OOGHE (2006).

performance, but so the CEO's fit with the corporate strategy.[604] Including the CEO's "hard skills" such as education or industry experience and "soft skills" such as intellectual, motivational, or interpersonal capabilities should extend insights into the effectiveness of replacing top executives on corporate turnaround. Although examining these contingencies exceeds the scope of this dissertation, future turnaround research on managerial restructuring should address these critical issues.

The third potential for future research is related to the explorative research setting of the third question. Most prior research on corporate turnaround is limited to comparing turnaround or non-turnaround companies. Successful companies have been only partially considered. This study is the first to compare single restructuring actions among turnaround, non-turnaround, and non-distressed companies. Its results show that distinct turnaround measures exist, but that not all "turnaround actions" are limited to application within turnaround situations. Hopefully, future researchers will include non-distressed firms in their samples to allow further testing and refinement of the explorative results in this research.

---

604 Compare for example BHAGAT ET AL. (2010) and KAPLAN ET AL. (2011).

APPENDIX

Appendix 1: Matched sample – Details per company.

Company Name	Status	DY Y_0	Region	ICB	Net revenue Y_{-1} (m USD)	Total assets Y_{-1} (m USD)
Aeolus Tyre Company	NT	2003	AP	3357	121.9	164.5
Ahresty Corp.	TA	2002	AP	3355	384.2	509.3
Aisin Seiki Company Ltd.	TA	2001	AP	3355	8,750.4	9,716.2
Akebono Brake Industry Company Ltd.	TA	2002	AP	3355	1,003.4	1,001.5
Alpine Electronics Inc.	ND	2000	AP	3355	979.3	1,466.9
American Axle & Manufacturing Holdings	NT	2005	AM	3355	2,532.0	3,599.6
Anhui Jianghuai Automobile	NT	2004	AP	3355	302.6	658.4
APM Automotive Holdings Berhad	ND	2002	AP	3355	120.5	173.6
Apollo Tyres Ltd.	TA	2004	AP	3357	223.9	338.3
Armour Group PLC	ND	2005	EA	3355	52.3	56.1
Asahi TEC Corp.	TA	2004	AP	3355	428.0	432.6
Ashimori Industry Company Ltd.	TA	2001	AP	3355	287.4	277.8
Aska Corp.	NT	2005	AP	3355	138.7	171.7
Astra International Terbuka	TA	2000	AP	3355	2,934.6	2,147.5
Autoliv Inc.	ND	2001	AM	3355	4,067.8	4,116.1
Balkrishna Industries Ltd.	NT	2004	AP	3357	56.8	62.4
Bandag Inc.	ND	2002	AM	3357	718.6	964.9
Brembo	ND	2001	EA	3355	421.6	432.0
Bridgestone Corp.	TA	2001	AP	3357	17,070.4	17,560.4
Car Mate Manufacturing Company Ltd.	TA	2003	AP	3355	91.2	97.7
Carraro	TA	2001	EA	3355	370.8	357.0
Cheng Shin Rubber Industries Company Ltd.	NT	2003	AP	3357	851.7	611.4
China Strategic Holdings Ltd.	NT	2000	AP	3357	892.7	482.4
Chongqing Zongshen Power Machinery	ND	2004	AP	3355	63.0	120.0
CIE Automotive SA	TA	2001	EA	3355	213.0	169.0
Clarion Company Ltd.	TA	2000	AP	3355	1,451.7	1,660.5
Collins Industries Inc.	TA	2000	AM	3355	66.4	196.4
Continental AG	TA	2001	EA	3357	7,031.5	9,533.5
Cooper Tire & Rubber Company	TA	2004	AM	3357	2,868.9	3,514.4
Daewon Kangup Company Ltd.	TA	2005	AP	3355	339.4	554.5
Daibea Company Ltd.	TA	2001	AP	3355	137.6	160.0
Dana Holding Corp.	NT	2004	AM	3355	9,288.0	7,964.0
Delphi Corp.	NT	2001	AM	3355	16,478.0	29,139.0
Denso Corp.	ND	2003	AP	3355	17,420.4	18,080.3
Depo Auto Parts Industry Company Ltd.	ND	2005	AP	3355	228.2	202.6
Diamond Electric Manufacturing Company Ltd.	TA	2005	AP	3355	204.8	236.5
Dongah Tire & Rubber Company Ltd.	ND	2003	AP	3357	212.4	150.3
Dongfeng Electronic Technology Company Ltd.	NT	2005	AP	3355	136.4	98.5
Dongwon Metal Company Ltd.	NT	2001	AP	3355	105.3	116.7
Double Coin Holdings Ltd.	NT	2003	AP	3357	651.5	400.1
Dura Automotive Systems Inc.	ND	2000	AM	3355	2,444.9	2,200.4
Edelbrock Corp.	ND	2000	AM	3355	94.3	108.9
Eidai Kako Company Ltd.	TA	2005	AP	3355	95.0	80.8
Exedy Corp.	ND	2001	AP	3355	966.7	1,015.8
F-Tech Inc.	TA	2002	AP	3355	402.4	633.8
Fangda Special Steel Technology Company	ND	2005	AP	3355	161.8	147.7
FCC Company Ltd.	ND	2002	AP	3355	414.0	500.2
Federal Corp.	TA	2004	AP	3357	238.9	143.4
Federal Mogul Corp.	NT	2000	AM	3355	9,796.4	6,487.5

Abbr.: TA Turnaround, NT Non-turnaround, ND Non-distressed

Appendix 1 (cont.): Matched sample – Details per company.

Company Name	Status	DY Y_0	Region	ICB	Net revenue Y_{-1} (m USD)	Total assets Y_{-1} (m USD)
Federal-Mogul Goetze India Ltd.	NT	2005	AP	3355	124.0	89.6
Fengfan Stock Company Ltd.	NT	2005	AP	3355	157.8	120.7
Finishmaster Inc.	ND	2001	AM	3355	216.4	337.2
Fuel Systems Solutions Inc.	NT	2001	AM	3355	95.0	112.8
Fuji Kiko Company Ltd.	NT	2002	AP	3355	276.5	459.4
Futaba Industrial Company Ltd.	NT	2005	AP	3355	2,158.0	2,102.7
Fuyao Glass Industry Group Company Ltd.	NT	2003	AP	3355	251.5	135.8
G-7 Holdings Inc.	TA	2003	AP	3355	121.0	180.5
Gentex Corp.	ND	2001	AM	3355	428.1	297.4
Genuine Parts Company	ND	2002	AM	3355	4,206.6	8,220.7
Gevelot	NT	2005	EA	3355	219.3	256.1
Giti Tire Corp.	ND	2005	AP	3357	413.0	204.2
Global & Yuasa Battery Company Ltd.	TA	2003	AP	3355	201.5	191.0
Grammer AG	ND	2005	EA	3355	505.3	1,118.9
GUI Zhou Tyre Company Ltd.	TA	2003	AP	3357	289.4	186.8
Guizhou Guihang Automotive	TA	2005	AP	3355	127.0	61.0
H-One Company Ltd.	NT	2004	AP	3355	296.2	315.8
Halla Climate Control Corp.	ND	2001	AP	3355	495.4	673.3
Hanil E-Hwa Company Ltd.	NT	2003	AP	3355	186.2	305.8
Hankook Tire Company Ltd.	TA	2000	AP	3357	2,123.1	1,307.3
Hayes Lemmerz International Inc.	NT	2000	AM	3355	2,648.1	2,296.4
HKS Company Ltd.	TA	2004	AP	3355	99.4	70.5
Hwa Fong Rubber Industry Company Ltd.	NT	2003	AP	3357	179.4	141.5
Hwaseung R & A Company Ltd.	NT	2005	AP	3355	772.4	889.9
Hwashin Company Ltd.	TA	2003	AP	3355	110.8	185.2
Ichikoh Industries Ltd.	NT	2004	AP	3355	738.7	991.7
Imasen Electric Industrial Company Ltd.	ND	2004	AP	3355	351.7	422.3
Industrias Arteb S/A	NT	2004	AM	3355	113.7	70.1
Inter Cars SA	NT	2005	EA	3355	107.5	203.7
Inter Groclin Auto SA	NT	2003	EA	3355	77.1	112.0
Iochpe-Maxion SA	TA	2002	AM	3355	190.6	161.7
Johnson Controls Inc.	ND	2003	AM	3355	10,923.9	20,103.4
Jtekt Corp.	TA	2001	AP	3355	3,841.4	3,505.9
Jui Li Enterprise Company Ltd.	NT	2005	AP	3355	136.7	134.4
Kasai Kogyo Company Ltd.	TA	2002	AP	3355	458.6	624.5
Kayaba Industry Company Ltd.	TA	2002	AP	3355	1,373.3	1,521.1
Keihin Corp.	TA	2001	AP	3355	1,045.6	1,734.0
Kinugawa Rubber Industrial Company Ltd.	TA	2002	AP	3357	334.4	459.2
Koito Manufacturing Company Ltd.	ND	2004	AP	3355	2,413.5	2,632.2
Kumho Tires Company Inc.	NT	2005	AP	3357	2,055.8	1,746.8
LE Belier	NT	2002	EA	3355	90.9	132.9
Lear Corp.	NT	2005	AM	3355	9,944.4	16,960.0
Lexington Precision Corp.	NT	2003	AM	3355	92.1	124.9
LG Balakrisnan & Brothers	NT	2005	AP	3355	53.5	72.3
Linamar Corp.	TA	2004	AM	3355	1,000.6	1,180.7
Magna International Inc.	ND	2001	AM	3355	7,312.0	10,412.0
Marujun Company Ltd.	NT	2003	AP	3355	138.5	139.5
Mekonomen AB	ND	2003	EA	3355	146.0	166.2
Metalart Corp.	TA	2001	AP	3355	147.3	118.4

Abbr.: TA Turnaround, NT Non-turnaround, ND Non-distressed

Appendix 1 (cont.): Matched sample – Details per company.

Company Name	Status	DY Y_0	Region	ICB	Net revenue Y_{-1} (m USD)	Total assets Y_{-1} (m USD)
Miba AG	ND	2002	EA	3355	231.6	262.7
Michelin	ND	2001	EA	3357	16,016.9	14,510.5
Mitsuba Corp.	TA	2001	AP	3355	1,024.3	1,105.7
Mitsuboshi Belting Ltd.	ND	2000	AP	3357	538.4	568.1
Motonic Corp.	ND	2005	AP	3355	183.1	215.8
MRF Ltd.	TA	2004	AP	3357	328.8	464.8
Murakami Corp.	TA	2002	AP	3355	257.8	323.8
Muraki Corp.	NT	2001	AP	3355	124.1	193.9
Musashi Company Ltd.	ND	2004	AP	3355	285.0	350.2
Musashi Seimitsu Industry Company Ltd.	TA	2002	AP	3355	366.2	511.1
Nankang Rubber Tire Corp. Ltd.	TA	2003	AP	3357	274.3	126.9
Nexen Corp.	NT	2004	AP	3357	433.0	373.8
Nexen Tire Corp.	NT	2004	AP	3357	277.1	241.3
NGK Spark Plug Company Ltd.	TA	2002	AP	3355	2,898.0	1,776.2
Nichirin Company Ltd.	TA	2001	AP	3355	209.9	510.5
Nidec Tosok Corp.	TA	2005	AP	3355	246.2	257.3
Nifco Inc.	ND	2001	AP	3355	1,174.6	895.3
Nihon Plast Company Ltd.	NT	2001	AP	3355	363.0	673.0
Nippon Piston Ring Company Ltd.	TA	2001	AP	3355	714.8	381.7
Nippon Seiki Company Ltd.	ND	2000	AP	3355	690.0	891.0
Nishikawa Rubber Company Ltd.	ND	2004	AP	3355	406.6	351.7
Nissin Kogyo Company Ltd.	ND	2001	AP	3355	495.2	765.0
Nittan Valve Company Ltd.	TA	2000	AP	3355	208.3	179.0
NOK Corp.	TA	2000	AP	3355	1,791.1	1,992.5
Nokian Renkaat OYJ	ND	2001	EA	3357	437.3	375.6
Ogura Clutch Company Ltd.	TA	2002	AP	3355	322.1	344.7
Ohashi Technica Inc.	ND	2003	AP	3355	118.1	174.6
Owari Precious Products Company Ltd.	TA	2002	AP	3355	77.7	87.5
Pacific Industrial Company Ltd.	TA	2001	AP	3355	450.6	382.6
Pacifica Group Ltd.	TA	2000	AP	3355	636.4	583.3
Phoenix AG	TA	2000	EA	3355	507.4	865.8
Pirelli & Co.	TA	2002	EA	3357	11,272.2	6,918.0
Plastic Omnium	TA	2001	EA	3355	1,095.6	1,098.5
Pyeong Hwa Automotive Company Ltd.	TA	2004	AP	3355	91.7	116.0
Renk AG	ND	2000	EA	3355	207.6	233.7
Riken Corp.	TA	2001	AP	3355	805.3	675.4
Sakurai Ltd.	ND	2005	AP	3355	61.7	65.7
Sanden Corp.	NT	2000	AP	3355	1,517.8	1,926.7
Sangsin Brake Industry Company Ltd.	TA	2005	AP	3355	68.0	97.5
Sanluis Corporacion SA De CV	TA	2001	AM	3355	869.7	532.3
Schaffer Corp. Ltd.	ND	2003	AP	3355	89.8	116.1
Schulz SA	TA	2004	AM	3355	57.0	64.2
Shanghai Jiao YUN Company Ltd.	NT	2005	AP	3355	189.2	107.4
Shiroki Corp.	TA	2001	AP	3355	758.3	1,030.3
Showa Corp.	ND	2002	AP	3355	768.6	1,225.4
SL Corp.	ND	2002	AP	3355	221.6	259.6
SNT Corp.	TA	2005	AP	3355	247.7	131.4
Sogefi	ND	2005	EA	3355	1,088.1	1,310.9
Spectra Premium Industries	TA	2003	AM	3355	203.1	147.4

Abbr.: TA Turnaround, NT Non-turnaround, ND Non-distressed

Appendix 1 (cont.): Matched sample – Details per company.

Company Name	Status	DY Y_0	Region	ICB	Net revenue Y_{-1} (m USD)	Total assets Y_{-1} (m USD)
SPK Corp.	ND	2001	AP	3355	97.3	275.0
Standard Motor Products Inc.	TA	2004	AM	3355	675.1	678.8
Stanley Electric Company Ltd.	ND	2002	AP	3355	1,719.8	1,723.7
Stoneridge Inc.	TA	2004	AM	3355	579.7	606.7
Strattec Security Corp.	ND	2002	AM	3355	101.5	203.0
Sumitomo Wiring Systems Ltd.	ND	2000	AP	3355	1,155.7	1,746.4
Suncall Corp.	ND	2001	AP	3355	275.2	276.0
Superior Industries International Inc.	TA	2005	AM	3355	744.5	901.8
Ta YIH Industrial Company Ltd.	ND	2003	AP	3355	72.1	76.8
Tachi-S Company Ltd.	TA	2003	AP	3355	596.3	969.7
Taiho Kogyo Company Ltd.	TA	2004	AP	3355	455.0	533.1
Taiwan Kai YIH Industrial Company Ltd.	NT	2005	AP	3355	157.9	152.0
TBC Corp.	ND	2000	AM	3357	348.4	743.1
Technomag AG	ND	2005	EA	3355	249.1	296.9
Teikoku Piston Ring Company	ND	2001	AP	3355	362.7	304.1
Tenneco Inc.	TA	2000	AM	3355	2,930.0	3,279.0
Thai Stanley Electric Public Company Ltd.	ND	2001	AP	3355	63.6	66.1
The Lead Company Inc.	TA	2001	AP	3355	107.7	141.8
Tiger Wheels Ltd.	TA	2003	EA	3355	181.9	245.9
Titan International Inc.	TA	2001	AM	3357	591.6	543.1
Tokai Rika Company Ltd.	ND	2001	AP	3355	1,462.6	1,898.4
Tokai Rubber Industries Ltd.	ND	2000	AP	3357	1,182.2	1,239.7
Tong Yang Industry Company Ltd.	TA	2005	AP	3355	427.6	288.5
Topre Corp.	ND	2000	AP	3355	448.9	393.9
Tower Automotive Inc.	NT	2000	AM	3355	2,552.6	2,170.0
Toyo Tire & Rubber Company Ltd.	TA	2004	AP	3357	2,180.4	2,158.6
Toyoda Gosei Company Ltd.	TA	2002	AP	3355	1,815.6	2,319.6
TYC Brother Industrial Company Ltd.	TA	2003	AP	3355	240.3	169.8
TYE Soon Ltd.	TA	2003	AP	3355	55.0	67.5
U-Shin Ltd.	NT	2001	AP	3355	472.6	351.3
Unipres Corp.	TA	2001	AP	3355	1,071.1	1,281.2
United Capital Corp.	ND	2000	AM	3355	133.7	59.7
Valeo	TA	2001	EA	3355	7,518.4	8,595.7
VBG Group AB	ND	2004	EA	3355	57.4	73.7
Visteon Corp.	NT	2001	AM	3355	11,225.0	19,467.0
Wanxiang Qiangchao Company Ltd.	NT	2001	AP	3355	192.4	148.6
Weds Company Ltd.	TA	2005	AP	3355	118.8	208.3
Weifu High Technology Group Company Ltd.	NT	2001	AP	3355	240.8	102.8
Wescast Industries Inc.	NT	2005	AM	3355	421.7	340.8
Xinyi Glass Holdings Ltd.	NT	2004	AP	3355	132.2	103.1
YHI International Ltd.	ND	2005	AP	3355	114.4	178.5
Yokohama Rubber Company Ltd.	TA	2000	AP	3357	3,537.3	3,337.8
Yokowo Company Ltd.	ND	2002	AP	3355	209.8	216.6
Yoo Sung Enterprise Company Ltd.	TA	2000	AP	3355	118.9	74.8
Yorozu Corp.	TA	2002	AP	3355	468.0	537.0
Yuan Feng Industrial Company Ltd.	NT	2003	AP	3355	91.2	106.5
Zypro Inc.	NT	2002	AP	3355	135.7	174.9

Abbr.: TA Turnaround, NT Non-turnaround, ND Non-distressed

Appendix 2: Matched sample – Profitability development.

		TA			NT			ND			Total		
In %		Mean[a]	Median	S.D.	Median	S.D.	S.D.	Mean[a]	Median	S.D.	Mean[a]	Median	S.D.
ROA	Y_{-1}	3.94	2.52	3.41	6.24	5.84	3.62	6.26	6.11	3.48	5.27	4.52	3.66
	Y_0	1.12	1.04	4.65	3.08	3.26	5.40	6.35	6.24	3.84	3.26	3.00	5.12
	Y_{+1}	2.44	2.20	3.19	3.07	2.83	4.99	6.60	6.15	3.66	3.90	3.22	4.28
	Y_{+2}	3.66	3.39	3.39	2.94	2.89	4.45	6.50	6.17	3.87	4.35	3.96	4.10
	Y_{+3}	4.14	3.68	3.10	1.99	1.52	4.95	6.44	6.11	3.42	4.27	4.01	4.12
ROI	Y_{-1}	5.60	3.51	4.88	9.13	7.87	5.34	9.24	8.47	5.18	7.66	6.75	5.37
	Y_0	1.66	1.42	6.41	4.35	4.71	7.49	9.24	8.92	5.48	4.73	4.46	7.18
	Y_{+1}	3.48	3.20	4.50	4.11	3.88	6.87	9.46	8.63	5.04	5.50	4.80	5.99
	Y_{+2}	5.30	5.25	4.55	4.19	4.48	5.41	9.32	9.42	5.18	6.28	5.85	5.39
	Y_{+3}	6.00	5.46	4.19	2.38	2.21	6.04	9.14	8.66	4.29	6.04	6.05	5.39
ROE	Y_{-1}	7.80	5.29	7.80	13.53	10.98	8.94	12.75	11.68	7.92	10.83	9.10	8.52
	Y_0	-1.42	0.88	11.81	3.81	5.81	13.48	12.05	10.73	7.18	4.15	5.61	12.44
	Y_{+1}	2.52	3.64	10.22	2.90	4.86	15.16	12.35	11.51	7.06	5.70	6.16	11.77
	Y_{+2}	7.36	6.71	7.92	5.18	5.57	10.68	12.13	12.06	7.41	8.33	8.00	8.93
	Y_{+3}	8.72	7.59	6.74	-0.07	3.44	12.78	11.48	11.31	5.87	7.44	8.25	9.48

a. All observations that lie ± 3 standard deviations from the mean are winsorized.
Abbr.: TA Turnaround, NT Non-turnaround, ND Non-distressed.

Appendix 3: Matched sample – Restructuring actions Y_{-1}-Y_{+3}.

		TA				N=82	NT				N=52	ND				N=60	Matched Sample				N=194
		Y_{-1}	Y_0	Y_{+1}	Y_{+2}	Y_{+3}	Y_{-1}	Y_0	Y_{+1}	Y_{+2}	Y_{+3}	Y_{-1}	Y_0	Y_{+1}	Y_{+2}	Y_{+3}	Y_{-1}	Y_0	Y_{+1}	Y_{+2}	Y_{+3}
Managerial restructuring																					
Top executive change – All	Frequency	-	0.159	0.085	0.085	0.024		0.077	0.077	0.038	0.135		0.033	0.050	0.050	0.050		0.098	0.072	0.062	0.062
Top executive change – Non-routine	Frequency	-	0.085	0.024	0.049	0.024		0.058	0.058	0.019	0.096		0.017	0.033	0.050	0.033		0.057	0.036	0.041	0.046
Operational restructuring																					
Revenue growth	Delta	-	-0.046	0.036	0.078	0.075		-0.144	-0.033	-0.018	-0.018		0.020	0.004	0.077	0.038		-0.052	0.008	0.052	0.039
Cost cutting	Ratio	0.951	0.962	0.961	0.955	0.952	0.935	0.954	0.962	0.964	0.964	0.926	0.925	0.928	0.925	0.931	0.939	0.949	0.951	0.948	0.949
Financial restructuring																					
Equity issue	Frequency	0.220	0.256	0.268	0.207	0.280	0.135	0.192	0.192	0.212	0.231	0.217	0.183	0.233	0.200	0.283	0.196	0.216	0.237	0.206	0.268
Dividend policy	Index	1	1.113	1.117	1.092	1.266	1	1.418	1.461	1.333	1.224	1	1.242	1.495	1.554	1.455	1	1.235	1.326	1.300	1.313
Debt restructuring	Ratio	0.275	0.294	0.286	0.279	0.253	0.293	0.328	0.337	0.331	0.362	0.200	0.181	0.170	0.158	0.160	0.257	0.268	0.264	0.256	0.253
Asset restructuring																					
Change in assets	Index	1	1.072	1.112	1.180	1.273	1	1.127	1.221	1.430	1.566	1	1.067	1.164	1.249	1.363	1	1.085	1.157	1.268	1.380
Capital expenditures	Ratio	0.168	0.223	0.173	0.171	0.169	0.175	0.250	0.207	0.213	0.196	0.203	0.206	0.195	0.202	0.215	0.181	0.225	0.189	0.192	0.191

Abbr.: TA Turnaround, NT Non-turnaround, ND Non-distressed

Appendix 4: Univariate logistic regression.

Variable		Coefficient β	s.e.	$R^{2\,a}$	LRT χ^2	sig.	Hypothesis
Managerial restructuring							
Top executive change –	MRA-ER	0.573	0.462	0.016	1.611	0.204⁺	✓
All	MRA-LR	-0.529	0.509	0.011	1.074	0.300	✓
Top executive change –	MRN-ER	-0.056	0.560	0.001	0.010	0.920	×
Non-routine	MRN-LR	-0.502	0.607	0.007	0.680	0.410	✓
Operational restructuring							
Revenue development	REV-ER	2.165	0.681	0.109	11.210	0.001***	×
	REV-LR	2.165	0.661	0.120	12.436	0.001***	✓
Operating expense ratio	EXP-ER	-17.711	5.649	0.104	10.668	0.001***	✓
	EXP-LR	-16.046	6.729	0.059	5.996	0.014**	×
Financial restructuring							
Equity issue	EQU-ER	0.353	0.382	0.009	0.863	0.353	×
	EQU-LR	-0.013	0.384	0.001	0.001	0.973	×
Dividend policy	DIV-ER	-0.328	0.178	0.036	3.559	0.059*	✓
	DIV-LR	0.073	0.235	0.001	0.096	0.756	×
Debt restructuring	DBT-ER	-0.654	0.478	0.019	1.895	0.169⁺	✓
	DBT-LR	-1.925	0.598	0.115	11.850	0.001***	×
Asset restructuring							
Total assets change	TAS-ER	-1.569	0.689	0.053	5.367	0.021**	✓
	TAS-LR	-1.514	0.531	0.086	8.730	0.003***	×
Capital expenditure intensity	CAP-ER	-0.680	0.362	0.036	3.632	0.057*	✓
	CAP-LR	0.297	0.378	0.006	0.622	0.430	×
Context							
Firm size	TA-CTX	0.123	0.131	0.009	0.897	0.344	×
Prior performance	PP-CTX	-0.096	0.041	0.056	5.682	0.017**	×
Distress severity	DS-CTX	0.006	0.042	0.001	0.020	0.889	×
Financial capacity	FC-CTX	0.032	0.224	0.001	0.020	0.887	×
Financial slack	FS-CTX	2.071	1.247	0.028	2.844	0.092*	✓
Distress year: 2000[b]	DY1-CTX	-	-	0.117	10.878	0.054*	×
2001	DY2-CTX	0.105	0.669	-	0.025	0.875	✓
2002	DY3CTX	0.821	0.831	-	0.976	0.323	✓
2003	DY4-CTX	-0.693	0.694	-	0.997	0.318	✓
2004	DY5-CTX	-0.421	0.692	-	0.370	0.543	✓
2005	DY6-CTX	-1.258	0.673	-	3.493	0.062*	×
Region Asia-Pacific	RG-CTX	0.320	0.395	0.007	0.653	0.419	✓
Industry subsector Tires	IN-CTX	-0.160	0.470	0.001	0.001	0.972	✓

a. Nagelkerke R^2
b. Wald statistic provided for categorical variable.
✓ as expected, × not as expected
Abbr.: s.e. standard error, LRT Likelihood-Ratio-Test, sig. significance level
⁺, *, **, *** indicate significance at the 25%, 10%, 5%, and 1% levels respectively

Appendix 5: Model 2 – Box-Tidwell transformation test.

Variable	Coef		Wald statistic			LRT		
	β	s.e.	Wald	df	sig.	χ^2	df	sig.
Constant	0.54	3.69	0.02	1	0.884	0.02	1	0.884
REV-ER	-2.62	1.00	6.96	1	0.008	7.88	1	0.005
REV-LR	-2.64	1.12	5.56	1	0.018	6.19	1	0.013
EXP-ER	27.04	37.43	0.52	1	0.470	0.52	1	0.471
EXP-LR	35.72	47.67	0.56	1	0.454	0.56	1	0.453
DBT-LR	1.60	1.27	1.61	1	0.205	1.77	1	0.183
CAP-ER	0.79	0.97	0.66	1	0.417	0.68	1	0.409
CAP-LR	1.79	1.25	2.03	1	0.154	2.17	1	0.141
FS-CTX	-7.34	5.23	1.97	1	0.160	2.02	1	0.156
REV-ER * LN(REV-ER)	2.04	1.93	1.12	1	0.290	1.14	1	0.285
REV-LR * LN(REV-LR)	-0.04	0.28	0.02	1	0.879	0.02	1	0.879
EXP-ER * LN(EXP-ER)	-2.04	20.11	0.01	1	0.919	0.01	1	0.919
EXP-LR * LN(EXP-LR)	10.07	22.03	0.21	1	0.648	0.21	1	0.649
DBT_LR * LN(DBT-LR)	-0.29	1.75	0.03	1	0.866	0.03	1	0.866
CAP-ER * LN(CAP-ER)	0.67	1.15	0.33	1	0.563	0.33	1	0.565
CAP-LR * LN(CAP-LR)	-0.87	1.35	0.41	1	0.521	0.42	1	0.517
FS-CTX * LN(FS-CTX)	9.56	10.96	0.76	1	0.383	0.76	1	0.384

Note: Adjustment for negative values
Abr.: s.e. standard error, df degrees of freedom, sig. significance level

Appendix 6: Model 2 – Multicollinearity analysis and diagnostics.

		Descriptives		**Collinearity statistics**		**Correlations (significance level in italics)**							
Variable		mean	s.d.	Tolerance	VIF	1	2	3	4	5	6	7	8
REV-ER	1	-0.075	0.285	0.86	1.17	1	0.16	-0.20	-0.14	-0.13	-0.01	0.18	-0.19
							0.06	*0.02*	*0.10*	*0.13*	*0.93*	*0.04*	*0.03*
REV-LR	2	0.080	0.311	0.84	1.19		1	0.10	-0.17	-0.32	0.03	0.06	0.07
								0.26	*0.05*	*0.00*	*0.75*	*0.51*	*0.45*
EXP-ER	3	0.018	0.034	0.88	1.14			1	-0.08	0.11	-0.06	-0.16	0.13
									0.38	*0.22*	*0.52*	*0.06*	*0.13*
EXP-LR	4	-0.004	0.028	0.88	1.14				1	0.18	0.11	-0.23	-0.12
										0.04	*0.21*	*0.01*	*0.18*
DBT-LR	5	0.000	0.334	0.84	1.19					1	0.10	-0.19	0.01
											0.26	*0.03*	*0.91*
CAP-ER	6	0.185	0.500	0.87	1.15						1	-0.33	-0.10
												0.00	*0.27*
CAP-LR	7	-0.017	0.476	0.79	1.27							1	0.09
													0.31
FS-CTX	8	0.084	0.148	0.92	1.09								1

Abbr.: VIF Variance Inflation Factor, s.d. standard deviation

Appendix 7: Model 2 – Durbin-Wu-Hausman test.

Omnibus Tests of Model		χ^2	df	sig.[a]
Step 1	Step	1.895	4	0.755
	Block	1.895	4	0.755
	Model	55.668	12	0.001***

a. Based on Likelihood-Ratio-Tests
Note: Reference category Non-turnaround
Abbr.: s.e. standard error, df degrees of freedom, sig. significance level
*, **, *** indicate significance at the 10%, 5%, and 1% levels respectively

Appendix 8: Model 2 – Outlier diagnostics.

A. Leverage (ht)

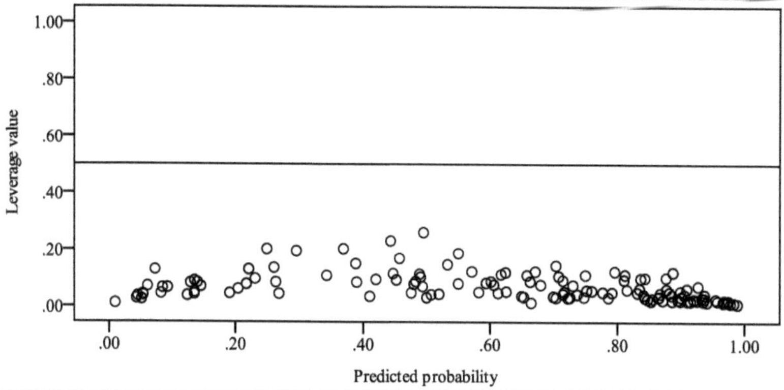

B. Cook's distance (CD)

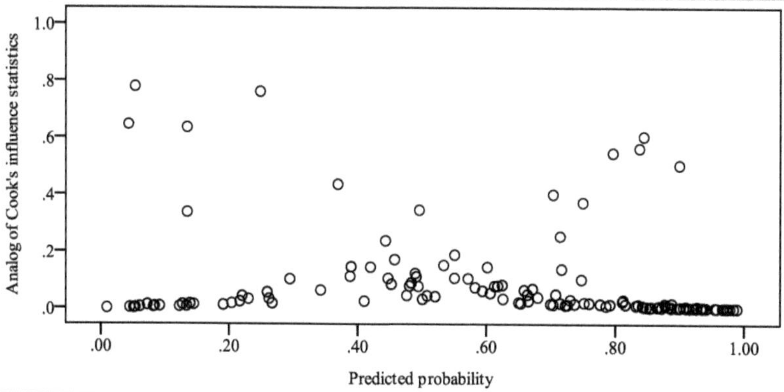

C. Standardized residual (e*)

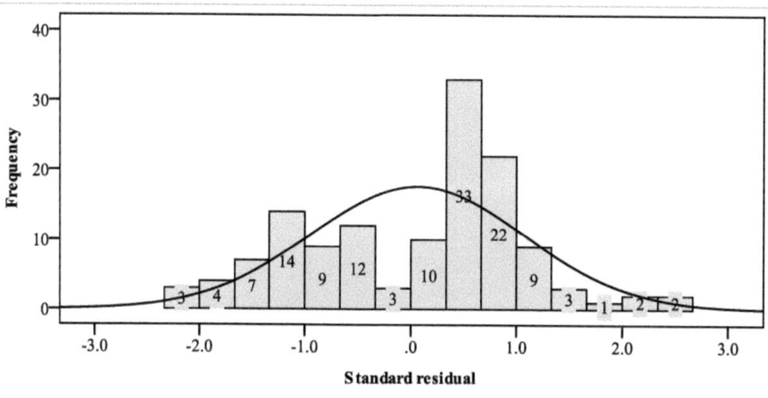

Appendix 9: Model 2 – Multivariate probit regression.

		Model 2 – Final (Probit)		
Variable		β	s.e.	sig.[a]
Constant		-0.559	0.170	0.001***
Revenue development	REV-ER	1.166	0.480	0.015**
	REV-LR	1.294	0.479	0.007***
Operating expense ratio	EXP-ER	-16.516	4.331	0.001***
	EXP-LR	-8.101	5.195	0.119
Debt restructuring	DBT-LR	-0.761	0.416	0.067*
Capital expenditure intensity	CAP-ER	-0.693	0.292	0.018**
	CAP-LR	-0.629	0.305	0.039**
Financial slack	FS-CTX	2.306	0.925	0.013**
Model evaluation		$\chi 2$	df	Sig.
Likelihood-Ratio-Test		53.361	8	0.001***
Nagelkerke R^2		0.446		
McFadden R^2		0.298		

a. Based on Wald test statistic
Note: Reference category Non-turnaround
Abbr.: s.e. standard error, df degrees of freedom, sig. significance level
*, **, *** indicate significance at the 10%, 5%, and 1% levels respectively

Appendix 10: Cluster analysis – Multicollinearity analysis.

Variable		Descriptives mean	s.d.	Pearson Correlation (significance level in italics) 2	3	4	5	6	7	8	9	10	11	12	13	14	15	16
MRA-ER	1	0.24	0.43	0.16	0.14	-0.08	0.11	-0.06	-0.02	0.18	0.10	0.03	0.04	0.10	0.09	-0.14	0.10	0.01
				0.14	*0.20*	*0.48*	*0.31*	*0.62*	*0.87*	*0.11*	*0.36*	*0.81*	*0.71*	*0.36*	*0.45*	*0.22*	*0.38*	*0.90*
MRA-LR	2	0.11	0.32	1	0.10	0.07	-0.05	0.18	-0.02	0.02	0.15	-0.02	0.07	0.05	0.34	-0.21	-0.09	-0.03
					0.37	*0.51*	*0.66*	*0.11*	*0.83*	*0.85*	*0.17*	*0.85*	*0.56*	*0.69*	*0.00*	*0.06*	*0.41*	*0.79*
REV-ER[a]	3	0.52	0.50		1	-0.04	0.13	0.01	0.01	0.10	0.24	0.03	0.20	0.06	0.25	-0.06	0.15	-0.15
						0.74	*0.23*	*0.93*	*0.90*	*0.37*	*0.03*	*0.81*	*0.07*	*0.61*	*0.02*	*0.61*	*0.18*	*0.19*
REV-LR[a]	4	0.80	0.40			1	-0.10	0.15	-0.20	-0.28	0.25	-0.02	-0.10	0.10	0.02	0.08	-0.22	0.05
							0.38	*0.18*	*0.07*	*0.01*	*0.03*	*0.83*	*0.38*	*0.35*	*0.88*	*0.49*	*0.05*	*0.66*
EXP-ER[a]	5	0.40	0.49				1	-0.02	-0.06	0.05	0.13	-0.08	0.29	0.24	0.06	-0.08	-0.02	-0.15
								0.88	*0.62*	*0.65*	*0.26*	*0.45*	*0.01*	*0.03*	*0.59*	*0.46*	*0.90*	*0.17*
EXP-LR[a]	6	0.65	0.48					1	0.03	-0.06	0.12	0.04	0.02	0.11	-0.02	0.08	-0.03	0.01
									0.77	*0.57*	*0.30*	*0.72*	*0.84*	*0.34*	*0.83*	*0.46*	*0.80*	*0.95*
EQU-ER	7	0.37	0.49						1	0.49	-0.04	-0.12	-0.10	-0.09	-0.16	0.08	0.06	0.17
										0.00	*0.71*	*0.30*	*0.39*	*0.43*	*0.16*	*0.50*	*0.62*	*0.13*
EQU-LR	8	0.30	0.46							1	0.05	-0.15	-0.08	0.00	-0.07	0.10	0.13	-0.01
											0.64	*0.17*	*0.45*	*1.00*	*0.54*	*0.39*	*0.25*	*0.93*
DIV-ER[a]	9	0.56	0.50								1	-0.04	-0.07	0.05	0.15	0.13	-0.02	0.13
												0.70	*0.56*	*0.66*	*0.18*	*0.26*	*0.89*	*0.26*
DIV-LR[a]	10	0.48	0.50									1	-0.40	-0.17	-0.10	0.00	-0.15	0.29
													0.00	*0.14*	*0.39*	*1.00*	*0.18*	*0.01*
DBT-ER[a]	11	0.46	0.50										1	0.09	0.08	-0.04	0.07	-0.22
														0.42	*0.49*	*0.72*	*0.54*	*0.05*
DBT-LR[a]	12	0.72	0.45											1	0.21	0.06	-0.02	-0.31
															0.06	*0.62*	*0.87*	*0.00*
TAS-ER[a]	13	0.33	0.47												1	-0.05	0.18	-0.22
																0.63	*0.10*	*0.05*
TAS-LR[a]	14	0.26	0.44													1	0.07	0.15
																	0.53	*0.17*
CAP-ER[a]	15	0.46	0.50														1	-0.32
																		0.00
CAP-LR[a]	16	0.49	0.50															1

a. Binned variables (cutpoint 0).

Appendix 11: Cluster analysis – Dendogram single linkage algorithm.

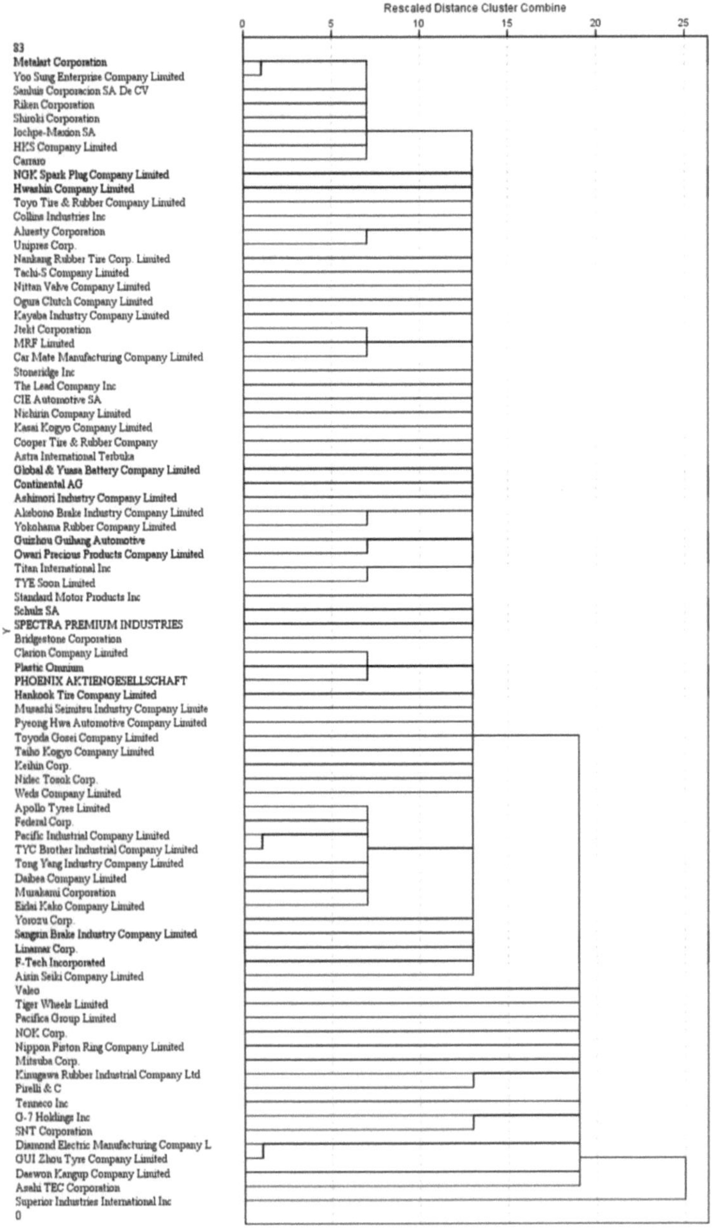

Appendix 12: Cluster analysis – Ward linkage algorithm.

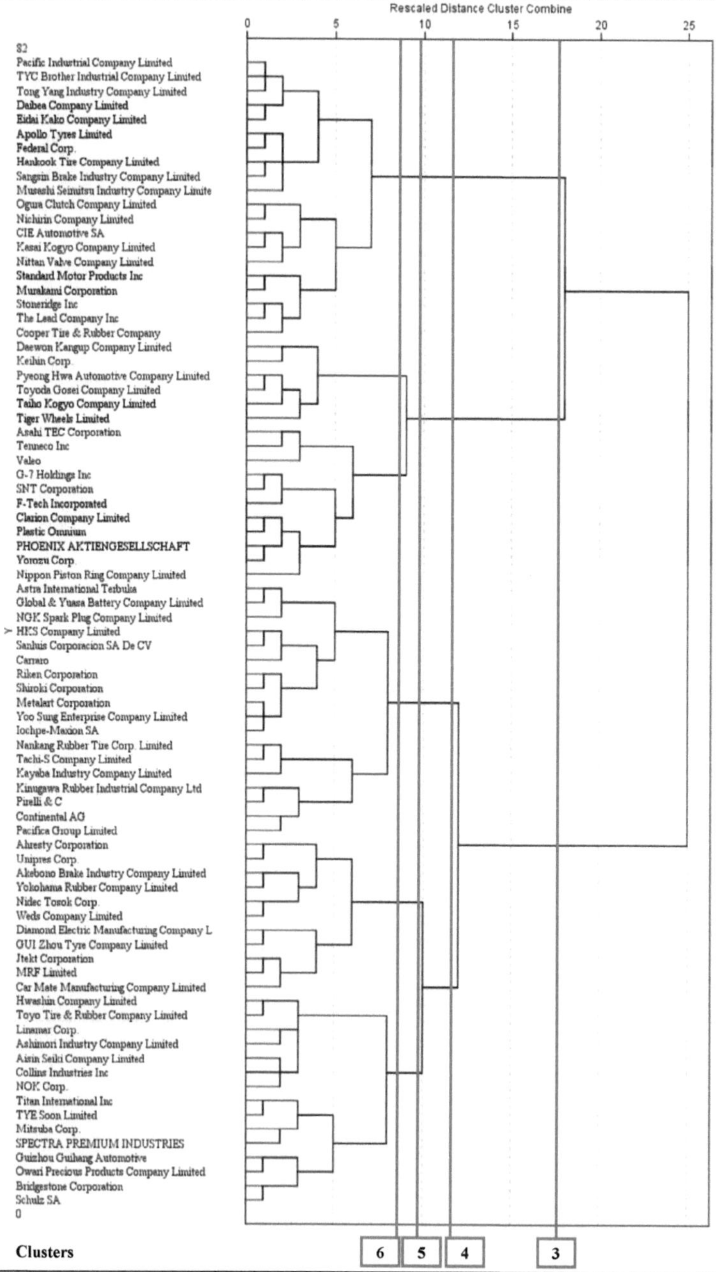

Appendix 13: Cluster analysis – F-statistics.

Cluster		Cluster 1	Cluster 2	Cluster 3	Cluster 4
		N=26	N=18	N=20	N=17
Managerial restructuring					
Top executive change –	MRA-ER	0.808	1.509	1.006	1.144
All[a]	MRA-LR	0.000	1.812	1.145	0.504
Top executive change –	MRN-ER	0.000	2.120	0.500	1.540
Non-routine[a]	MRN-LR	0.000	1.793	1.159	0.720
Operational restructuring					
Revenue development[a]	REV-ER	0.654	0.272	0.840	0.605
	REV-LR	0.740	0.604	0.177	1.500
Expense ratio[a]	EXP-ER	0.000	1.000	1.000	0.000
	EXP-LR	0.000	1.000	1.000	0.000
Financial restructuring					
Equity issue[a]	EQU-ER	0.471	1.044	0.876	0.262
	EQU-LR	0.346	1.178	0.234	0.514
Dividend policy[a]	DIV-ER	0.254	1.768	0.167	0.654
	DIV-LR	0.218	0.566	0.152	0.617
Debt restructuring[a]	DBT-ER	0.900	0.350	0.929	1.086
	DBT-LR	0.696	0.223	1.027	1.196
Asset restructuring					
Total assets change[a]	TAS-ER	0.486	0.243	1.314	0.714
	TAS-LR	0.659	0.203	0.488	1.106
Capital expenditures[a]	CAP-ER	1.020	1.248	0.732	0.324
	CAP-LR	0.646	0.743	0.836	0.832
Context					
Firm size	TA-CTX	1.317	0.977	0.444	0.670
Prior profitability	PP-CTX	1.000	1.000	1.500	1.000
Distress severity	DS-CTX	1.000	1.000	1.000	1.000
Financial capacity	FC-CTX	0.724	1.430	0.421	1.711
Financial slack	FS-CTX	1.136	0.909	0.818	0.864
Region Asia-Pacific	RG-CTX	0.818	1.071	0.848	1.116
Industry subsector Tires	IN-CTX	1.294	1.280	1.175	0.000
Average F-statistic	Cluster variables	0.494	0.860	0.745	0.691
Average F-statistic	All variables	0.607	1.014	0.791	0.787

a. Clustering variable

Appendix 14: ANCOVA – Levene's test of equality.

Dependent variable[a]	F	df1	df2	sig.
1 REV-ER	2.353	2	191	0.098*
2 REV-LR	1.896	2	191	0.153
3 EXP-ER	1.878	2	191	0.156
4 EXP-LR	2.230	2	191	0.110
5 DBT-LR	1.785	2	191	0.171
6 CAP-ER	1.485	2	191	0.229
7 CAP-LR	1.643	2	191	0.196

a. Design: Intercept + TA_CTX + PP_CTX + FS_CTX + STATUS

Appendix 15: ANCOVA – Normal Q-Q plots.

Early restructuring phase **Late restructuring phase**

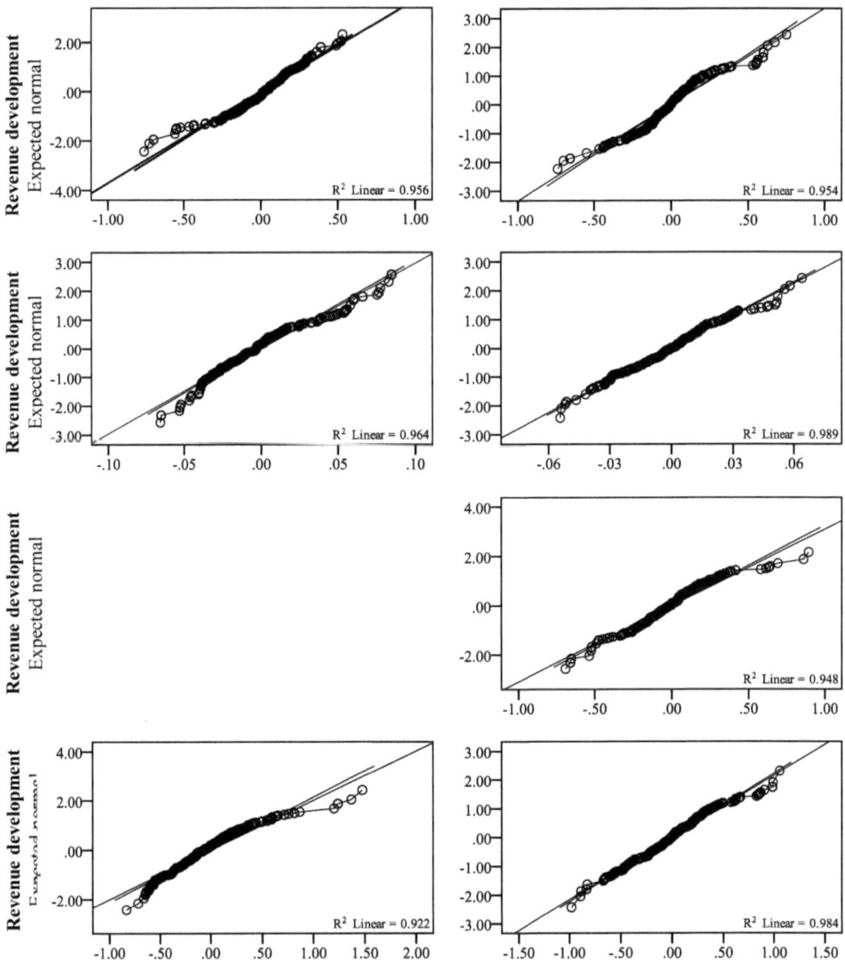

Appendix 16: ANCOVA – Scatterplots firm size.

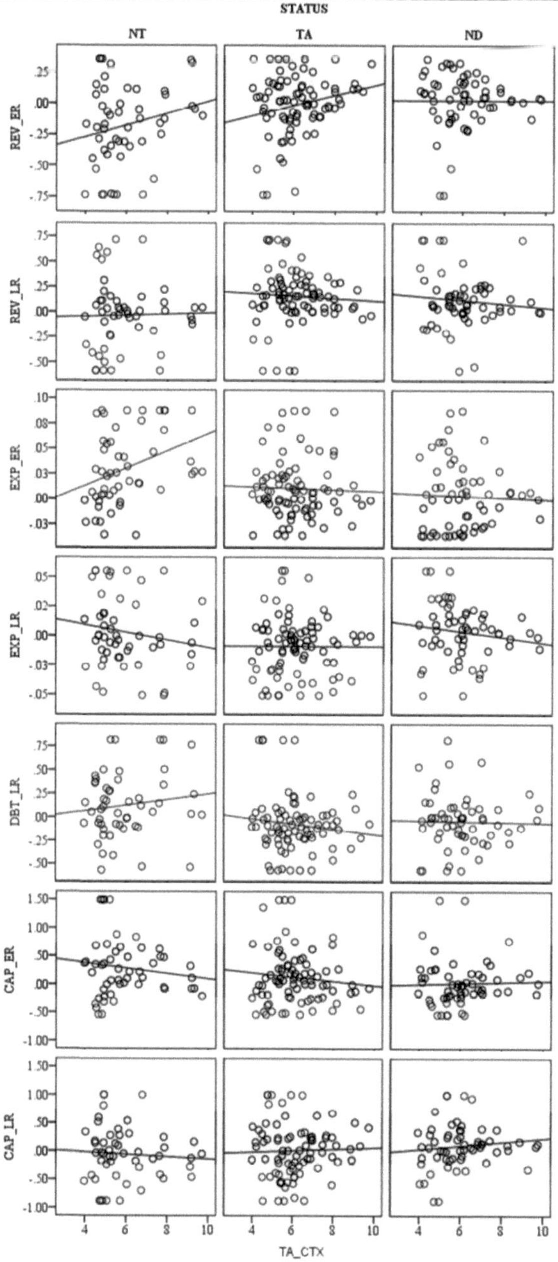

Appendix 17: ANCOVA – Scatterplots prior profitability.

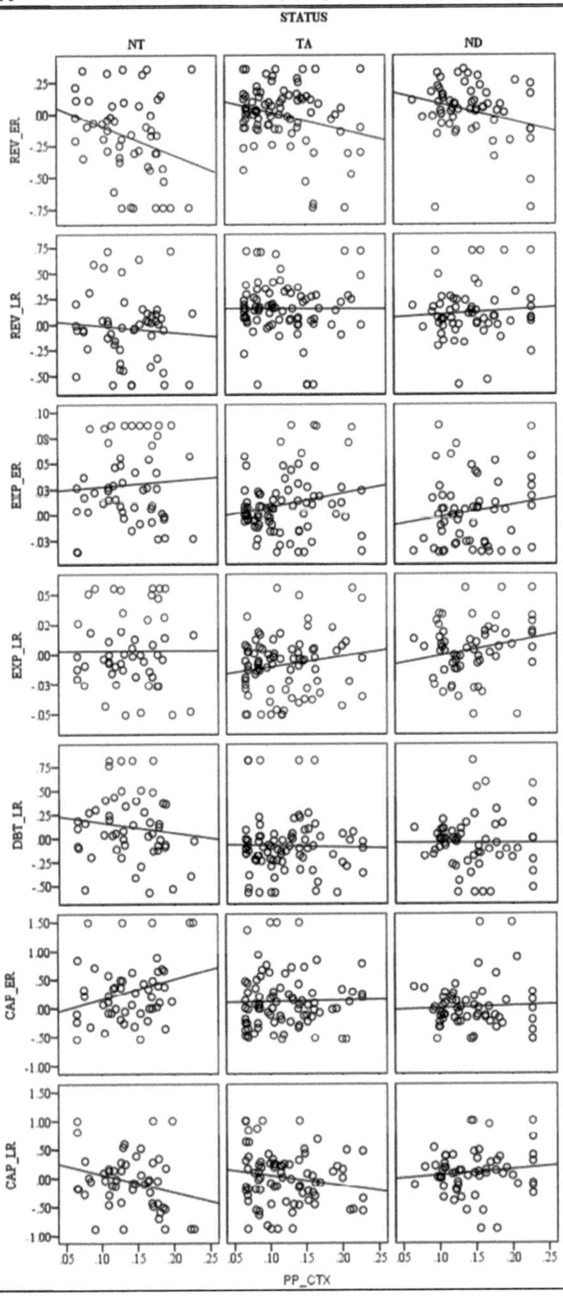

Appendix 18: ANCOVA – Scatterplots financial slack.

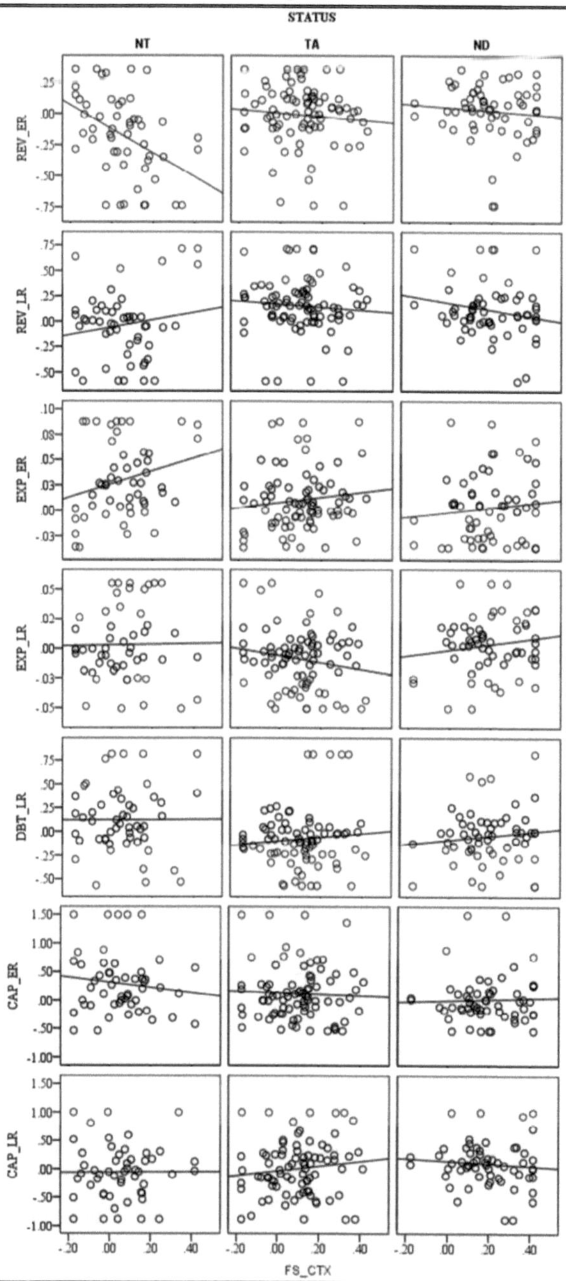

References

ABEBE, MICHAEL A. (2009): Leadership characteristics of declining firms attempting turnaround - An empirical examination. In: Journal of Strategy and Management, Vol. 2, No. 3, pp. 201-216.

ACHARYA, VIRAL V. / BHARATH, SREEDHAR T. / SRINIVASAN, ANAND (2007): Does industry-wide distress affect defaulted firm? Evidence from creditor recoveries. In: Journal of Financial Economics, Vol. 85, No. 3, pp. 787-821.

ACHLEITNER, ANN-KRISTIN / BASSEN, ALEXANDER / WAHL SIMON (2003): Corporate Restructuring: Instrumente und deren Anwendung in Deutschland. In: Finanz Betrieb, Vol. 5, No. 7-8, pp. 432-447.

AGARWAL, VINEET / TAFFLER, RICHARD J. (2007): Twenty-five years of the Taffler z-score model: Does it really have predictive ability. In: Accounting and Business Research, Vol. 37, No. 4, pp. 285-300.

AGUINIS, HERMAN / WERNER, STEVE / ABBOTT, JÉANNA L. / ANGERT, CORY / PARK, JOON H. / KOHLHAUSEN, DONNA (2010): Customer-centric science - Reporting significant research results with rigor, relevance and practical impact in mind. In: Organizational Research Methods, Vol. 13, No. 3, pp. 515-539.

ALBERS, SÖNKE / HILDEBRANDT, LUTZ (2006): Methodische Probleme bei der Erfolgsfaktorenforschung - Messfehler, formative versus reflektive Indikatoren und die Wahl des Strukturgleichungs-Modells. In: Zeitschrift für betriebswirtschaftliche Forschung, Vol. 58, No. 1, pp. 2-33.

ALTMAN, EDWARD I. (1968): Financial ratios, discriminant analysis and the prediction of corporate bankruptcy. In: Journal of Finance, Vol. 23, No. 4, pp. 589-609.

ALTMAN, EDWARD I. (2000): Predicting financial distress of companies: Revisiting the Z-Score and ZETA models. Working Paper. New York University 2000.

ALTMAN, EDWARD I. / HALDEMAN, ROBERT G. / NARAYANAN, P. (1977): ZETA analysis - A new model to identify bankruptcy risk of corporations. In: Journal of Banking and Finance, Vol. 1, No. 1, pp. 29-54.

ALTMAN, EDWARD I. / HOTCHKISS, EDITH S. (2006): Corporate financial distress and bankruptcy, 3rd edition. Hoboken.

ALVES, PAULO / BEEKES, WENDY / YOUNG, STEVEN (2007): A comparison of UK firms' financial statement data from six sources. Working Paper. Lancaster University 2007.

AROGYASWAMY, KAMALA (1992): Organizational turnaround: A two-stage strategy-contingency model. Dissertation. University of Wisconsin-Milwaukee 1992.

AROGYASWAMY, KAMALA / BARKER, VINCENT L. III / YASAI-ARDEKANI, MASOUD (1995): Firm turnarounds: An integrative two-stage model. In: Journal of Management Studies, Vol. 32, No. 4, pp. 493-525.

AROGYASWAMY, KAMALA / YASAI-ARDEKANI, MASOUD (1997): Organizational turnaround: Understanding the role of cutbacks, efficiency improvements, and investment in technology. In: IEEE Transactions on Engineering Management, Vol. 44, No. 1, pp. 3-11.

ASQUITH, PAUL / GERTNER, ROBERT / SCHARFSTEIN, DAVID (1994): Anatomy of financial distress: An examination of junk-bond issuers. In: Quarterly Journal of Economics, Vol. 109, No. 3, pp. 625-658.

ATIASE, ROWLAND K. / PLATT, DAVID E. / TSE, SENYOY Y. (2004): Operational restructuring charges and post-restructuring performance. In: Contemporary Accounting Research, Vol. 21, No. 3, pp. 493-522.

AUTOMOTIVE NEWS (2011): Top 100 global suppliers - The Top 100 global OEM parts suppliers ranked by 2010 global OEM parts sales. URL: http://www.automotivenews.com, 15.07.2012.

BACKHAUS, KLAUS / ERICHSON, BERND / PLINKE, WULFF / WEIBER, ROLF (2008): Multivariate Analysemethoden - Eine anwendungsorientierte Einführung, 12th edition. Berlin.

BALCAEN, SOFIE (2009): Explaining distress-related firm exit: Analysis of exit paths. Dissertation. Ghent University 2009.

BALCAEN, SOFIE / OOGHE, HUBERT (2006): Thirty five years of studies on business failure: An overview of the classic statistical methodologies and their related problems. In: British Accounting Review, Vol. 38, No. 1, pp. 63-93.

BALGOBIN, ROLF / PANDIT, NARESH R. (2001): Stages in the turnaround process: The case of IBM UK. In: European Management Journal, Vol. 19, No. 3, pp. 301-316.

BARKER, VINCENT L. III / BARR, PAMELA S. (2002): Linking top manager attributions to strategic reorientation in declining firms attempting turnarounds. In: Journal of Business Research, Vol. 55, No. 12, pp. 963-979.

BARKER, VINCENT L. III / DUHAIME, IRENE M. (1997): Strategic change in the turnaround process: theory and empirical evidence. In: Strategic Management Journal, Vol. 18, No. 1, pp. 13-38.

BARKER, VINCENT L. III / MONE, MARK A. (1994): Retrenchment: Cause of turnaround or consequence of decline. In: Strategic Management Journal, Vol. 15, No. 5, pp. 395-405.

BEMMANN, MARTIN (2005): Improving the comparability of insolvency predictions. Working Paper. Technische Universität Dresden 2005.

BERGER, PHILIP G. / OFEK, ELI (1999): Causes and effects of corporate refocusing programs. In: Review of Financial Studies, Vol. 12, No. 2, pp. 311-345.

BHAGAT, SANJAI / BOLTON, BRIAN J. / SUBRAMANIAN, AJAY (2010): CEO education, CEO turnover, and firm performance. Working Paper. University of Colorado (Boulder) 2010.

BIBEAULT, DONALD B. (1982): Corporate turnaround - How managers turn losers into winners. New York.

BORTZ, JÜRGEN (2005): Statistik für Human- Sozialwissenschaftler, 6th edition. Berlin.

BORTZ, JÜRGEN / DÖRING, NICOLA (2006): Forschungsmethoden und Evaluation - Für Human- und Sozialwissenschaftler, 4th edition. Berlin.

BOWMAN, EDWARD H. / SINGH, HARBIR (1993): Corporate restructuring: Reconfiguring the firm. In: Strategic Management Journal, Vol. 14, Special Issue: Corporate Restr, pp. 5-14.

BOWMAN, EDWARD H. / SINGH, HARBIR / USEEM, MICHAEL / BHADURY, RAJA (1999): When does restructuring improve economic performance? In: California Management Review, Vol. 41, No. 2, pp. 33-54.

BRUTON, GARRY D. (1989): Performance differences between related and unrelated acquisitions of turnaround candidates. Dissertation. Oklahoma State University 1989.

BRUTON, GARRY D. / AHLSTROM, DAVID / WAN, JOHNNY C. (2003): Turnaround is east asian firms: Evidence from ethnic overseas communities. In: Strategic Management Journal, Vol. 24, No. 6, pp. 519-540.

BRYMAN, ALAN / BELL, EMMA (2007): Business research methods, 2nd edition. Oxford.

BUSCHMANN, HOLGER (2006): Erfolgreiches Turnaround-Management - Empirische Untersuchung mit Schwerpunkt auf dem Einfluss der Stakeholder. Dissertation. Universität St. Gallen 2006.

CARLILE, PAUL R. / CHRISTENSEN, CLAYTON M. (2005): The cycles of theory building in management research. Working Paper. Boston University 2005.

CASTROGIOVANNI, GARY J. / BRUTON, GARRY D. (2000): Business turnaround processes following acquisitions: Reconsidering the role of retrenchement. In: Journal of Business Research, Vol. 48, No. 1, pp. 25-34.

CEGLAREK, D. / HUANG, W. / ZHOU, S. / DING, Y. / KUMAR, R. / ZHOU, Y. (2004): Time-Based Competition in multistage manufacturing: Stream-of-Variation Analysis (SOVA) methodology review. In: The International Journal of Flexible Manufacturing Systems, Vol. 16, No. 1, pp. 11-44.

CHAKRAVARTHY, BALAJI S. (1986): Measuring strategic performance. In: Strategic Management Journal, Vol. 7, No. 5, pp. 437-458.

CHAUDHURY, MO (2011): The financial crisis and the behvior of stock prices. Working Paper. McGill University 2011.

CHENHALL, ROBERT H. / MOERS, FRANK (2007): The issue of endogeneity within theory-based, quantitative management accounting research. In: European Accounting Review, Vol. 16, No. 1, pp. 173-196.

CHOWDHURY, SHAMSUD D. (2002): Turnarounds: A stage theory perspective. In: Canadian Journal of Administrative Science, Vol. 19, No. 3, pp. 249-266.

CHOWDHURY, SHAMSUD D. / LANG, JAMES R. (1993): Crisis, decline and turnaround: A test of competing hypotheses for short-term performance improvement in small firms. In: Journal of Small Business Management, Vol. 31, No. 4, pp. 8-17.

CHOWDHURY, SHAMSUD D. / LANG, JAMES R. (1994): Turnaround actions, contingency influences, and profitability: The case for slack and capital intensity. In: Canadian Journal of Administrative Science, Vol. 11, No. 3, pp. 205-213.

CHOWDHURY, SHAMSUD D. / LANG, JAMES R. (1996): Turnaround in small firms: an assessment of efficiency strategies. In: Journal of Business Research, Vol. 36, No. 2, pp. 169-178.

CHRISTIE, ANDREW A. / JOYE, MARC P. / WATTS, ROSS L. (2003): Decentralization of the firm: theory and evidence. In: Journal of Corporate Finance, Vol. 9, No. 1, pp. 3-36.

CRESWELL, JOHN W. (2009): Research design - Qualitative, quantitative, and mixed methods approaches, 3rd edition. Thousand Oaks.

DAS, SOMNATH / LECLERE, MARC (2003): The survival of marginally distressed firms: evidence on the duration of turnaround. Working Paper. University of Illinois (Chicago) 2003.

D'AVENI, RICHARD A. (1989a): Dependability and organizational bankruptcy: An application of agency and prospect theory. In: Management Science, Vol. 35, No. 9, pp. 1120-1138.

D'AVENI, RICHARD A. (1989b): The aftermath of organizational decline: A longitudinal study of the strategies and managerial characteristics of declining firms. In: Academy of Management Journal, Vol. 32, No. 3, pp. 577-605.

DEANGELO, HARRY / DEANGELO, LINDA (1990): Dividend policy and financial distress: An empirical investigation of troubled NYSE firms. In: Journal of Finance, Vol. 45, No. 5, pp. 1415-1431.

DENIS, DIANE K. / KRUSE, TIMOTHY A. (2000): Mangerial discipline and corporate restructuring following performance declines. In: Journal of Financial Economics, Vol. 55, No. 3, pp. 391-424.

DENIS, DIANE K. / SHOME, DILIP K. (2005): An empirical investigation of corporate asset downsizing. In: Journal of Corporate Finance, Vol. 11, No. 3, pp. 427-448.

DIEZ, WILLI / REINDL, STEFAN (2005): Das Management der automobilen Wertschöpfungskette, in: Diez, W. et al. (Eds.), Grundlagen der Automobilwirtschaft, München 2005, pp. 71-104.

DIEZ, WILLI / REINDL, STEFAN (2005): Die Automobilindustrie im Zeichen der Globalisierung, in: Diez, W. et al. (Eds.), Grundlagen der Automobilwirtschaft, München 2005, pp. 105-128.

EICHNER, TOBIAS (2008): Restructuring and turnaround of distressed manufacturing firms - An international empirical study. Dissertation. Ulm University 2008.

EMMERICH, HUGO (1929): Die Sanierung. Mannheim.

FALKENBERG, ALEXANDER D. / CHONG, LI-CHOY / PRINZ, PASCAL P. (2004): Asset and cost retrenchment in turnaround strategies - A large-sample study of corporate responses to the Asian crisis in Singapur. Working Paper. Universität St. Gallen 2004.

FAN, JOSEPH P. / HUANG / JUAN / ZHU, NING (2011): Institutions, ownership structures, and firm distress resolution. Working Paper. Chinese University (Hong Kong) 2011.

FIELD, ANDY (2005): Discovering Statistics Using SPSS. London.

FILATOTCHEV, IGOR / TOMS, STEVE (2006): Corporate governance and financial constraints on strategic turnarounds. In: Journal of Management Studies, Vol. 43, No. 3, pp. 407-433.

FOLEY & LARDNER (2008): Survival in today's automotive industry - How to manage relationships with financially distressed companies. URL: http://www.foley.com/publications/pub_detail.aspx?pubid=3786, 15.07.2012.

FRANCIS, JOHN D. / DESAI, ASHAY B. (2005): Situational and organizational determinants of turnaround. In: Management Decision, Vol. 43, No. 9, pp. 1203-1224.

FRANCIS, JOHN D. / MARIOLA, ELENI (2005): Decline, turnaround, and managerial ownership. Working Paper. Iona College 2005.

FRANCIS, JOHN D. / PETT, TIMOTHY L. (2004): Retrenchment in declining organizations: Towards an integrative understanding. In: Journal of Business and Management, Vol. 10, No. 1, pp. 39-52.

FURRER, OLIVIER / PANDIAN, J. R. / THOMAS, HOWARD (2007): Corporate strategy and shareholder value during decline and turnaround. In: Management Decision, Vol. 45, No. 3, pp. 372-392.

GILSON, STUART C. (1989): Management turnover and financial distress. In: Journal of Financial Economics, Vol. 25, No. 2, pp. 241-262.

GLESS, SVEN-ERIK (1996): Unternehmenssanierung - Grundlagen, Strategien, Maßnahmen. Dissertation. Humboldt-Universität Berlin 1996.

GOPAL, R. (1991): Turning around sick companies - the Indian experience. In: Long Range Planning, Vol. 24, No. 3, pp. 79-83.

GRINYER, PETER H. / MAYES, DAVID G. / MCKIERNAN, PETER (1990): The Sharpbenders: achieving a sustained improvement in performance. In: Long Range Planning, Vol. 23, No. 1, pp. 116-125.

GULATI, RANJAY (2007): Tent poles, triabalism, and boundary spanning: The rigor-relevance debate in management research. In: Academy of Management Journal, Vol. 50, No. 4, pp. 775-782.

HAENECKE, HENRIK (2002): Methodenorientierte Systematisierung der Kritik an der Erfolgsfaktorenforschung. In: Zeitschrift für Betriebswirtschaft, Vol. 72, No. 2, pp. 165-183.

HAMBRICK, DONALD C. (1994): What if the academy actually mattered? - 1993 presidential address. In: Academy of Management Review, Vol. 19, No. 1, pp. 11-16.

HAMBRICK, DONALD C. / SCHECTER, STEVEN M. (1983): Turnaround strategies for mature industrial-product business units. In: Academy of Management Journal, Vol. 26, No. 2, pp. 231-248.

HAMILTON, BARTON H. / NICKERSON, JACKSON A. (2003): Correcting for endogeneity in strategic management research. In: Strategic Organization, Vol. 1, No. 1, pp. 51-78.

HARKER, MICHAEL (2001): Market manipulation: A necessary strategy in the company turnaround process? In: Qualitative Market Research, Vol. 4, No. 4, pp. 197-206.

HARRIGAN, KATHRYN R. (1985): An application of clustering for strategic group analysis. In: Strategic Management Journal, Vol. 6, No. 1, pp. 55-73.

HAUGH, DAVID / MOUROUGANE, ANNABELLE / CHATAL, OLIVIER (2010): The automobile industry in and beyond crisis. Working Paper. OECD Economics Department 2010.

HAUSCHILDT, JÜRGEN (2000): Unternehmenskrisen - Herausforderungen an die Bilanzanalyse, in: Hauschildt, J. / Leker, J. (Eds.), Krisendiagnose durch Bilanzanalyse, Köln 2000, pp. 1-17.

HAUSCHILDT, JÜRGEN (2006): Theorie-Orientierung oder Problem-Orientierung in der empirischen betriebswirtschaftlichen Forschung? In: Journal für Betriebswirtschaft, Vol. 56, No. 1, pp. 61-63.

HAUSCHILDT, JÜRGEN / GRAPE, CHRISTIAN / SCHINDLER, MARC (2006): Typologien von Unternehmenskrisen im Wandel. In: Die Betriebswirtschaft, Vol. 66, No. 1, pp. 7-25.

HOETKER, GLENN (2007): The use of logit and probit models in strategic management reserach: critical issues. In: Strategic Management Journal, Vol. 28, No. 4, pp. 331-343.

HOFER, CHARLES W. (1980): Turnaround strategies. In: Journal of Business Strategy, Vol. 1, No. 1, pp. 19-31.

HOFFMAN, RICHARD C. (1989): Strategies for corporate turnaround: what do we know about them? In: Journal of General Management, Vol. 14, No. 3, pp. b46-66.

HOLDER-WEBB, LORI / LOPEZ, THOMAS J. / REGIER, PHILIP R. (2005): The performance consequences of operational restucturings. In: Review of Quantitative Finance and Accounting, Vol. 25, No. 4, pp. 319-339.

HOPFMUELLER, LISA K. (2010): The role of the board of directors in turnaround situations - Empirical studies of Swiss listed companies. Dissertation. Universität St. Gallen 2010.

HOSMER, DAVID / LEMESHOW, STANLEY (2000): Applied logistic regression, 2nd edition. New York.

HOTCHKISS, EDITH S. (1995): Postbankruptcy performance and management turnover. In: Journal of Finance, Vol. 50, No. 1, pp. 3-21.

HURRLE, BEATRICE / KIESER, ALFRED (2005): Sind Key Informants verlässliche Datenlieferanten? In: Die Betriebswirtschaft, Vol. 65, No. 6, pp. 584-602.

HURRY, DILEEP (1993): Restructuring in the global economcy: The consequences of strategic linkages between Japanese and U.S. firms. In: Strategic Management Journal, Vol. 14, No. 1, pp. 69-82.

JOHN, KOSE / LANG, LARRY H. / NETTER, JEFFREY (1992): The voluntary restructuring of large firms in response to performance decline. In: Journal of Finance, Vol. 47, No. 3, pp. 891-917.

JOHN, KOSE / OFEK, ELI (1995): Asset sales and increase in focus. In: Journal of Financial Economics, Vol. 37, No. 1, pp. 105-126.

JOSTARNDT, PHILIPP (2007): Financial distress, corporate restructuring and firm survival - An empirical analysis of German panel data. Dissertation. Ludwig Maximilians-Universität München.

KAHL, MATTHIAS (2002): Economic distress, financial distress, and dynamic liquidation. In: Journal of Finance, Vol. 57, No. 1, pp. 135-168.

KALL, FLORIAN T. (1999): Controlling im Turnaround-Prozeß - Theoretischer Bezugsrahmen, empirische Fundierung und handlungsorientierte Ausgestaltung einer Controlling-Konzeption für den Turnaround-Prozeß. Dissertation. Europa-Universität Viadrina 1999.

KALMBACH, RALF (2007): The automotive power play moves into its next round, in: Gottschalk, B. / Kalmbach, R. (Eds.), Mastering automotive challenges, London 2007, pp. 25-45.

KANE, GREGORY D. / RICHARDSON, FREDERICK M. (2002): The relationship between changes in fixed plant investment and the likelihood of emergence from corporate financial distress. In: Review of Quantitative Finance and Accounting, Vol. 18, No. 3, pp. 259-272.

KANE, GREGORY D. / RICHARDSON, FREDERICK M. / VELURY, UMA (2006): The relevance of stock and flow-based reporting information in assessing the likelihood of emergence from corporate financial distress. In: Review of Quantitative Finance and Accounting, Vol. 26, No. 1, pp. 5-22.

KANG, JUN-KOO / SHIVDASANI, ANIL (1997): Corporate restructuring during performance declines in Japan. In: Journal of Financial Economics, Vol. 46, No. 1, pp. 29-65.

KAPLAN, STEVEN N. / KLEBANOV, MARK M. / SORENSEN, MORTEN (2011): Which CEO characteristics and abilities Matter? Working Paper. University of Chicago 2011.

KEASEY, KEVIN / WATSON, ROBERT (1987): Non-financial symptoms and the prediction of small company failure: a test of Argenti's hypotheses. In: Journal of Business Finance & Accounting, Vol. 14, No. 3, pp. 335-353.

KELLE, UDO (2008): Die Integration qualitativer und quantitativer Methoden in der empirischen Sozialforschung - Theoretische Grundlagen und methodologische Konzepte, 2nd edition. Wiesbaden.

KETCHEN, DAVID J. JR. / SHOOK, CHRISTOPHER L. (1996): The application of cluster analysis in strategic management research: An analysis and critique. In: Strategic Management Journal, Vol. 17, No. 6, pp. 441-458.

KIESER, ALFRED / NICOLAI, ALEXANDER T. (2005): Success factor research - Overcoming the trade-off between rigor and relevance. In: Journal of Management Inquiry, Vol. 14, No. 3, pp. 275-279.

KIRSCH, WERNER (1981): Über den Sinn der empirischen Forschung in der angewandten Betriebswirtschaftslehre, in: Witte, E. (Ed.), Der praktische Nutzen empirischer Forschung, Tübingen 1981, pp. 189-229.

KPMG (2009): Global location strategy for automotive suppliers. URL: http://www.kpmg.de/docs/Global_Location.pdf, 15.07.2012.

KRAUS, KARL-J. / HAGHANI, SASCHA (2004): Krisenverlauf und Krisenbewältigung - der aktuelle Stand, in: Bickhoff, N. et al. (Eds.), Die Unternehmenskrise als Chance, Berlin 2004, pp. 13-37.

KRYSTEK, ULRICH (1987): Unternehmungskrisen - Beschreibung, Vermeidung und Bewältigung überlebenskritischer Prozesse in Unternehmungen. Wiesbaden.

LAABS, JAN-PETER (2009): The long-term success of mergers and acquisitions in the international automotive supply industry. Dissertation. European Business School Oestrich-Winkel 2009.

LACEY, RUSSEL / SUH, JAEBEOM / MORGAN, ROBERT M. (2007): Differential Effects of Preferential Treatment Levels on Relational Outcomes. In: Journal of Service Research, Vol. 9, No. 3, pp. 241-256.

LAFRENZ, KARSTEN (2004): Shareholder Value-orientierte Sanierung - Ansatzpunkte und Wertsteigerungspotenzial beim Management von Unternehmenskrisen. Dissertation. Europa-Universität Viadrina.

LAI, CHEE C. (1997): Corporate restructuring and turnaround: an exploratory study of the determinants and effectiveness of corporate restructuring strategies by troubled UK firms. Dissertation. City University 1997.

LAI, JIM / SUDARSANAM, SUDI (1997): Corporate restructuring in response to performance decline: impact of ownership, governance and lenders. In: European Finance Review, Vol. 1, No. 2, pp. 197-233.

LANG, LARRY H. / POULSEN, ANNETTE B. / STULZ, RENÉ (1995): Asset sales, firm performance, and the agency costs of managerial discretion. In: Journal of Financial Economics, Vol. 37, No. 1, pp. 3-37.

LAWRENCE, PAUL R. (1992): The challenge of problem-oriented research. In: Journal of Management Inquiry, Vol. 1, No. 2, pp. 139-142.

LEE, CHUN I. / MATHUR, IKE / GLEASON, KIMBERLY C. (1998): Corporate response to poor performance. In: Journal of General Management, Vol. 24, No. 1, pp. 69-80.

LEE, PICHENG (2000): Earnings management at different stages of financial distress. Dissertation. State University of New Jersey 2000.

LIN, BEIXIN / LEE, ZU-HSU / GIBBS, LANCE G. (2008): Operational restructuring: Reviving an ailing business. In: Management Decision, Vol. 46, No. 4, pp. 539-552.

LIN, BEIXIN / LEE, ZU-HSU / PETERSON, RICHARD (2006): An analytical approach for making management decisions concerning corporate restructuring. In: Managerial and Decision Economics, Vol. 27, No. 8, pp. 655-666.

LIOU, DAH-KWEI / SMITH, MALCOM (2007): Financial distress and corporate turnaround: A review of the literature and agenda for fesearch. In: Accounting, Accountability & Performance, Vol. 13, No. 1, pp. 74-114.

LO, ANDREW W. (1986): Logit versus discriminant analysis - A specification test and application to corporate bankruptcies. In: Journal of Econometrics, Vol. 31, No. 2, pp. 151-178.

LONG, JOHN S. (1997): Regression models for categorical and limited dependent variables. Thousand Oaks.

MAHESHWARI, SUNIL K. (2000): Organisational decline and turnaround management: A contingency framwork. In: Vikalpa, Vol. 25, No. 4, pp. 39-50.

MARCH, JAMES G. / SUTTON, ROBERT I. (1997): Organizational performance as a dependent variable. In: Organization Science, Vol. 8, No. 6, pp. 698-706.

MCGAHAN, ANITA M. / PORTER, MICHAEL E. (1997): How much does industry matter, really? In: Strategic Management Journal, Vol. 18, Summer special issue, pp. 15-30.

MENARD, SCOTT (1995): Applied logistic regression. Thousand Oaks.

MENTZ, MARKUS (2006): Mergers & acquisitions in der Automobilzulieferindustrie - Wertschöpfungspotentiale durch internationale Positionierung. Dissertation. European Business School Oestrich-Winkel 2006.

MOLDENHAUER, RALF / SEAGON, CHRISTOPHER (2008): Unternehmensrestrukturierung die ungenutzte Chance: Möglichkeiten und Grenzen des Unternehmenserhaltes durch Sanierung außerhalb bzw. im Insolvenzverfahren. Heidelberg.

MORROW, J. L. JR. / JOHNSON, RICHARD A. / BUSENITZ, LOWELL W. / LOWELL W. (2004): The effects of cost and asset retrenchment on firm performance: the overlooked role of a firm's competitive environment. In: Journal of Management, Vol. 30, No. 2, pp. 189-208.

MORROW, J. L. JR. / SIRMON, DAVID G. / HITT, MICHAEL A. / HOLCOMB, TIM R. (2007): Creating value in the face of declining performance: firm strategies and organizational recovery. In: Strategic Management Journal, Vol. 28, No. 3, pp. 271-283.

MÜLLER, RAINER (1985): Corporate crisis management. In: Long Range Planning, Vol. 18, No. 5, pp. 38-48.

NAUJOKS, MARCEL B. (2012): Restructuring strategies and post-bankruptcy performance. Dissertation. Technische Universität München.

NEUMAN, LAWRENCE W. (2005): Social research methods - Quantitative and qualitative approaches. London.

NICOLAI, ALEXANDER T. / KIESER, ALFRED (2002): Trotz eklatanter Erfolglosigkeit: Die Erfolgsfaktorenforschung weiter auf Erfolgskurs. In: Die Betriebswirtschaft, Vol. 62, No. 6, pp. 579-596.

NORUSIS, MARIJA J. (2009): PASW Statistics 18 statistical procedures companion. Upper Saddle River.

NOTHARDT, FRANZ (2001): Corporate turnaround and corporate stakeholders: an empirical examination of the determinants of corporate turnaround in Germany with a focus on financial stakeholder theory. Dissertation. Universität St. Gallen.

OFEK, ELI (1993): Capital structure and firm response to poor performance. In: Journal of Financial Economics, Vol. 34, No. 1, pp. 3-30.

OLIVER, NICK / HOLWEG, MATTHIAS / CARVER, MIKE (2008): A systems perspective on the death of a car company. In: International Journal of Operations & Production Management, Vol. 28, No. 6, pp. 562-583.

O'NEILL, HUGH M. (1986a): An analysis of the turnaround strategy in commercial banking. In: Journal of Management Studies, Vol. 23, No. 2, pp. 165-188.

O'NEILL, HUGH M. (1986b): Turnaround and recovery: what strategy do you need? In: Long Range Planning, Vol. 19, No. 1, pp. 80-88.

OUTECHEVA, NATALIA (2007): Corporate financial distress: An empirical analysis of distress risk. Dissertation. Universität St. Gallen 2007.

PAJUNEN, KALLE (2005): Comparative causal analysis in processual strategy research: A study of causal mechanisms in organizational decline and turnarounds. In: Advances in Strategic Management, Vol. 22, pp. 415-456.

PANDIT, NARESH R. (2000): Some recommendations for improved research on corporate turnaround. In: M@n@gement, Vol. 3, No. 2, pp. 31-56.

PANT, LAURIE W. (1991): An investigation of industry and firm structural characteristics in corporate turnarounds. In: Journal of Management Studies, Vol. 28, No. 6, pp. 623-643.

PEARCE, JOHN A. II (2007): The value of corporate financial measures in monitoring downturn and managing turnaround: an exploratory study. In: Journal of Managerial Issues, Vol. 19, No. 2, pp. 253-270.

PEARCE, JOHN A. II / DOH, JONATHAN P. (2002): Improving the management of turnaround with corporate financial measures. In: Academy of Management Proceedings, pp. B1-B6.

PEARCE, JOHN A. II / ROBBINS, DON K. (1993): Toward improved theory and research on business turnaround. In: Journal of Management, Vol. 19, No. 3, pp. 613-636.

PENG, CHAO-YING J. / SO, TAK-SHING H. (2002): Logistic regression analysis and reporting: A primer. In: Understanding Statistics, Vol. 1, No. 1, pp. 31-70.

PETTIGREW, ANDREW M. (1987): Researching strategic change, in: Pettigrew, A. (Ed.), The management of strategic change, Oxford 1987, pp. 1-13.

PETTIGREW, ANDREW M. (1992): The character and significance of strategy process research. In: Strategic Management Journal, Vol. 13, Special Issue: Fundamental Themes in Strategy Process Research, pp. 5-16.

PRESS, JAMES S. / WILSON, SANDRA (1978): Choosing between logistic regression and discriminant analysis. In: Journal of American Statistical Association, Vol. 74, No. 364, pp. 699-705.

PRETORIUS, MARIUS (2009): Defining business decline, failure and turnaround: a content analysis. In: South African Journal of Entrepreneurship and Small Business Management, Vol. 2, No. 1, pp. 1-16.

PRETORIUS, MARIUS (2010): Drivers and moderators of business decline. In: Acta Commerci, Vol. 10, No. 1, pp. 218-233.

PUNJI, GIRISH / STEWART, DAVID W. (1983): Cluster analysis in marketing research: Review and suggestions for application. In: Journal of Marketing Research, Vol. 20, No. 2, pp. 134-148.

RASHEED, HOWARD S. (2005): Turnaround strategies for declining small business: The effects of performance and resources. In: Journal of Developmental Entrepreneurship, Vol. 10, No. 3, pp. 239-252.

RIESENHUBER, FELIX (2007): Großzahlige empirische Forschung, in: Albers, S. et al. (Eds.), Methodik der empirischen Forschung, Wiesbaden 2007, pp. 1-16.

ROBBINS, DON K. / PEARCE, JOHN A. II (1992): Turnaround: retrenchment and recovery. In: Strategic Management Journal, Vol. 13, No. 4, pp. 287-309.

ROBBINS, DON K. / PEARCE, JOHN A. II (1993): Entrepreneurial retrenchment among small manufacturing firms. In: Journal of Business Venturing, Vol. 8, No. 4, pp. 301-318.

RÖDERSTEIN, RENÉ (2009): Erfolgsfaktoren im Supply Chain Management der DIY-Branche. Dissertation. Universität Siegen 2009.

ROHRLACK, CHRISTIAN (2007): Logistische und Ordinale Regression, in: Albers, S. et al. (Eds.), Methodik der empirischen Forschung, Wiesbaden 2007, pp. 199-214.

ROSSER, BRUCE A. / CANIL, JEAN M. (2011): Stock versus options in financially distressed firms. Working Paper. University of Adelaide 2011.

ROUTLEDGE, JAMES / GADENNE, DAVID (2004): An exploratory study of the company reorganisation decision in voluntary administration. In: Pacific Accounting Review, Vol. 16, No. 1, pp. 31-56.

RUNKEL, PHILIP J. / MCGRATH, JOSEPH E. (1972): Research on human behavior - A systematic guide to method. New York.

SCHENDEL, DAN / PATTON, G. R. (1976): Corporate stagnation and turnaround. In: Journal of Economics and Business, Vol. 28, No. 3, pp. 236-241.

SCHENDEL, DAN / PATTON, G. R. / RIGGS, JAMES (1976): Corporate turnaround strategies: a study of profit decline and recovery. In: Journal of General Management, Vol. 3, No. 3, pp. 3-11.

SCHLEY, LENNART (2010): Erfolgsfaktoren von Sanierungen; eine kausalanalytische Untersuchung mit dem Partial-Least-Squares-Verfahren. Dissertation. Technische Universität Chemnitz 2010.

SCHMALEN, CAROLINE / KUNERT, MATTHIAS / WEINDLMAIER, HANNES (2005): Erfolgsfaktorenforschung: Theoretische Grundlagen, methodische Vorgehensweise und Anwendungserfahrungen in Projekten für die Ernährungsindustrie. Working Paper. Technische Universität München 2005.

SCHMALENBACH, EUGEN (1932): Beteiligungs-Finanzierung, 5th edition. Leipzig.

SCHMIDT-GOTHAN, HANNO (2008): Holistisches Sanierungs- und Wertmanagement. Wiesbaden.

SCHMITT, ACHIM (2009): Innovation and growth in corporate restructurings - Solution or Contradiction. Dissertation. University of Geneva.

SCHNELL, RAINER / HILL, PAUL B. / ESSER, ELKE (2005): Methoden der empirischen Sozialforschung, 7th edition. München.

SCHWAIGER, MANFRED / ZIMMERMANN, LORENZ (2009): Quantitative Forschung: Ein Überblick, in: Schwaiger, M. / Meyer, A. (Eds.), Theorien und Methoden der Betriebswirtschaft, München 2009, pp. 419-437.

SHAH, SONALI K. / CORLEY, KEVIN G. (2006): Building better theory by bridging the quantitative-qualitative divide. In: Journal of Management Studies, Vol. 43, No. 8, pp. 1821-1835.

SINGH, HARBIR (1993): Challenges in researching corporate restructuring. In: Journal of Management Studies, Vol. 30, No. 1, pp. 147-172.

SLATTER, STUART (1984): Corporate recovery - Successful turnaround strategies and their implementation. London.

SLATTER, STUART / LOVETT, DAVID (1999): Corporate turnaround. London.

SMITH, MALCOM / GRAVES, CHRISTOPHER (2005): Corporate turnaround and financial distress. In: Managerial Auditing Journal, Vol. 20, No. 3, pp. 304-320.

STARBUCK, WILLIAM H. (2005): Performance measures: Prevalent and important but methodologically challenging. In: Journal of Management Inquiry, Vol. 14, No. 3, pp. 280-286.

SUDARSANAM, SUDI / LAI, JIM (2001): Corporate financial distress and turnaround strategies: an empirical analysis. In: British Journal of Management, Vol. 12, No. 3, pp. 183-199.

SUDARSANAM, SUDI / WRIGHT, MIKE / HUANG, JIAN (2011): Target bankruptcy risk and its impact on going private buyout performance and exit. In: Corporate Governance: An International Review, Vol. 19, No. 3, pp. 240-258.

TAFFLER, RICHARD J. (1983): The assessment of company solvency and performance using a statistical model. In: Accounting and Business Research, Vol. 13, No. 52, pp. 295-307.

TAFFLER, RICHARD J. (1984): Empirical models for the monitoring of UK corporations. In: Journal of Banking and Finance, Vol. 8, No. 2, pp. 199-227.

TAIMER, LARS (2007): Verhaltensorientiertes Sanierungsmanagement. Düsseldorf.

THAIN, DONALD H. / GOLDTHORPE, RICHARD L. (1989): Turnaround management: causes of decline. In: Business Quarterly, Vol. 54, No. 1, pp. 55-62.

THIÉTART, RAYMOND-ALAIN (1988): Success strategies for businesses that perform poorly. In: Interfaces, Vol. 18, No. 3, pp. 32-45.

THOMSON REUTERS: Worldscope database - Data definitions guide 2010. URL: http://cdnete.lib.ncku.edu.tw/93cdnet/libref/handout/20110107_worldscopedatadefinitionsguideseptember2010.pdf, 15.07.2012.

TRIMBATH, SUSANNE (2006): Financial ratios in quantitative data analysis: A pratical guide, in: Hoque, Z. (Ed.), Methodological issues in accounting research; theories, methods and issues, London 2006, pp. 411-525.

TSIKRIKTSIS, NIKOS (2005): A review of techniques for treating missing data in OM survey research. In: Journal of Operations Management, Vol. 24, No. 1, pp. 53-62.

ULBRICHT, NIELS / WEINER, CHRISTIAN (2005): Worldscope meets Compustat: A comparison of financial databases. Working Paper. Humboldt-Universität Berlin 2005.

VENKATRAMAN, N. / RAMANUJAM, VASUDEVAN (1986): Measurement of business performance in strategy research: A comparison of approaches. In: Academy of Management Review, Vol. 11, No. 4, pp. 801-814.

VENKATRAMAN, N. / RAMANUJAM, VASUDEVAN (1987): Measurement of business economic performance: an examination of method convergence. In: Journal of Management, Vol. 13, No. 1, pp. 109-122.

WAD, PETER (2008): The development of automotive parts suppliers in Korea and Malaysia: A global value chain Perspective. In: Asia Pacific Business Review, Vol. 14, No. 1, pp. 47-64.

WAD, PETER (2009): Impact of the global economic and financial crisis over the automotive indutry in developing countries. Working Paper. Copenhagen Business School 2009.

WAHRENDORFF, MATTHIAS (2008): Automotive industry: High performance business in the era of the 'multi-polar' world - Accenture Research. URL: http://download.microsoft.com/download/e/b/6/eb6a75d9-b368-4b91-a7c0-22f1270ba57d/T11_DI_1530_C.pdf, 15.07.2012.

WALLENTOWITZ, HENNING / FREIALDENHOVEN, ARNDT / OLSCHEWSKI, INGO (2009): Strategien in der Automobilindustrie - Technologietrends und Marktentwicklungen. Wiesbaden.

WEITZEL, WILLIAM / JONSSON, ELLEN (1989): Decline in organisations: a literature integration and extension. In: Administrative Science Quarterly, Vol. 34, No. 1, pp. 91-109.

WHITAKER, RICHARD B. (1999): The early stages of financial distress. In: Journal of Economics and Finance, Vol. 23, No. 2, pp. 123-133.

WHITING, ROSALIND / GILKISON, SIMON (2000): Financial leverage and firm response to poor performance. In: Pacific Accounting Review, Vol. 12, No. 2, pp. 1-35.

WINN, JOAN (1993): Performance measures for corporate turnarounds. In: Journal of General Management, Vol. 19, No. 2, pp. 48-63.

WINN, JOAN (1997): Asset productivity turnaround: the growth/efficiency challenge. In: Journal of Management Studies, Vol. 34, No. 4, pp. 585-600.

WITTE, EBERHARD (1981a): Die Unternehmenskrise - Anfang vom Ende oder Neubeginn, in: Bratschitsch, R. / Schnellinger, W. (Eds.), Unternehmenskrisen - Ursachen, Frühwarnung, Bewältigung, Stuttgart 1981, pp. 7-24.

WITTE, EBERHARD (1981b): Nutzungsanspruch und Nutzungsvielfalt, in: Witte, E. (Ed.), Der praktische Nutzen empirischer Forschung, Tübingen 1981, pp. 13-40.

WOLFF, GERHARDT / HERRMANN, MARCO / NIGGEMANN, MARKUS (2004): Quo vadis Erfolgsfaktorenforschung? In: Jahrbücher für Nationalökonomie und Statistik, Vol. 224, 1-2, pp. 263-269.

WOYWODE, MICHAEL (2004): Wege aus der Erfolglosigkeit der Erfolgsfaktorenforschung, in: KfW-Bankengruppe (Ed.), Was erfolgreiche Unternehmen ausmacht, Heidelberg 2004, pp. 15-48.

YAWSON, ALFRED (2009): Interaction effects of restructuring decisions on operating profit following performance shocks. In: Journal of Economics and Business, Vol. 61, No. 3, pp. 216-237.

ZIMMERMANN, FREDERICK M. (1989): Managing a successful turnaround. In: Long Range Planning, Vol. 22, No. 3, pp. 105-124.

MIX
Papier aus verantwortungsvollen Quellen
Paper from responsible sources
FSC® C105338

If you have any concerns about our products,
you can contact us on
ProductSafety@springernature.com

In case Publisher is established outside the EU,
the EU authorized representative is:
Springer Nature Customer Service Center GmbH
Europaplatz 3, 69115 Heidelberg, Germany

Printed by Libri Plureos GmbH
in Hamburg, Germany